KOIZUMI DIPLOMACY

TOMOHITO SHINODA

UNIVERSITY OF WASHINGTON PRESS | *Seattle and London*

KOIZUMI DIPLOMACY

Japan's Kantei Approach to Foreign and Defense Affairs

Koizumi Diplomacy is published with the assistance of a grant from the Japanese Ministry of Education.

University of Washington Press
P.O. Box 50096, Seattle, WA 98145 U.S.A.
www.washington.edu/uwpress

The paper used in this publication is acid-free
and 90 percent recycled from at least 50 percent
post-consumer waste. It meets the minimum
requirements of American National Standard
for Information Sciences—Permanence of Paper
for Printed Library Materials, ANSI Z39.48–1984.

LIBRARY OF CONGRESS
CATALOGING-IN-PUBLICATION DATA

Shinoda, Tomohito, 1960–
Koizumi diplomacy : Japan's kantei approach
to foreign and defense affairs /
Tomohito Shinoda.
    p. cm.
    Includes bibliographical references and index.
ISBN-13: 978-0-295-98699-9 (pbk. : alk. paper)
ISBN-10: 0-295-98699-9 (pbk. : alk. paper)
1. Japan—Foreign relations—1989–   2. Koizumi,
Jun'ichiro, 1942–   3. National security—Law and
legislation—Japan.   I. Title.
DS891.2.S48 2007
327.52009'0511—dc22
2006100674

TO GRETCHEN AND ERIKA

CONTENTS

ACKNOWLEDGMENTS

I n the early 1990s, I began my research on changes in Japanese political institutions and the impact such changes have had on the national leader. I closely followed the 1994 electoral changes, the 1999 political changes, and especially the 2001 central-government reforms, which strengthened the Cabinet Secretariat, a supporting organ for the prime minister. These changes had a significant impact on Japan's policy-making process. Another major theme in my research is the leadership role of politicians in the area of foreign and national security policy. A friend suggested combining the two topics to create this book, which encompasses all of my research for the last fifteen years.

The book's completion would not have been possible without the support of many individuals. I am particularly indebted to Sohei Nakayama, a

Japanese senior business leader who guided me in my professional and personal life. He passed away in November 2005 during the last part of this project. I cannot thank him enough for his contributions to my career and life. I also owe a significant debt to George R. Packard, who provided guidance through my academic and professional career. Without him, this work would not have even begun.

Over the years, I have been fortunate enough to interview many important policy makers. I am particularly grateful to the three former prime ministers who granted me interviews: Morihiro Hosokawa, Tomiichi Murayama, and Yasuhiro Nakasone. Their valuable comments helped me understand the thoughts behind their critical decisions. I also had three opportunities to interview former chief cabinet secretary Masaharu Gotoda, who passed away in September 2005. His comments significantly contributed to my understanding of the Cabinet Secretariat.

I had the good fortune to conduct a three-hour interview with Teijiro Furukawa, who, as deputy chief cabinet secretary, played an instrumental role in developing many Japanese government policies between 1995 and 2003, including the national-security policies described in this book. I would like to thank him and former chief cabinet secretary Yasuo Fukuda, who kindly introduced me to him.

In addition to these top policy makers, I conducted interviews with many current and former government officials who were involved in foreign- and national-security policy making or had worked at the Cabinet Secretariat. They provided me with firsthand knowledge of the prime ministers and their involvement in the foreign-policy process. These officials include Tatsuo Arima, Kenji Eda, Yoshihiro Handa, Keiichi Konaga, Michihiko Kunihiro, Junzo Matoba, Raisuke Miyawaki, and Ken Moroi. I would like to thank them and all those other government officials who preferred to remain anonymous. If the reader finds this work unique and concrete, it is due to their invaluable and lively comments.

I enjoy friendships with many Diet members who offer me insider views on Japanese politics. They include Yoshimasa Hayashi, Yutaka Kobayashi, Taro Kono, Yoriko Madoka, Akihisa Nagashima, Yasutoshi Nishimura, Nobumori Ohtani, Takuya Tasso, and Tsuyoshi Yamaguchi.

I would like to express my gratitude to the following scholars for their valuable input: Robert Angel, James Auer, Kent Calder, I. M. Destler, Glenn Hook, Chihiro Hosoya, Carl Jackson, Takashi Inoguchi, Richard Katz, Ellis

Krauss, Seigen Miyasato, Henry Nau, Robert Pekkanen, T. J. Pempel, Richard Samuels, James Schoff, Michael Smitka, Yoshihide Soeya, Akihiko Tanaka, Nathaniel Thayer, and several anonymous readers.

My sincere gratitude goes to the editors at the University of Washington Press, Michael Duckworth, Laura Iwasaki, and Marilyn Trueblood, for their support of this book project. Doug Jackson of Fresh Eyes deserves special thanks for his superb professional editing of an earlier version of my manuscript. Research and publication support for this study came from the Japan Society for the Promotion of Science's Grants-in-Aid for Scientific Research and for Publication of Scientific Research Results.

Finally, I dedicate this work to the two most important women in my life, my wife Gretchen and daughter Erika, who brought new meaning to my life and gave me the motivation to finish this project.

A NOTE ON CONVENTIONS

Japanese words and personal names are romanized according to the modified Hepburn system. Japanese personal names are normally presented in Western order with the exception of Japanese scholars whose Japanese-language publications give their names in Japanese order.

ABBREVIATIONS AND JAPANESE TERMS

anti-terrorism legislation The Special Measures Law Concerning Measures
Taken by Japan in Support of the Activities of Foreign Countries Aim-
ing to Achieve the Purposes of the Charter of the United Nations in
Response to the Terrorist Attacks Which Took Place on 11 September 2001
in the United States of America as well as Concerning Humanitarian Measures Based on Relevant Resolutions of the United Nations

CCS chief cabinet secretary

DPJ Democratic Party of Japan

DSP Democratic Socialist Party

GP Conference Government Parties Conference on National Emergency Legislation for Diet Operation

GP Council Government Parties Council for Iraq and North Korea

GP Project Team Government Parties National Security Project Team

INF Intermediate-range Nuclear Forces

Iraq legislation: Law Concerning the Special Measures for Humanitarian and Reconstruction Assistance in Iraq

JCP Japan Communist Party

JDA Japan Defense Agency

jimujikan kaigi administrative vice-ministerial meeting

JSP Japan Socialist Party

kacho division director

kacho hosa deputy director

kanbo chokan chief cabinet secretary

kanbo fukuchokan deputy chief cabinet secretary

kanbo fukuchokanho assistant chief cabinet secretary

Kantei The prime minister's official residence

Keidanren Japan Federation of Economic Organizations, or Keizai Dantai Rengokai

keiretsu A set of companies with interlocking business relationships and shareholdings

Keizai Doyukai Japan Association of Corporate Executives

kiki kanrikan deputy chief cabinet secretary for crisis management

Komeito Clean Government Party

LDP Liberal Democratic Party

METI Ministry of Economy, Trade, and Industry

MITI Ministry of International Trade and Industry

MOC Ministry of Construction

MOF Ministry of Finance

MOFA Ministry of Foreign Affairs

MOSS talks Market-Oriented Section-Specific talks

MOT Ministry of Transportation

MOU memorandum of understanding

MPT Ministry of Post and Telecommunications

Naimusho Ministry of Home Affairs (before World War II)

nemawashi log-rolling

NHK Nippon Hoso Kyokai

NPA National Policy Agency

NSC National Security Council (United States)

NTT Nippon Telegraph and Telephone

PKF peacekeeping force

PKO peacekeeping operations

PMO Prime Minister's Office, or *sorifu*

Rengo Japan Trade Union Confederation, or Nihon Rodo Kumiai Sorengokai

SDF Self-Defense Forces

SDP Social Democratic Party (formerly Japan Socialist Party)

seifu shuno top official of the government

SII Structural Impediments Initiative

UN United Nations

zoku policy tribe at the Liberal Democratic Party's Policy Research Council

KOIZUMI DIPLOMACY

W ith the end of the Cold War, the security environment surrounding Japan changed drastically. Japan's security is protected by the Japan-U.S. Security Treaty, which is asymmetric
by nature. The United States is obliged to protect Japan, and Japan provides
bases for U.S. forces but has no obligation to protect them unless they are
in its territory. During the Cold War, the arms race and ideological con-
frontation with the Soviet Union were justification enough for Americans
to maintain such an arrangement with Japan.

As the end of the Cold War virtually removed the Soviet military threat,
the U.S. Congress began questioning the value of the asymmetric alliance
with Japan. Since security affairs in East Asia were no longer perceived as

Table I-1 Japan's National Security Chronology

1946	McArthur orders SCAP to draft a model Japanese constitution (February)
1947	Japan's Peace Constitution goes into effect (May)
1950	McArthur orders Japan to form the National Police Reserve (July)
1951	San Francisco Peace Treaty, U.S.-Japan Security Treaty signed (September)
1952	Occupation ends, Japan becomes independent (April)
1955	JDA and SDF established (July)
1960	Revision of U.S.-Japan Security Treaty (January)
1972	Reversion of Okinawa (May)
	GOJ declares that Japan cannot exercise collective self-defense (October)
1978	Guidelines for U.S.-Japan Security Cooperation established (November)
1979	USSR invades Afghanistan, the new Cold War begins (December)
1981	Suzuki-Reagan Summit; the word "alliance" becomes controversial (May)
1983	Prime Minister Nakasone makes "unsinkable aircraft carrier" statement (January)
	Williamsburg Summit (May)
1989	Berlin Wall comes down; end of the Cold War (October)
1990	Iraq invades Kuwait (August)
	U.N. Peace Cooperation bill dies (November)
1991	Gulf War starts, Japan contributes $13 billion (January)
	Japan dispatches minesweepers to the Persian Gulf (April)
	USSR collapses (December)
1992	International Peace Cooperation Law enacted (June)
	SDF sent to Cambodia for PKO (September)
1993–94	Korean Peninsula Crisis
1995	Nye Report (February)
	Okinawa rape incident (September)
1996	Hashimoto-Clinton Summit, Joint Defense Declaration (April)
1997	Agreement on new U.S.-Japan Defense Guidelines (September)
1998	Taepodong flies over Japan (August)
1999	New Guidelines Law enacted (August)
2000	Negotiation over Japanese subsidy to USFJ
2001	9/11 terrorist attacks on New York and Washington, D.C. (September)
	Anti-terrorism legislation enacted (November)
	SDF dispatched to Indian Ocean for rear-echelon support (December)
2002	Contingency legislation introduced in the Diet (April)
	Koizumi visit to Pyongyang; five abductees return to Japan (September)
	North Korea admits its violation of the 1994 framework agreement (October)
	UN begins inspections of Iraq for WMD (November)
2003	North Korea withdraws from NPT (January)
	Contingency legislation enacted (June)
	Special law on Iraq reconstruction enacted (July)
2004	Ground SDF sent to Iraq (January)
	More contingency-related legislation enacted (June)

directly connected to the safety of the United States, the bases provided by Japan were not seen as significant as they had been.

The 1990 Gulf crisis happened in this political climate. Officials of the George H. W. Bush administration had high expectations: Japan was to provide a substantial contribution to show Congress that it was a very reliable ally. Knowing Japan's constitutional restriction on external use of its military forces, the United States nevertheless requested that Tokyo contribute personnel to the multinational forces in the region. The Toshiki Kaifu government failed to pass legislation that would have sent Self-Defense Forces (SDF) overseas but provided $13 billion in financial support. Although Japan was one of the two largest donors, its effort was criticized as "checkbook diplomacy."

In order to overcome this criticism, the Kaifu cabinet submitted another bill to the Diet that would allow the SDF to participate in peacekeeping operations under United Nations command. This bill passed in June 1992, one and a half years after the Gulf War, and the Japanese government sent the SDF to Cambodia. Although the new law did not serve the original objective, it provided Tokyo with a new diplomatic tool for contributing personnel to the international community.

In spring 1993, the North Korean nuclear crisis created a serious concern for officials in Tokyo and Washington, D.C. The 1992 legislation authorized the Japanese government to dispatch the SDF only for UN operations, and Tokyo still had no legal basis for taking action in a regional crisis near Japan. Washington had severely criticized Tokyo for not contributing forces for the Gulf War. If Japan could not offer more than bases for U.S. forces in the event of a contingency on the Korean Peninsula, the U.S. Congress would question the value of the U.S.-Japan alliance and might demand termination of the bilateral security arrangement. This strong concern, shared by officials on both sides of the Pacific, motivated the two governments to create new defense cooperation guidelines for regional crises. The initiative was announced by Prime Minister Ryutaro Hashimoto and President Bill Clinton at the April 1996 summit meeting, and Tokyo and Washington reached an agreement in September 1997. In May 1999, the Japanese Diet finally enacted the U.S.-Japan defense guidelines bills, which authorize the government to mobilize the SDF to provide rear-echelon support to U.S. forces in the event of a regional crisis. (The development of Japan's national security policies is shown in table I-1.)

Enter Koizumi

Throughout the 1990s, Japan made slow but steady progress in the area of national security in order to become a more responsible member of the international community and a more reliable ally to the United States. But when Prime Minister Junichiro Koizumi entered onto the political scene, Japan's policy-making strategy underwent major changes. The prime example is the Koizumi administration's response to the September 11 terrorist attacks in the United States. Within two months, the Koizumi cabinet enacted a major piece of legislation for the purpose of dispatching the SDF into active combat for the first time in Japan's post–World War II history. In 2003, the Koizumi cabinet crafted and enacted two major pieces of legislation on national security. The first was an emergency law passed in June 2003 providing a legal framework for defending the nation against external attack— legislation once considered politically taboo. Then, in late July, Koizumi successfully pushed through the Iraq legislation, which allows Japan's Self-Defense Forces to offer humanitarian and reconstruction assistance in Iraq. These moves showed the Koizumi administration's determination to strengthen Japan's role in its alliance with the United States and to bolster Japan's security.

There is no doubt that Koizumi had a strong political will, and he exercised his leadership skills to convince the Japanese public to accept major policy changes in defense and foreign affairs. During the November 2003 general election, opposition parties were unable to attack the ruling parties using these policy changes as election issues. In fact, the Socialist and Communist parties, which had criticized the changes as blind support for the Bush administration, actually lost ground in the election. The Democratic Party of Japan (DPJ), however, acted realistically in its opposition to the anti-terrorist and emergency legislation and increased its seats in the House of Representatives, the lower house.

Despite his limited diplomatic experience, Koizumi has achieved significant policy outcomes in defense and foreign affairs. He established a strong, trusting relationship with U.S. president George W. Bush during his first official trip to the United States in June 2001. In September 2001, Koizumi also became the first Japanese prime minister to visit Pyongyang, North Korea; he even brought home an apology from North Korean leader Kim Jong Il for the abductions of Japanese nationals. The latter accomplishment contributed to a significant increase in the Koizumi cabinet's approval rating. Some journalists have described these achievements as "Koizumi magic," as if the prime minister were producing such results out of nothing.[1]

While Koizumi's campaign to become a national leader focused on domestic reform, he appeared to be even prouder of his diplomatic triumphs. His confidence in handling foreign affairs was reflected in the number of days he spent overseas: during his first sixteen months in office, he was abroad for more than a hundred days—40 percent more than former prime minister Ryutaro Hashimoto, who openly boasted of his diplomatic prowess.[2]

Koizumi always had a surprisingly weak power base within the Liberal Democratic Party (LDP), compared to past prime ministers, before taking the leadership position. He was not even an LDP faction leader but belonged instead to the Mori faction, which represented just a sixth of all LDP Diet members. Within the faction itself, he was viewed as a lone wolf and had few supporters; there was no guarantee that he would even receive solid backing from his own faction during his tenure.

Different Explanations

How was Koizumi able to exercise leadership in foreign and defense affairs despite his weak power base within the LDP and his limited diplomatic experience? Scholars offer different explanations.[3] Some emphasize the role of public opinion in the formulation of Japan's postwar security policy. For a long time, intense pacifism supported Japan's strict interpretation of Article 9 and prevented serious debate on national security issues.[4] Many Japanese, however, felt embarrassed about their country's inability to provide anything more than financial assistance for the 1991 Gulf War. Ichiro Ozawa, who experienced the crisis as LDP secretary-general, stressed the need for Japan to become a "normal nation," which assumes responsibilities not only as an economic power but as a political and military one as well.[5] According to Cabinet Office opinion polls on foreign policy, only 34.7 percent of respondents in October 1990 identified "Japan's role in the international community" as "contribution to maintaining international peace, including personnel assistance." This answer came in third, after "global environment issues" and "contribution to the development of world economy." However, in the same poll taken in October 2004, the response on "contribution to international peace" came in first, identified by 51.9 percent of respondents.[6]

With greater public support for personnel contribution, the Koizumi government faced less political resistance to dispatching the SDF to join multinational forces in the Indian Ocean.[7]

While such public support can create a favorable political environment, this does not explain why the Koizumi government could enact those important pieces of national security legislation in such short periods of time. Especially in the case of the 2003 Iraq legislation, public support for the Koizumi cabinet was hovering around 40–45 percent, not as high as in 2001 when the anti-terrorism legislation was enacted. Disapproval of Koizumi's support for the U.S. attack on Iraq was higher than approval among the Japanese public (49 percent to 40 percent, according to a *Nihon Keizai Shimbun* poll of March 22, 2003).

Japan's more active role in the area of security may also be explained by weakening objections from Asian countries. When Prime Minister Kaifu introduced legislation to dispatch the SDF to assist multinational forces in the Middle East in 1990, some Asian countries reacted strongly against the initiative, viewing it as a step toward Japan's remilitarization. Among the most vocal were China, the Philippines, South Korea, and Singapore, which had suffered at the hands of the Japanese Imperial Army during World War II. However, the SDF's successful and honorable performance in UN peacekeeping operations in Cambodia, the Golan Heights, and Mozambique reduced these concerns.[8] Opposition from Asian countries to the 2001 anti-terrorism legislation was almost nonexistent. China even endorsed Japan's decision to send the SDF to the Indian Ocean. However, reaction from Asian countries cannot be the most important determinant in Japan's security decisions, and the Miyazawa administration passed legislation to send the SDF overseas for peacekeeping operations in 1992, despite objections from Asian countries.

Realist scholars view the post–Cold War international environment as the most important factor in the shift in Japan's security policy. During the Cold War, the Soviet military threat was a global concern for the United States. Americans widely viewed protection of Japan as essential for U.S. global strategy. As the Soviet threat diminished, however, Japan began to face an increasing threat from China and North Korea, which can be considered regional security matters. In order to assure its own security, Japan needs to play a more important role in its security ties with the United States.[9] This view, however, leaves domestic politics outside its scope and does not explain why the Koizumi government could enact important security laws in such a timely manner.

Yet another explanation is party politics. Tomohiko Taniguchi focuses on factional politics in the LDP. Each LDP faction had its own foreign-policy orientation. The largest faction, founded by Prime Minister Kakuei Tanaka, who was succeeded by Prime Ministers Noboru Takeshita, Keizo Obuchi, and Ryutaro Hashimoto, had long played an influential role in intra-party politics, especially when the party elected its leader. After Tanaka successfully normalized diplomatic relations with China in 1972, this faction became "the most Beijing-friendly" within the LDP. Under the Koizumi administration, however, the faction lost influence, enabling Koizumi to take a tougher stance against China while cementing Japan's alliance with the United States.[10]

Robert Pekkanen and Ellis Krauss, while noting the changing dynamics of intra-party politics, emphasize the importance of interparty politics.[11] The end of the Cold War brought an end to the traditional framework of Japan's interparty politics, the so-called 1955 system. Under this system, the LDP strongly promoted the security partnership with the United States, while the largest opposition party, the Japan Socialist Party, opposed the alliance and claimed it was illegal for Japan to maintain the SDF. The old system closed down when the Socialist party formed a coalition government with the LDP and approved the U.S.-Japan alliance and the SDF. Partly because of this change in policy stance, the Socialist party lost its traditional supporters. The current largest opposition party, the Democratic Party of Japan, has taken a more realistic line toward the Koizumi government's security policies.

Although the changing dynamics of intra- and interparty politics are important factors, they likewise do not provide an answer to the question, Why could the Koizumi government, given Koizumi's weak political base within the LDP and limited experience, swiftly deliver important pieces of security legislation? The answer lies in a key phrase that frequently appeared in the media throughout Koizumi's tenure: "Kantei-led" policy making.

What Is the Kantei?

The Kantei is the prime minister's official residence, the Japanese equivalent of the United States' White House or Britain's 10 Downing Street. Completed in April 2002 at a cost of 70 billion yen, the new residence, located in Tokyo's Nagata-cho district, has five stories aboveground and one floor underground.

The number of government officials working at the official residence is relatively small, even though the building itself is two and a half times larger than the old residence. The fifth floor houses only the offices of the prime minister, the chief cabinet secretary (*kanbo chokan*), and the three deputy chief cabinet secretaries (*kanbo fukuchokan*)—one administrative and two parliamentary. On the fourth floor are the offices of the deputy chief cabinet secretary for crisis management (*kiki kanrikan*), three assistant chief cabinet secretaries (*kanbo fukuchokanho*), the director general of the Cabinet Affairs Office, the cabinet public relations secretary, the director of Cabinet Intelligence, and special advisers to the prime minister. However, many of the officials on the fourth floor have their main offices elsewhere and do not work at the Kantei full-time. The third floor is basically an entrance hall, and the second and first floors have a press-conference room and reception halls. The underground floor houses the Crisis Management Center, where about a hundred people can gather in the event of an emergency, and the Situation Center of the Cabinet, where five groups, each containing four staffers, take turns gathering information from all over the world twenty-four hours a day; however, these staffers usually are not included when media people talk about the Kantei.

By its narrowest definition, the Kantei includes only the prime minister, the chief cabinet secretary (CCS), and three deputy CCSs. The broader definition used in this book, however, includes the entire body of the Cabinet Secretariat along with the prime minister. Across the street from the prime minister's official residence is the Cabinet Office building, which houses the rest of the secretariat. There are individual offices for three assistant chief cabinet secretaries and their staff room for about a hundred staffers; the Cabinet Intelligence and Research Office, which has 165 staffers; the Cabinet Public Relations Office; and the Cabinet Affairs Office. In addition, there are fifteen ad hoc policy rooms under the Cabinet Secretariat, although some are located in separate buildings. The official number of secretariat staffers as of the end of March 2006 was 655.

Until recently, the Kantei had a very limited role in policy making. Ichiro Ozawa, who served as deputy CCS in the Takeshita administration (1987–89), wrote in his 1994 book *Blueprint for a New Japan* that strong leadership was unnecessary in Japan. Political decisions required complete consensus, and there was extreme diffusion of political power at the national level. The policy-making system lacked coherence, while the governmental bureaucracy was relied upon to draft policy, so control was divided between the party in power and the bureaucracy. The Kantei was therefore inherently weak, Ozawa argues, with the prime minister being "nothing more than master of ceremonies for the ritual at hand."[12]

Prime Minister Ryutaro Hashimoto (1996–98) shared that viewpoint and was very concerned about the Kantei's weakness. One of his major reform goals was to strengthen the cabinet and the Kantei. He and his cabinet implemented wide-ranging administrative reform that culminated in a series of institutional changes in January 2001. Koizumi is the first prime minister to enjoy the fruits of Hashimoto's reform efforts in conducting his own diplomacy.

Although there is abundant academic literature on the role of the bureaucracy and the ruling party in foreign affairs, the role of the Kantei has been largely neglected.[13] The Kantei's direct involvement in foreign and defense affairs is a relatively recent phenomenon, although past prime ministers had not stayed out of the foreign-policy realm. While the statutory top officer of the Ministry of Foreign Affairs (MOFA) is the foreign minister, MOFA officials have always required the involvement of the prime minister and the CCS in major foreign policies. In fact, postwar prime ministers have often demonstrated leadership in foreign- and defense-policy making.

However, the Kantei did not have any real institutional mechanisms by which to support the national leader's agenda until July 1986, under the Nakasone administration, and its ability to provide major backing arose only after the 2001 Cabinet Secretariat reorganization. MOFA played the dominant role in traditional foreign- and defense-policy making, while the prime minister, acting as "the first foreign minister," made political decisions.

Without the institutional support of the Cabinet Secretariat, however, prime ministerial leadership in foreign affairs could not be described as "Kantei diplomacy." North Korean policy under the Koizumi cabinet, for example, is not classified as such since the Cabinet Secretariat as an organization was not involved in making policy. Instead, an initiative developed by a MOFA official guided the prime minister to make the historic visit to Pyongyang in September 2002.[14] In this book, "Kantei diplomacy" is defined as a phenomenon in which the Cabinet Secretariat offers institutional support as a core executive for political decisions and policy-making coordination that MOFA cannot provide.

Framework of Analysis

Many scholars have attempted to explore the role of national leaders in policy making. American presidents are among the most explored national leaders, and Richard Neustadt's *Presidential Power* (1960) is a classic study. Neustadt emphasizes the limitations of presidential power and identifies presidential power as "the power to persuade."[15] Graham Allison's *Essence of Decision* (1971) introduced the bureaucratic politics model that includes Neustadt's concept.[16] According to Neustadt and Allison, the president is an influential actor, but he is not a dominant figure in policy making. The large and powerful bureaucracies are the most important determinant of policy outcomes. Robert Art and Stephen Krasner criticize the bureaucratic politics model, pointing out that the president and his advisers matter a great deal, that there is a clear hierarchy in the process, and that presidents trump bureaucracies.[17]

Before Allison presented his model, Roger Hilsman introduced a government politics model in his book *To Move a Nation* (1967).[18] Hilsman portrays the policy process as a series of concentric circles, with the president and his staff as the innermost circle. Beyond this core are other departments and agencies of the executive branch. The "attentive public," which includes Congress, the press, and interest groups, exist outside these circles. It is assumed that actors in the inner circle have direct influence in the decision making, and those in the outside circles can influence policy outputs only indirectly. As Allison points out, Hilsman's model exhibits three characteristics: (1) "a diversity of goals and values that must be reconciled before a decision can be reached," (2) "the presence of competing clusters of people within the main group who are identified with each of the alternative goals and policies," and (3) "the relative power of these different groups of people included is as relevant to the final decision as the appeal of the goals they seek or the cogency and wisdom of their arguments." Policy making is portrayed as a process of "conflict and consensus building."[19]

As his original model did not put enough emphasis on the roles of Congress, interest groups, and the media, Hilsman introduced a revised model in 1987.[20] In the revised model, the president and presidential staff, politi-

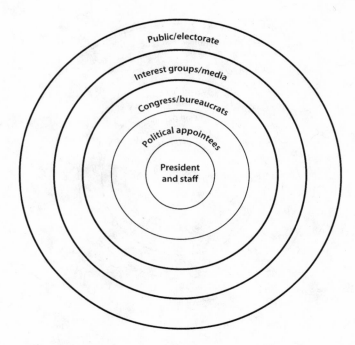

Fig. I.1 Hilsman's model, 1987

cal appointees, and the Congress and bureaucrats belong to "the inner ring of power," with different levels of influence. Interest groups and the media fall into the "second ring of power," while public opinion and the electorate are placed in "the outer ring of power" (see fig. I-1).

This revision changed Hilsman's model from its original government politics model to a more comprehensive political process model, with the president and his staff at the core of the process. It does not reflect the institutional arrangements that exist under the U.S. system but simply assumes that those in the innermost circle most directly influence policy making and those in the outer rings have less impact on policy outcomes. With some modifications, therefore, this model can be applied to any nation with a parliamentary system, including Japan.

In formulating Japan's foreign and national security policies, both MOFA and the prime minister traditionally played primary roles. To implement their policies, however, they had to acquire agreement from the ruling party, especially the LDP's policy subcommittees, and other governmental agencies.

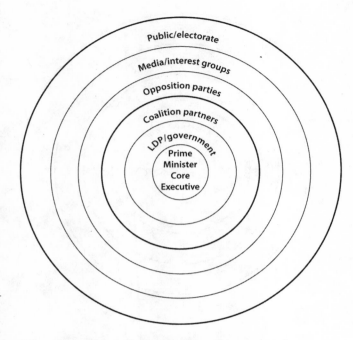

Fig. I.2 Hilsman's model applied to the Koizumi government

After the ruling party reached a consensus on the issue, the cabinet sought approval from coalition partners. When the cabinet officially decided on a policy, the policy was introduced in the Diet, where it faced scrutiny from the opposition parties. Throughout this policy process, the public observed and reacted to the policy, which affected the political process.

The reforms instituted under the Hashimoto administration (1996–98), however, gave the Cabinet Secretariat new authority to draft and plan policies (see chapter 3). The three examples of policy making presented in this book show that the Kantei has supplanted MOFA in formulating legislation. The political process model used in this book shows the innermost circle occupied by the Kantei, which consists of the prime minister and the Cabinet Secretariat as well as the top executives of the LDP who serve as the prime minister's agents vis-à-vis the LDP, coalition partners, and the opposition parties.[21]

The order of the rings, from the inside to the outside, corresponds to the traditional policy process, with those closest to the center involved in the earlier stages of policy making and those farther out more active during the latter stages. Just outside the core is a layer consisting of LDP members and the government. The Koizumi government was originally a coalition with Komeito (Clean Government Party) and the Conservative Party (later merged into the LDP), so the second ring includes these two coalition partners. The opposition parties occupy the third ring, interest groups and the media are in the fourth ring, and the public makes up the outermost ring.

This book does not widely cover the role of special interest groups and the media, both of which are included as elements of the "attentive public" in Hilsman's original model. Rather, the focus here is on the policy process within the government and the legislative branch. As Hilsman points out, the role of interest groups is much less important in foreign affairs than in domestic matters. Many economic interest groups participate in the politics of trade issues, for example. However, interest groups exert a minor influence in national security issues, the subject of this book. Hilsman notes that some ideological groups "seem to be involved in foreign policy issues only episodically and never very intensely."[22] Such ideologically oriented interest groups in Japan would be represented within the ruling and opposition parties. This book only refers to some outstanding activities in foreign and defense affairs on the part of business groups and labor unions.

In Japanese society, the mass media have considerable social power. As Ikuo Kabashima and Jeffrey Broadbent found when conducting their opinion survey of different political groups, such power can translate into political influence.[23] John C. Campbell notes that the Japanese media are influential because Japanese decision makers "take press attention as a surrogate for public opinion."[24] However, it would be difficult to identify the media's impact on certain policy outcomes. This book, therefore, covers the most traceable opinions expressed in the editorials of Japan's five major newspapers: *Asahi, Mainichi, Nihon Keizai, Sankei,* and *Yomiuri.*

Goal and Structure of This Book

This book examines the role the Kantei plays, or should play, in Japan's foreign- and defense-policy making and demonstrates that the Kantei has become Japan's new policy center in defense and foreign affairs. Chapter 1 looks at the earlier stage of the Kantei's involvement in foreign-policy making between the Nakasone and Kaifu administrations. It explains how Prime

Minister Yasuhiro Nakasone tried to exercise stronger political leadership as the "president-like" prime minister and to develop his own style of diplomacy independent of MOFA. Under the Nakasone cabinet, the new Cabinet Office on External Affairs was established in the Kantei, with the intent that it would provide support for the prime minister. The chapter also explores the Kantei's role in trade negotiations with the United States under the Takeshita and Kaifu cabinets.

Chapter 2 shifts focus and examines the Kaifu cabinet's reaction to the 1990–91 Gulf crisis. The Japanese government's inadequate responses drew international criticism, creating a trauma within the Japanese government and leading to a consensus that the Kantei should be strengthened for international emergencies.

Chapter 3 analyzes how Hashimoto's administrative reform elevated the Kantei's status within the Japanese government. It examines the increasing power of the CCS and the administrative deputy CCS, who fulfill a crucial function in linking the prime minister and the bureaucracy, as well as the Kantei's new organization and strengthened statutory authority to initiate policies. Augmented in this manner, the Kantei helped establish the Koizumi cabinet's top-down style of policy making, generating several major pieces of legislation.

Chapters 4–6 present examples of how the new system has been operating on a practical policy level in national security affairs. Chapter 4 analyzes the policy process for the first of three major pieces of legislation on national security that the Kantei initiated and prepared. It illustrates how the Kantei responded to the September 11 attacks and initiated the 2001 anti-terrorism legislation that enabled the government to send SDF units abroad in a period of armed conflict for the first time since World War II. Chapter 5 describes the process surrounding the first post–World War II attempt to pass new bills governing the nation's response to an external military attack. It explores the Kantei's role in the preparation of the emergency legislation, which used to be considered a political taboo. Chapter 6 deals with the 2003 Iraq legislation, which permitted the dispatch of SDF ground units to Iraq for active contribution to humanitarian and reconstruction activities. These examples highlight the Kantei's role in making national security policy.

Chapter 7 evaluates the phenomenon of top-down decision making in foreign and defense affairs. It reapplies the concentric circles model to the three examples studied in chapters 4–6. It then examines the merits and demerits of Kantei diplomacy by comparing it with the U.S. process, which has been marked by fierce battles between the White House and the State Department. Although there are some drawbacks similar to those found in American examples, such as the possibility of conflict between the Kantei and MOFA, the positives far outweigh the negatives.

There is limited information on what happens inside the Kantei, and the actual workings of the institution are kept very much out of sight. It is my hope that this book will shed light on Japan's new style of top-down decision making in foreign and defense affairs.

THE ROOTS OF KANTEI DIPLOMACY

Article 73 of Japan's Constitution provides the cabinet the authority to "manage foreign affairs." As head of the cabinet, the prime minister represents the nation internationally and attends annual summit meetings as Japan's chief diplomat. The ruling parties and the government recognize his authority to represent the nation, and these summit meetings often set the goals of national policies. Therefore, although the Ministry of Foreign Affairs (MOFA) has a minister, it requires the prime minister's agreement or involvement in decisions on major foreign policies. Given the national leader's deep involvement in diplomacy, MOFA was said to have two ministers: the prime minister as the first minister and the foreign minister as the second. As long as his foreign policy objectives do not conflict with domestic interests, the prime minister is given relative freedom in foreign affairs.

Although their degree of interest and involvement in foreign affairs has varied, all of Japan's postwar prime ministers have recognized their responsibilities in this area. When the political decision must be made to prioritize an international goal above domestic interests, the prime minister must take the lead. Former chief cabinet secretary (CCS) Masaharu Gotoda summarizes the prime minister's situation: "[The government] needs to make political decisions within the framework of the Constitution, considering external relations. Otherwise, [Japan] cannot survive this severe international society. Needless to say, such political decisions are made by the prime minister."[1]

Several prime ministers demonstrated leadership in the policy-making process. Among them are Shigeru Yoshida, who concluded the 1951 San Francisco Peace Treaty; Ichiro Hatoyama, who normalized Japan-Soviet relations in 1955; Nobusuke Kishi, with his revision of the U.S.-Japan security treaty in 1960; Eisaku Sato, who successfully negotiated the 1972 reversion of Okinawa; and Kakuei Tanaka, who normalized Japan-China relations in 1972.[2] These examples cannot be considered Kantei diplomacy, however, since the Kantei did not provide organizational support for foreign affairs.

Before 1998, the CCS and the parliamentary deputy CCS were the only other political figures, aside from the prime minister, at the Kantei (in 1998, the number of parliamentary deputies increased to two). These positions were reserved for members of the prime minister's faction who served as his personal assistants. The administrative deputy CCS functioned as a liaison between the Kantei and the entire bureaucracy. With only small offices to support him, his coordination capability was very limited. Furthermore, since the administrative deputy CCS was chosen from the domestically oriented ministries and agencies such as the Ministry of Home Affairs, the Ministry of Health and Welfare, and the National Police Agency, he was not familiar with foreign affairs. Therefore, MOFA provided the necessary logistical assistance. The national leader is often considered the government's "first foreign minister," so MOFA constantly required his involvement in its policy making.

In this book, the term "Kantei diplomacy" refers to the phenomenon in which the Cabinet Secretariat—as the core in the concentric circle model—

Table 1.1 Postwar Prime Ministers

	Term	Days in Office
Naruhiko Higashikuni	8/17/45–10/9/45	54
Kijuro Shidehara	10/9/45–5/22/46	226
Shigeru Yoshida	5/22/46–5/24/47	368
Tetsu Katayama	5/24/47–3/10/48	292
Hitoshi Ashida	3/10/48–10/19/48	220
Shigeru Yoshida	10/19/48–12/10/54	2,248
Ichiro Hatoyama	12/10/54–12/23/56	745
Tanzan Ishibashi	12/23/56–2/25/57	65
Nobusuke Kishi	2/25/57–7/19/60	1,241
Hayato Ikeda	7/19/60–11/9/64	1,575
Eisaku Sato	11/9/64–7/7/72	2,798
Kakuei Tanaka	7/7/72–12/9/74	886
Takeo Miki	12/9/74–12/24/76	747
Takeo Fukuda	12/24/76–12/7/78	714
Masayoshi Ohira	12/7/78–6/12/80*	576
Zenko Suzuki	7/17/80–11/27/82	864
Yasuhiro Nakasone	11/27/82–11/6/87	1,806
Noboru Takeshita	11/6/87–6/2/89	576
Sosuke Uno	6/2/89–8/8/89	69
Toshiki Kaifu	8/8/89–11/5/91	818
Kiichi Miyazawa	11/5/91–8/6/93	644
Morihiro Hosokawa	8/6/93–4/28/94	265
Tsutomu Hata	4/28/94–6/29/94	63
Tomiichi Murayama	6/29/94–1/11/96	561
Ryutaro Hashimoto	1/11/96–7/30/98	932
Keizo Obuchi	7/30/98–4/5/2000	616
Yoshiro Mori	4/5/2000–4/26/01	387
Junichiro Koizumi	4/26/01–9/26/06	1,980
Shinzo Abe	9/26/06–	

*After Ohira's death, Masayoshi Ito served as acting prime minister for thirty-five days.

proactively supports the prime minister in making political decisions and carries out policy coordination that MOFA is unequipped to handle. Kantei diplomacy started under the Nakasone administration, which reorganized the secretariat in order to deliver institutional support in the foreign-policy arena. Before analyzing the roots of the Kantei's involvement in foreign affairs, let us look into the basic structure of the Japanese government and the traditional policy-making process.

The Structure and Tradition of the Government

Japan's Constitution embodies a British-style parliamentary system. The national parliament, the Diet, has the legislative power and is composed of two houses, the House of Representatives (the lower house, with 480 members) and the House of Councillors (the upper house, with 242 members); members of both houses are publicly chosen in nationwide elections. The Diet also selects the prime minister from among its members. When the prime minister forms the cabinet, he must choose at least half of his cabinet ministers (up to seventeen after 2001) from among Diet members. The cabinet has the executive power to run the government and is collectively responsible to the Diet for its executive operations. While the lower house can remove the prime minister and his cabinet by a vote of no-confidence, the national leader also can dissolve the lower house when he wishes.

In order to run the government, the cabinet delegates its executive authority to ministries and agencies. After the 2001 central government reorganization, Japan has the Cabinet Office and ten ministries. The National Public Safety Commission and the Defense Agency are headed by cabinet ministers but are under the Cabinet Office.

Each ministry is staffed by a group of highly competent elite bureaucrats. The majority are graduates of top national universities—most are from the Universities of Tokyo and Kyoto—and have passed a highly competitive civil service entrance examination. Although there are occasional interagency personnel exchange programs, the career patterns of the bureaucrats are dominated by service in a single ministry.[3] In the postwar era, each individual ministry has created its jurisdiction and become empowered through various laws.

Although ministries are technically subordinate to the cabinet, bureau-

Table 1.2 Ministries of the Central Government

Cabinet Office
    National Public Safety Commission
    Defense Agency
Ministry of Internal Affairs and Communications
Ministry of Justice
Ministry of Foreign Affairs
Ministry of Finance
Ministry of Education, Culture, Sports, Science, and Technology
Ministry of Health, Labor, and Welfare
Ministry of Agriculture, Forestry, and Fisheries
Ministry of Economy, Trade, and Industry
Ministry of Land, Infrastructure, and Transport
Ministry of the Environment

crats are responsible only to their ministers. Because Japan's longtime ruling party, the Liberal Democratic Party (LDP), reshuffled the cabinet almost once a year before the Koizumi administration, an individual serving as minister generally had little time to accumulate the experience and knowledge necessary to become influential in actual decision making within his ministry.

A top civil service official, the administrative vice minister, is in charge of coordinating the activities of the various branches of the ministry, preparing ministerial decisions, and supervising their implementation, just like the British Permanent Secretary. Although the minister holds appointive authority, the appointments of the vice minister as well as other positions were almost always decided within the bureaucracy, with the minister rubber-stamping the decision.[4] During his short tenure, the minister more often than not represents the interests of the ministry vis-à-vis the cabinet and the ruling party. As minister, an elected legislator has an excellent opportunity to build personal relations with the bureaucracy and related industries. Unlike in France, the minister in Japan does not have elite bureaucrats who serve as his private advisers and watchdogs. In order to gain trust and administrative assistance from elite bureaucrats, the minister is often expected to be loyal to his ministry, which makes it difficult for the prime minister to coordinate conflicting interests in the cabinet.

As a result, Japan's policy-making system has for long been decentralized, bottom-up style.

Traditional Bottom-up Policy Process

In traditional decision making within the Japanese government, each section of the bureaucracy worked for its own interests and the industry sectors it oversaw administratively. Since the prime minister's authority to initiate policy was not clearly defined, the national leader rarely initiated policies or championed them through the approval process. When the prime minister did provide policy direction, he usually instructed the related cabinet minister. The minister in turn gave instructions to his vice minister, the bureau chief, and the director of the related section. If an officer in the chain of command sabotaged the measure, however, the policy did not survive.

In the traditional bottom-up policy process, the main working-level officers are deputy directors (*kacho hosa*) and in their late thirties to early forties.[5] Their original proposals are discussed within the section. A proposal accepted at that level is brought to a working-level meeting with other sections within the same bureau. If the other sections approve the proposal, it is finalized as a bureau decision with the approval of all the bureau's directors. Before the decision is made, however, the officers in charge are expected to have coordinated with officials in other ministry bureaus and related ministries as well as completed legal and budget examination through the ministry secretariat.

Former administrative deputy CCS Nobuo Ishihara states, "The bureau meetings are the actual decision-making organ within the bureaucracy."[6] Of course there are official meetings at higher levels: ministry meetings, administrative vice-ministerial meetings, and ultimately cabinet meetings. The decisions made at the cabinet meeting represent the end of a long, formal process within the government. However, the policy process steps taken after the bureau meeting are really nothing more than confirmation. "The bureau chief is expected to be able to finalize the policy. If he cannot, he is no longer qualified for his position," explains Ishihara.[7]

The bottom-up policy process also existed within the ruling party. The LDP's Policy Research Council had seventeen subcommittees (the number was reduced to thirteen in 2001) and more than thirty research commissions. Traditionally, the subcommittees served as the first forum the government

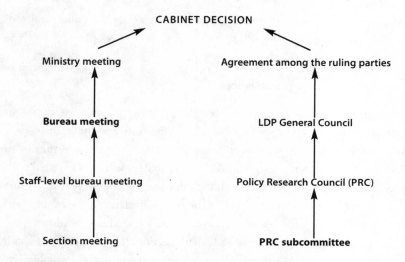

Fig. 1.1 Traditional Bottom-up Policy Process

consulted on its proposals. Members of these subcommittees earning the *zoku* (policy tribe) label—such as construction *zoku* and agricultural *zoku*—were the ultimate arbiters of political power on a specific issue and were instrumental in policy making. They examined the government's policies and often amended them. According to Ishihara, the subcommittees dominated policy making within the ruling party: "Since the LDP controlled the government for a long time after the war, an approval at the subcommittee level was virtually the same to the bureaucrats as a de facto approval in the Diet."[8] It was the typical bottom-up, decentralized policy process.

Once the subcommittee approved a policy, it was brought to the full Policy Research Council and finally to the LDP General Council, where the decision had to be unanimous. The coalition government requires agreement from the coalition partners. But when the LDP was stable and in charge, Ishihara testifies, "We only needed to seek approval from the powerful figures within the subcommittees and the party. The deliberation at the Diet was close to a ceremony."[9]

Aurelia George Mulgan describes such a bottom-up process as the "Un-Westminster" system. In Westminster systems, the "cabinet under the prime minister conducts substantive policy debate and takes charge of policy-making. Ministers both collectively in cabinet and individually as heads of ministries are the source and authority of all major government policies."[10] Ruling party members outside the government have little direct influence on the policy making. In contrast, in Mulgan's view, the Japanese bureaucracy has "formidable control over the function of policy advice, initiation, formulation and implementation. . . . The ruling party, not the executive, is the only political institution with sufficient power to bargain and negotiate with bureaucrats." In Japan's Un-Westminster system, the role of the prime minister and his cabinet is very limited.

Nakasone's Ambition to Promote Top-down Decision Making

When Prime Minister Yasuhiro Nakasone took office in 1982, his stated aim was to change this bottom-up policy process and become a "president-style prime minister." He believed postwar Japanese prime ministers had more potential power than their British counterparts but less than American presidents. The prewar Meiji constitution limited the prime minister's control over the cabinet, as its Article 55 instructed each minister to directly advise the emperor, who held all governing authority, including executive power. The postwar constitution, however, recognized the prime minister as head of the cabinet, which is vested with all executive powers. In addition, he has appointive power over cabinet members and Supreme Court judges and control of the Self-Defense Forces (SDF). However, Nakasone argued that his predecessors had not taken advantage of their greater statutory authority because "they could not get out of the prewar passivity." He also felt that bureaucrats had weakened the national leader because "they do not like a leader who would disturb the existing harmony while they try hard to protect their ministerial interests in turf battles [within the government]."[11]

As Nakasone indicates, leaders who emphasized consensus building were preferred in Japan's postwar politics. The status quo was bolstered by legal arrangements such as Article 6 of the Cabinet Law, which denies the prime minister executive power independent of what the cabinet approves. He can direct the ministries only when backed by a unanimous cabinet decision, forcing him to build a consensus among different groups within the ruling parties and the government so as to ensure cabinet approval.

This mechanism has proved unwieldy and problematic, especially in major emergencies. During the Hashimoto administration's reform efforts in 1996–98, the Administrative Reform Council—which functioned as an advisory organ to the prime minister—suggested revising the law to allow the prime minister to act more independently of the cabinet. The council proposed that the cabinet pre-authorize the prime minister to act in emergencies. It also recommended a more flexible interpretation of the Cabinet Law in peacetime and urged the government to continue studying the issue. The Cabinet Legislation Bureau strongly opposed the revisions, however, stating that the collective responsibility described in Article 66 of the constitution did not allow such independent actions.[12]

Since cabinet decisions require unanimous consent, each cabinet member holds de facto veto power on any issue, as do the ministries through their ministers. As a result, the Japanese government's decision making traditionally followed a bottom-up style, which requires consensus building.

Nakasone wanted to establish true political control over the bureaucracy-led government by "exercising top-down style leadership in governing as a president-like national leader by avoiding the traditional way of the prime minister influenced by the old customs under the prewar constitution."[13] He promoted top-down policy making through the following political strategies: (1) creating power centers to counter the political parties and the bureaucracy by establishing many official and unofficial advisory councils, consisting mainly of civilians, to stimulate public opinion and obtain popular support; (2) emphasizing international cooperation by regularly appointing powerful political figures as the ministers of MOFA, the Ministry of Finance (MOF), the Ministry of International Trade and Industry (MITI), and the Japan Defense Agency (JDA); and (3) strengthening the Kantei by appointing more competent staff.[14]

Nakasone and Koizumi both used the first strategy mentioned, and for similar reasons. Neither had held a senior cabinet position, such as foreign or finance minister, which was commonly viewed as a crucial step to becoming the nation's leader. In addition, their ties with the bureaucracy were limited, and their power bases within both the government and the LDP were weak, making public support a key political resource. Nakasone established the second Ad Hoc Commission for Administrative Reform in order to gain popular support for his move to privatize the national railways.[15] Koizumi, in turn, used the newly established Council on Economic and Fiscal Policy to promote domestic reform.

Nakasone aggressively pursued the second strategy of appointing powerful figures to important cabinet posts. He named Shintaro Abe as foreign minister and Noboru Takeshita as finance minister for the unusually long period of four years, and Yuko Kurihara and Koichi Kato served as defense agency director general for two years each. Abe became a power as the head of MOFA and promoted his own brand of diplomacy, often termed "Abe diplomacy." As Nakasone observed, "I saw that my successor would be either Mr. Takeshita or Mr. Abe. Appointing them to important cabinet positions for long periods had the purpose of educating the next leader."[16]

The first strategic attempt at strengthening the Kantei itself was Nakasone's surprise appointment of Masaharu Gotoda, a former administrative deputy CCS and Tanaka faction member, as CCS. The CCS post was usually reserved for a member of the prime minister's own faction. But Nakasone, with his limited bureaucratic experience, needed Gotoda's skill and experience in controlling the bureaucracy as he pursued administrative reform. A former MOF official who served Nakasone and Gotoda as cabinet councillor for domestic affairs describes their relationship:

I think Mr. Nakasone and Mr. Gotoda were the best combination of prime minister and chief cabinet secretary in postwar political history. Mr. Nakasone presented policy ideas and Mr. Gotoda followed up on them using his administrative skills. Mr. Gotoda himself used to be a senior bureaucrat and was well aware of the bureaucratic system and its limitations. Mr. Gotoda's knowledge, experience, and control over the bureaucracy more than supplemented Mr. Nakasone's shortcomings.[17]

Nakasone also ordered the ministries to send more senior officials to serve as his personal secretaries. He told them he would not take anyone who was not capable and directed them to choose senior directors whom they regarded as future ministry leaders. MOF, MOFA, MITI, and the National Police Agency (NPA) each sent one administrative secretary. The ministries usually selected these individuals from among officers at the *kacho* (division director) level. Nakasone instructed former deputy CCS Hiromori Kawashima to select the candidates from the ministries and the agency, and Nakasone then made the final picks himself.[18] Nakasone had high expectations for his new staff: "You are important assistants to me as well as secretaries," he told them, "I am an aggressive person who makes many mistakes. I expect you to give warning and suggest anything to me."[19]

Other prime ministers had selected their own secretaries; Kakuei Tanaka, for one, brought in an official who had served as his secretary while he was MITI minister to advise him on trade and industrial issues. By handpicking all his secretaries, however, Nakasone broke with tradition and showed how determined he was to strengthen his office.

"Handcrafted Diplomacy"

Nakasone wanted to use his staff to develop what he called "handcrafted diplomacy," or *tezukuri gaiko*, rather than follow the scenarios MOFA prepared. One demonstration of his strategy is the resolution of a dispute he inherited from his predecessor, Zenko Suzuki, involving South Korea. The dispute was sparked by Japanese-history textbooks that described Japanese military actions in the 1930s as "the advancement" instead of "the invasion." Japan's economic assistance to Korea had somehow become entangled with this emotionally charged issue. Nakasone saw improvement of relations between the two countries as his top diplomatic priority. At his first cabinet meeting on November 30, 1982, he told his foreign minister, finance minister, and CCS, "I'd like to start by bettering relations with South Korea."[20] He made the country his first overseas destination.

Rather than turn to the usual MOFA contacts, Nakasone opened up his own diplomatic channel, persuading his friend, Itochu Corporation chairman Ryuzo Sejima, to go on a secret mission to South Korea. Sejima, who served on Nakasone's advisory council for administrative reform, had been a top aide on the wartime general staff, so he knew many influential Korean figures who had attended military academies in Japan. He had traveled frequently to Seoul to give talks on Japanese politics. Moreover, he had advised former Korean president Park Chung Hee, his junior at the academy, and knew Korean president Chun Doo Hwan.[21]

Nakasone said of the mission:

Upon assuming office in November 1982, I made a phone call
to President Chun and told him of my determination to improve
our relations with South Korea. President Chun told me that
he would cooperate with me. Judging from this conversation, I
felt that secret diplomacy would be a better way. Furthermore,
I planned to visit the United States in January. Going through

normal diplomatic channels would not solve the economic assistance issue by then.[22]

Sejima visited Seoul several times to negotiate with a close associate of President Chun's. According to Sejima, his mission was so top-secret that only six high officials were involved in addition to the prime minister and CCS: MOFA's minister, vice minister, and Asian bureau chief and MOF's minister, vice minister, and international finance bureau chief.[23] Nakasone's secret diplomacy proved a great success: Chun subsequently agreed on the amount of economic aid.[24] On January 5, 1983, Nakasone surprised the media by announcing that in six days he would be the first postwar Japanese prime minister to visit South Korea. The media still did not know about the secret negotiations that had resolved the issue.

When Nakasone arrived in Seoul, however, the Korean people gave him a cold reception. As Nakasone's secretary described it: "When the Japanese mission drove into the city, there were Korean people along the road in cold weather watching us without expression. There were no smiles or applause."[25]

Nakasone met twice with Chun to discuss a variety of global issues, and the two leaders got to know each other. He gave a speech at a state dinner reception Chun hosted, demonstrating his Korean-language skills for a total of five minutes at the start and the end of his presentation. Attendees at the reception and those who listened to a television broadcast were very impressed by Nakasone's speech. In contrast to the unenthusiastic greeting Nakasone and his mission received on their arrival, many Koreans came out to the street to wave as the group was leaving for the airport. Nakasone felt that "the ice that had separated the people of the two countries had suddenly melted."[26]

Nakasone enjoyed a close relationship with President Chun after this historic visit and has said that the secret diplomacy helped establish "comradeship with President Chun."[27] This experience made Nakasone realize that "trust and friendship between the two nations depend largely on personal friendship and trust between the top leaders."[28]

"Ron-Yasu" Relationship

The most famous example of Nakasone's diplomatic style, however, is his close relationship with U.S. president Ronald Reagan. His successful visit to

Seoul had pleased the Reagan administration, which wanted to establish a stronger alliance in East Asia to help the United States confront the Soviet Union. The U.S. government had been asking Tokyo for a 7 percent increase in Japanese defense spending to confront Soviet military expansionism in the Far East. In December 1982, Nakasone instructed Finance Minister Noboru Takeshita to expand defense spending.

Citing the stringent budget policy imposed by administrative reform efforts, MOF budget bureau chief Mitsuhide Yamaguchi offered only a 5.1 percent increase. Nakasone pushed hard for a 6.5 percent expansion, but Yamaguchi refused, arguing that "the budget was a result of negotiations with all the ministries." Nakasone told Yamaguchi, "The budget must be made by the cabinet. Consult with Finance Minister Takeshita." As Nakasone proudly relates, "I heard that Mr. Takeshita told Yamaguchi, 'The prime minister is stubborn, we have to follow his instructions.'"[29] The defense budget was eventually increased by 6.5 percent in late December 1982.

Nakasone prepared other "gifts" for his first visit to Washington, D.C., opening the market for American chocolates and cigarettes and allowing military technology transfers to the United States (the latter is described in detail below). Nakasone explained his thinking at the time: "I wanted to impress on President Reagan that the new Japanese prime minister is different from the past ones. To do that, I could not visit Washington with empty hands. I had to show my achievements."[30]

His efforts to improve U.S.-Japan relations did help Nakasone establish a personal and more equable relationship with the American president. Nathaniel Thayer, a scholar and longtime friend of Nakasone, describes the first Nakasone-Reagan meeting:

Nakasone met President Ronald Reagan at 11:25 A.M. [on January 18, 1983] in the Oval Office. No aides attended. President Reagan took from his pocket three-by-five cards. "I want to talk about beef and oranges," he is remembered as saying. Japan was blocking the import of these agricultural products. "Let's leave that discussion to the experts," replied Nakasone, "I wish to talk about global issues." Reagan again said that he wanted to talk about beef and oranges. Nakasone repeated that he preferred to address global issues. Reagan repocketed his cards, and the two men talked about global issues.[31]

Meanwhile, Nakasone's personal assistant from MOFA, Kazutoshi Hasegawa, suggested to Gaston Sigur, a senior adviser at the National Security Council, that the two leaders should have a less formal relationship. At the White House breakfast the next day, Reagan suggested to Nakasone that they call each other by their first names.[32] As a result, their partnership was often described as the "Ron-Yasu" relationship.

The partnership proved to be a potent one at the May 1983 summit in Williamsburg, Virginia. President Reagan was trying to persuade European leaders to agree to the deployment of Pershing II missiles with thermonuclear warheads in Western Europe in order to deter the Soviets' SS-20 nuclear threat. Nakasone's active support for Reagan's proposal helped build a consensus, which Nakasone calls his greatest diplomatic achievement:

> Since it was the height of the Cold War, it was important for the Western nations to be united against the Soviet nuclear deployment. But President François Mitterrand was a very independent person, and opposed Mr. Reagan's proposal to issue a joint statement that included their unified intention on U.S. missile deployment in Europe. I said to the French president, "Japan had never voiced an opinion on security affairs at the summit because we have the peace constitution. But we cannot separate security issues between Europe and Asia. When I get back to Japan, I will be attacked from everywhere for this statement. However, I would like to take the risk. If our nations are not united, it would only benefit the Soviet Union. Please understand my position and true feeling." President Mitterrand could not say a word. At that time, President Reagan announced he would make a political statement along my argument.[33]

As a result of Nakasone's comment, the political statement at the Williamsburg Summit specifically mentioned the missile deployment: "Our nations express the strong wish that a balanced INF [Intermediate-range Nuclear Forces] agreement be reached shortly. . . . It is well known that should this not occur, the countries concerned will proceed with the planned deployment of the U.S. systems in Europe at the end of 1983."[34] According to Nakasone, "President Reagan was so grateful for my statement that he sent Secretary of State George Schultz to thank me the following morning."[35] Nakasone's achievement at the summit was widely reported by the Japanese media. In a *Mainichi Shimbun* opinion poll taken immediately after the summit, the cabinet's approval rating jumped from 34 to 40 percent.[36]

The Influential CCS Masaharu Gotoda

Under the Nakasone administration, the Kantei also became a true player in the foreign-policy-making game. CCS Masaharu Gotoda, for example, showed his negotiation skills in the revision of three arms export measures. Since 1980, the U.S. government had repeatedly asked Japan to share its military technology. Prime Minister Zenko Suzuki, however, could not act on the request because of intense opposition within the government. This opposition was based on the three principles of 1967 prohibiting the export of arms and military-related technology to countries that could be involved in an international conflict or to communist countries.

Soon after Nakasone succeeded Suzuki, he instructed CCS Gotoda to persuade the opposition of the need to share this technology with the United States. Gotoda suggested to the new MITI minister, Sadanori Yamanaka, that Japan could export military technology to the United States within the framework of the 1960 U.S.-Japan Mutual Defense Assistance Agreement. Yamanaka, responsible for protecting domestic technology, agreed to Gotoda's idea, which would permit the transfer to the United States alone. At a cabinet meeting on January 14, 1982, Nakasone made an official exception to the arms export principles, thus allowing the transfer of Japan's technology to the United States.[37]

CCS Gotoda did not always follow Prime Minister Nakasone's instructions, however. He remarked without hesitation, "I would oppose any plan of the prime minister's if it went against national interests."[38] Gotoda blocked Nakasone's 1987 plan to send SDF minesweepers to the Persian Gulf to support U.S. Navy vessels guarding Kuwaiti oil tankers. He opposed the idea because it would involve Japan in the ongoing Iran-Iraq war.[39] He told Nakasone he would not sign a cabinet decision if it were presented. Nakasone would not be able to proceed with the plan unless he dismissed Gotoda—a radical step the prime minister was not prepared to take. Nakasone dropped the plan.[40]

Five Cabinet Offices Introduced by Gotoda

Gotoda's unparalleled administrative skills empowered the Kantei. Atsuyuki Sassa, his assistant for crisis management, recalled Gotoda's actions following the September 1983 downing of Korean Air Flight 007 over Sakhalin: "Without any assistant but his own secretaries, he managed to coordinate with related ministries, handled diplomatic matters with the United States, the Soviet Union, and South Korea, and dealt with the mass media and Diet operations."[41]

Gotoda's long experience as a bureaucrat, including service as deputy CCS in the Tanaka administration, had made him an expert at handling crises. Poor information exchange between the ministries and the JDA hampered him, however, leading Gotoda to wonder whether future CCSs would be equipped to do the same. As a result, he "strongly felt the need to establish an organ within the cabinet to handle crisis management."[42]

Gotoda's original plan was to create five vice-ministerial posts that would assist the CCS on domestic affairs, foreign affairs, national security, intelligence, and public affairs, respectively. With experienced, high-level assistants, the CCS would play a central role in managing crises. The old Cabinet Law, however, gave the Kantei only the authority of "passive" policy coordination—a ministry had to specifically request the Kantei's involvement. In a bid to further strengthen the Kantei, Gotoda sought the authority to initiate and assign policy.[43] Virtually all the ministries and agencies opposed this idea, the most vehement being MOFA and the JDA. The JDA vice minister openly stated that he would take the unusual step of vetoing the proposal at the sub-cabinet meeting.[44]

Forced to withdraw his original plan, Gotoda proposed creating three policy offices within the Kantei: the Cabinet Office on Internal Affairs (headed by a MOF official), the Cabinet Office on External Affairs (headed by a MOFA official), and the Cabinet Office on Security Affairs (headed by a JDA official). In addition, he gave the public relations section in the Prime Minister's Office a new name, the Cabinet Public Relations Office (headed by an NPA official), and reorganized it to work closely with the prime minister and the CCS. The Cabinet Research Office became the Cabinet Information and Research Office (headed by an NPA official), and its analytical functions were enhanced.

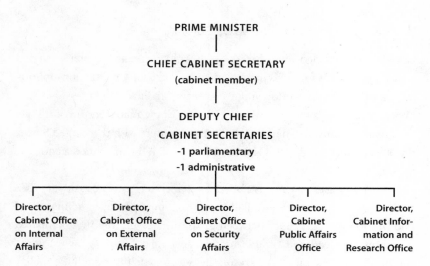

Fig. 1.2 The Five-Office System, 1986–2000

When Gotoda established this system, he instructed the five directors to think of national interests first. One of the directors, Junzo Matoba, recalled:

> Kantei officials were instructed to change their basic disposition
> once they entered their new office. In the case of the Nakasone
> cabinet, the prime minister and CCS Gotoda specifically told us
> that we should work for the cabinet, not for our home ministries.
> I think all five directors did work for the national interest. When
> we had to push hard on other ministries, we could not be soft on
> our home ministries. I had to be harder on MOF, where I was from,
> than on other ministries. If I had worked to save my home ministry,
> I would not have been as effective.[45]

At first, Nakasone was not very supportive of Gotoda's proposal. He remarked, "If the prime minister was powerful, I believed, it was not necessary to create a supporting organization within the cabinet."[46] But Nakasone did back the idea of strengthening the Kantei to handle national security and crisis management issues. Once the five-office system was set, Nakasone instructed Gotoda to bring in the best people that could be found and advised that "the directors of the five offices need to be strong candidates for vice-minister postings."[47]

Nakasone took full advantage of the new officers. The first director of the Cabinet Public Relations Office, Raisuke Miyawaki, explained that Nakasone always asked to meet him on a one-on-one basis. "The prime minister is shielded from raw information; what he receives is filtered by the bureaucracy. My role was to provide the raw information, and then to make impartial recommendations independent of the interests of the ministry."[48]

The first director of the Cabinet Office on External Affairs, Michihiko Kunihiro, was also asked to meet Nakasone privately. "I talked with the prime minister for thirty minutes every week," Kunihiro stated. "I never told anyone what I talked to him about."[49] Nakasone explained why he asked to meet the directors alone: "I listened to Miyawaki and Kunihiro as individuals. I never trusted the information the bureaucracy brought me."[50] The directors were invaluable to Nakasone as windows on the realities of Japanese society.

The five directors felt they directly served the prime minister and the CCS. Kunihiro explained, "Of course, we directors were under the administrative deputy CCS in the cabinet organizational chart. But the two deputy CCSs under whom I served, Shoichi Fujimori and Nobuo Ishihara, did not act as our bosses. I reported to them the same information I provided to the prime minister and the CCS. Often they helped me, but they never tried to control us."[51] (After Hashimoto's administrative reforms, however, the three cabinet offices were abolished; their directors were made assistant CCSs and placed under the deputy CCS.)

The ministries, though, were not supportive of the new cabinet offices. The Cabinet Security Affairs Office got a particularly cold welcome from the JDA, the National Land Agency, the Fire and Disaster Agency, which dealt with natural and other disasters, and the National Police Agency, which handled criminal activities such as hijackings. During the Diet's deliberations, the opposition parties strongly criticized establishment of the Security Affairs Office, saying it represented centralization of the government in case of emergency. Nakasone and Gotoda had both served in the prewar Home Ministry, and they were accused of reviving the powerful old ministry that had controlled a wide range of citizens' lives.[52]

Asked in the Diet about what the Security Affairs Office would oversee, Gotoda said it would "manage major emergencies that threaten national security." He gave four examples: (1) hijackings, (2) incidents similar to the 1986 MiG-25 exile case, (3) special international emergencies like the downing of Korean Air Flight 007, and (4) major earthquakes. Rather than treating these as examples, the opposition parties and the ministries interpreted Gotoda's statement literally, effectively limiting the office's scope of operations. Furthermore, the National Land Agency strenuously objected to letting the new office handle major earthquakes, so that portfolio was taken away. The first director of Security Affairs, Atsuyuki Sassa, said these conditions crippled his office and rendered it ineffective in later emergencies such as the Great Hanshin Earthquake of January 1995 and the sarin gas attack perpetrated by the Aum Shinrikyo cult in March 1995.[53]

MOFA was concerned that the new Cabinet Office on External Affairs might serve as a back channel for diplomacy. As a result, the cabinet office was limited to dealing with issues related to economic friction. Its first director, Kunihiro, said, "MOFA officials wanted to handle political and security affairs between themselves and the prime minister or the CCS. Since jurisdiction over economic matters goes beyond MOFA, it was considered appropriate for the cabinet office to handle them."[54]

There were five *kacho*-level officers seconded from MOFA and four economic ministries—MITI, MOF, the Ministry of Agriculture, Forestry, and Fisheries, and the Economic Planning Agency—handling trade issues in the office. "While those officers were expected to assist me, their home ministries often told them to persuade us to act in their favor. They had a very difficult time between the office and their ministries," Kunihiro recalled.[55]

The main function of the office was to coordinate domestic policies among different ministries rather than to handle negotiations with foreign governments. "In the policy-making process, we were often in the middle of conflicting interests," Kunihiro stated. "Not necessarily likable positions. The related ministries were not always cooperative." When they were unwilling to cooperate, Kunihiro often took advantage of the "lion's skin" of CCS Gotoda. "Sometimes I told ministry representatives that they needed to see Mr. Gotoda to explain directly to him. This was a very effective threat. Using this tactic, we were able to solve many issues without actually going to see Mr. Gotoda."[56]

Since the Cabinet Office on External Affairs was also part of the Prime Minister's Office (PMO), or *sorifu*, its staff engaged mostly in PMO-related tasks, such as payments to Taiwanese who had served in the Japanese army. Kunihiro often worked alone to carry out the prime minister's instructions. He saw the following as his three major functions: (1) gathering necessary information in foreign affairs for the prime minister, (2) offering the prime minister his situational assessments, and (3) following instructions from the prime minister or the CCS on coordinating with related ministries.[57] Although Gotoda's original scheme of establishing assistants to the CCS met with strong opposition, the directors of the cabinet offices actually functioned as Gotoda had envisioned, at least under the Nakasone cabinet.

The Takeshita Cabinet and Deputy CCS Ozawa

The Kantei expanded its role in foreign affairs under the Takeshita administration. When Noboru Takeshita became prime minister in 1987, a year after the five-office system was established, he appointed former minister of Home Affairs Ichiro Ozawa as deputy CCS. As Ozawa's negotiation and coordination skills and political influence strengthened the Kantei, the Cabinet Office on External Affairs and its director were directly involved in foreign affairs to support Ozawa.

However, the Takeshita administration's most important policy goal was not a foreign policy issue but a domestic one, the introduction of a new indirect tax. Nakasone had failed to introduce the sales tax, and he appointed Takeshita—a well-known political insider and experienced finance minister—as his successor to build on his efforts. Although Takeshita knew it was unusual to appoint a former cabinet member to deputy CCS, which is a sub-cabinet position, he needed the negotiation and coordination skills and experience in tax issues that Ozawa had acquired under the Nakasone administration.[58] During the final stage of Nakasone's push to establish the sales tax, the opposition parties agreed to establish a new committee to discuss tax reform if the sales tax proposal was withdrawn. Ozawa brokered this agreement as chairman of the lower house's Rules and Administration Committee. Takeshita recalled: "His negotiation skills were outstanding. . . . That was why I asked Mr. Ozawa to act behind the scenes."[59]

Ozawa's colleague, former administrative deputy CCS Nobuo Ishihara, observed: "Mr. Ichiro Ozawa was in charge of Diet operation regarding the tax reform. He was very active, and never stayed in his own office. In particular, he worked exhaustively on persuading the opposition parties."[60] Ozawa helped Takeshita successfully introduce the consumption tax.

With his negotiation and coordination skills, Ozawa also played a central role in foreign affairs at the Kantei.[61] Michihiko Kunihiro, who served as director of the Cabinet Office on External Affairs under Nakasone and

Takeshita, explained Ozawa's role: "Prime Minister Takeshita recognized the importance of the office as it was established by Mr. Nakasone, but he never gave me detailed instructions on foreign affairs. CCS Keizo Obuchi was very interested in foreign affairs, but he delegated the tasks to Mr. Ozawa."[62] According to Kunihiro, Deputy CCS Ishihara—who was later heavily involved in foreign affairs—stayed out of that area during Ozawa's tenure in the Kantei. "When Mr. Ozawa was the minister of Home Affairs, Mr. Ishihara was vice minister. I guess that Mr. Ishihara did not want to intervene in policy matters in which his former boss was involved."[63] As a result, Ozawa took the lead at the Kantei in dealing with issues related to U.S.-Japan economic friction. Negotiations on construction, the FSX aircraft, and telecommunications, described in the following pages, illustrate the Kantei's new role in foreign affairs.

U.S.-Japan Construction Negotiations

In spring 1985, U.S.-Japan trade issues hit the headlines in both countries. While economic disputes between the two usually focused on Japanese exports to the U.S. market, this time Americans were paying more attention to their lack of access to the Japanese market.

The construction sector is one high-profile example. In March 1986, U.S. construction companies wanting to bid on the new Kansai International Airport project ran into a catch-22 roadblock: A corporation had to be licensed in Japan and have considerable construction experience there to bid on public construction projects. Since U.S. corporations did not meet these conditions, they were effectively barred from the bidding, and the Japanese government rejected a U.S. request to soften these requirements. The issue was eventually brought to the September 1987 summit meeting between Prime Minister Nakasone and President Reagan, starting a long series of bilateral negotiations.

After the summit, the Japanese government offered to make the Kansai Airport project an exception to traditional bidding practices by treating companies' experience abroad as equivalent to experience in Japan. Although satisfied with the Kansai Airport deal, the U.S. government demanded the same treatment for other public works projects, such as the Tokyo Bay Bridge, the Tokyo Teleports, and Kansai Science City. The Americans further expanded their requests to include projects for public corporations, local governments, and the third sector (joint ventures between the private sector and local governments).

Initially, the Japanese government rejected the U.S. demands, arguing that the national government should not violate the principle of local autonomy by intervening in local government projects. It would also be reverse discrimination if foreign companies could apply their construction experience outside Japan, but Japanese corporations could not count their experience in other countries. Negotiations between Japanese and U.S. officials broke down.

The construction market issue was very complicated. The Japanese construction industry was a politically strong lobbying force, and major construction corporations had subsidiaries all over the nation. There was a great sense of unease in the government that market openings might weaken those corporations, creating social instability nationwide. There were complex procedural concerns as well. The director of MOFA's Second North America Division, who was in charge of the bilateral negotiations, recalled: "The Japanese government was asked to secure access for foreign enterprises while maintaining smooth execution of tens of thousands of public works projects within the fiscal year. It was a very delicate matter."[64]

Prime Minister Takeshita was planning a summit meeting with President Reagan in January 1988. He instructed Deputy CCS Ozawa to solve the problem by that time, making the Kantei central to Japan's policy making on the matter. Ozawa called a series of meetings with high officials from MOFA, the Ministry of Construction (MOC), and the Ministry of Transportation (MOT) to draft a Japanese counterproposal. Kunihiro, who assisted Ozawa on this, testified:

> The media often portrayed Mr. Ozawa as a forceful decision maker, but as far as I know, he never made decisions unilaterally or forcefully imposed them on others. He often discussed U.S.-Japan economic issues with me and came up with possible solutions. Once his plans were developed to be acceptable to the related ministries, he called upon high officials to consider them. After he acquired agreement from the ministries, he reported to the prime minister and the CCS. He conducted elaborate *nemawashi* [or log-rolling].[65]

Ozawa and his group came up with a plan to extend the special treatment in the Kansai Airport deal to other large-scale public works projects, such as the Tokyo Bay Bridge and the Nippon Telegraph and Telephone (NTT) headquarters building.[66] On November 4, 1987, the Japanese government proposed Ozawa's plan in a letter handed to Commerce Secretary William Verity by Ambassador Nobuo Matsunaga. However, Verity was not satisfied with the limited list of public works projects U.S. corporations could bid on. Later that month, Verity visited Japan to meet with Foreign Minister Sosuke Uno and Construction Minister Ihei Ochi to urge an early resolution of this issue.

Knowing that Takeshita wanted a solution in place by the January 1988 summit meeting in Washington, Kunihiro contacted his longtime friend Commerce Undersecretary Bruce Smart and visited Washington in mid-December. This was quite unusual, since the Cabinet Office on External Affairs traditionally handled domestic policy coordination, not negotiations with foreign governments. Kunihiro met with Smart as well as with Deputy Undersecretary of Commerce Michael Farren to explain the Takeshita cabinet's positions. In the unofficial meeting, Kunihiro proposed that U.S. construction corporations form a consortium with Japanese corporations and participate in bidding on the Japanese public works projects.

Kunihiro's efforts broke the deadlock. At the beginning of January, Farren and Deputy U.S. Trade Representative Michael Smith came to Japan to hold another unofficial meeting with Kunihiro. Afterward, Deputy CCS Ozawa met with the two American officials and gained a basic understanding of their proposal. Ozawa then reported to Prime Minister Takeshita and requested that he officially present the proposal to the U.S. government. The result: One day before the Reagan-Takeshita summit, Foreign Minister Uno and Secretary of State George Schultz agreed to restart construction negotiations.

Negotiations by government officials followed the summit, but Japanese and American negotiators clashed again. The latter could not accept the Japanese nomination bid system and insisted that the same treatment should apply to all public works projects. Many U.S. congressmen had a very negative view of the Japanese construction market. They pointed out that American companies earned construction contracts in Japan valued at just one-tenth of what Japanese companies earned in the United States. They believed that the imbalance was due to Japan's opaque bidding system. Pressured by Congress, the U.S. government threatened to invoke section 301 of the 1974 Trade Act to counter Japan's "unfair practices." The deadline was set at the end of March 1988, just three weeks away. This action moved the negotiations from the bureaucratic to the political level.

Kunihiro arrived in Washington on March 19 as the head of the Japanese negotiation team. Farren had left the government, so Deputy U.S. Trade Representative Smith became the chief U.S. negotiator. Smith asked Kunihiro if they could meet alone for the first session; Smith and Kunihiro met twice. A large group negotiation was set for March 23. On the following day, Ozawa came to Washington as a representative of the Japanese government. It was quite exceptional for a deputy CCS to lead diplomatic negotiations, since this role was usually taken by a cabinet minister from MOFA or another relevant ministry (in this case, MOC). Prime Minister Takeshita's choice of Ozawa indicates his high opinion of the latter's negotiation skills.

Since Ozawa's appointment might have caused legal problems, his meetings with American officials were regarded as unofficial. After the negotiations, Ozawa met with Commerce Secretary Verity and U.S. Trade Representative Clayton Yeutter. These meetings were arranged for political considerations. Ozawa, former minister of Home Affairs and current deputy CCS, was considered a cabinet-level officer. A cabinet-level officer should not visit Washington for the purpose of negotiating with a sub-cabinet-level officer. According to the official record, therefore, the purpose of Ozawa's trip was to make courtesy calls to Verity and Yeutter.

The selection of Deputy U.S. Trade Representative Smith as chief negotiator was also exceptional because the construction issue fell under the Commerce Department's jurisdiction, and the department's views often conflicted with those of the trade representative. A MOFA official commented, "This unusual appointment showed that the U.S. government had a strong determination to reach an agreement in this issue."[67]

But Ozawa showed firm determination of his own. He explained:

As a politician, I can show the bottom line. Bureaucrats often make gradual concessions, not because of their negotiation tactics but because of their worry of criticism against compromises. As a result, negotiations take time without any concrete outcome. In the end, bureaucrats often fall back on "external pressure" as an excuse to persuade domestic constituents. It was the way that the government handled negotiations. Instead, I wanted to guide my counterpart to understand my thinking. I was also willing to make concessions to the furthest extent possible. If my counterpart could not accept what I had to offer, I was ready to break off negotiations. That was how I approached the situation.[68]

Ozawa told his American counterpart that he had come to the session to reach an agreement and that he would not make a proposal if his counterpart was not willing to conclude the negotiations.[69]

This statement surprised Smith. According to an American observer, "Americans considered his [Ozawa's] no-nonsense manner a refreshing contrast to the conventional Japanese foot-dragging and indirectness."[70] Smith was widely known as a tough negotiator. Ozawa, however, did not yield and rejected some of Smith's counterproposals.[71] During the negotiations, a MOFA official observed that some kind of personal relationship was forming between Ozawa and Smith, and the two did finally reach an agreement.[72] The Japanese government maintained the nomination bidding system, but American corporations were allowed to participate in a wider variety of public works projects. According to Smith, "[Ozawa] just got to the heart of the matter. . . . The negotiations had gone on for two years, but he and I reached an agreement in eight hours."[73]

The bilateral construction negotiations are the first example of the Kantei playing a central role in easing major economic friction. Deputy CCS Ozawa showed strong administrative and negotiation skills, and the Cabinet Office on External Affairs provided him with very useful and timely support. Since the issue cut across the jurisdictions of the Ministries of Construction, Transportation, and Foreign Affairs, the Kantei was the best government institution to coordinate their different interests.

The FSX Negotiations

Since the early 1980s, there had been fierce competition between Japanese and U.S. manufacturers over procurement for the next generation of SDF fighter planes. Japanese manufacturers called for domestic production, while American aircraft makers were lobbying for joint development and utilization of existing U.S.-made fighter planes. The Reagan administration pressed the Japanese government hard on this issue. The Takeshita government eventually decided to use the American F-16 fighter as a basis for joint development. In November 1988, the two governments concluded a memorandum of understanding (MOU) stating that Japan would bear the entire cost of the joint development. The United States was to provide the F-16 technology, and U.S. manufacturers would be in charge of 40 percent of the total development budget.[74]

Unfortunately, things did not end there. Clyde Prestowitz, one of the so-called revisionists, argued in a *Washington Post* op-ed that giving aviation technology to Japan would later pose a commercial threat.[75] At his 1989 Senate confirmation hearing, future secretary of state James A. Baker III subsequently faced requests to review the MOU from hawkish senators such as Jesse Helms. Baker agreed to this request in order to gain confirmation. Separately, the Commerce Department also requested a review. Although this department was authorized to receive information on joint defense-development programs under the 1988 Department of Defense Appropriations Act, its officials had not received any information on the FSX project, and they were skeptical of the White House's commitment to putting priority on American commercial interests.[76]

The Defense Department was in charge of concluding the MOU and was in a position to support it. However, the department was in the midst of political turmoil. The candidate for Defense Secretary, Senator John Tower, had been rejected by the Senate, so no leader was in place to champion the FSX deal.

At the same time, new commerce secretary Robert Mosbacker called for reopening bilateral negotiations, with the agenda to include the establishment of technology transfer safeguards. On March 20, 1989, the National Security Council approved Mosbacker's request. The George H. W. Bush administration also wanted to strengthen intellectual property rights protection for computer software and to clarify the U.S. production share for the jet fighters. Three days later, JDA vice minister Seiki Nishihiro came to Washington to reopen negotiations. His meeting with Secretary Baker brought no agreement, however, nor did a subsequent meeting during Baker's April visit to Japan.

With the process deadlocked, Takeshita appointed Deputy CCS Ozawa as chief negotiator. In the words of Noboru Hojuyama, former director of the Defense Facilities Administration Agency, Ozawa took over "the issue that nobody wanted to deal with."[77]

After holding meetings with related officials in the Japanese government, Ozawa flew to Washington at the end of April to meet with Secretary Baker.

He followed the same bottom-line strategy he had used in the construction deal, and an agreement was soon reached. The United States would be in charge of 40 percent of production, and some technology—such as computer software for aviation control—would be excluded from the U.S. technology transfer package. In return, Japan would provide the United States with technology it developed during the project. Many in the U.S. government knew very well that Ozawa was offering the best compromise and were happy with the clarified MOU. Congress felt differently, however, and the Senate passed a resolution demanding that the government renegotiate more favorable conditions. President Bush vetoed this resolution, and his veto was supported by a one-vote margin, sustaining the negotiated MOU.

Telecommunications Negotiations

In the mid-1980s, Motorola, Inc., a major American manufacturer of cell phones, was eager to enter the Japanese market. Japan followed the technical standard created by NTT, but Motorola was unwilling to modify its products to meet the NTT standard. Motorola lobbied the U.S. government to pressure Japan into accepting Motorola's standard.

The telecommunications negotiations began in 1985 with this car cell phone issue at the Market-Oriented Sector-Specific (MOSS) talks. As a result of the talks, Motorola was granted market access with the significant exception of the Tokyo and Nagoya regions in 1986. Motorola was satisfied at first but soon realized that the Tokyo and Nagoya markets were too valuable to pass up and filed a formal complaint with the Bush administration claiming unfair treatment.

In April 1989, the U.S. government demanded that Japan provide access to the Tokyo and Nagoya areas. If access was denied, the U.S. threatened to impose economic sanctions based on Article 1377 of the 1988 Omnibus Trade Act, which allows retaliation against a country that is violating its bilateral trade agreements.

The Japanese government argued that since the MOSS agreement addressed geographic allocation of markets, there was no violation. The U.S. government insisted that Motorola's exclusion from the Tokyo and Nagoya markets was unfair, and if the Japanese government did not allocate radio frequency for the Motorola-system car phone, Washington would impose sanctions. On April 28, U.S. Trade Representative Carla Hills announced that the U.S. government would charge 100 percent duties on unspecified Japanese goods by July 10 if Japan did not live up to an earlier telecommunications agreement.[78]

Although the Japanese government, then under the leadership of Prime Minister Sosuke Uno, refused to accept these claims, it decided to begin negotiations over the matter. Ozawa was no longer a government official. Because he had been involved with this issue under the Takeshita administration, however, he was appointed to lead the negotiations as a special envoy representing the Kantei. He again adopted his bottom-line approach.[79] Ozawa's U.S. counterpart was Deputy U.S. Trade Representative Linn Williams, who had spent a few years as a lawyer in Japan.

The negotiations were tough. The focal issue was broadcast bandwidth: The U.S. government demanded a 5–megahertz band for service in the Tokyo and Nagoya regions. The Japanese government refused, citing limited capacity. Ozawa asked the Ministry of Posts and Telecommunications (MPT) to make a concession, and the MPT agreed to reallocate 2 megahertz from the 10–megahertz band assigned to the NTT system and an additional 3 megahertz in the future. The U.S. negotiators pressed for a contiguous 5–megahertz band. To meet that demand, however, Japan would have to totally reallocate the broadcast spectrum already assigned. In the eyes of the Japanese government, that was logistically impossible.

Negotiations broke off at 4 A.M. on June 27. After returning to his hotel, Ozawa held a press conference and stated bluntly: "Despite the maximum effort of the Japanese government, we did not reach an agreement. The American side is totally responsible for this result."[80] The U.S. side realized that Ozawa had control, and that if he said no, the Japanese government was saying no. The two sides met again two hours after that, and the U.S. negotiators conceded that the assigned band would not have to be contiguous if it was within the range of 27 megahertz. Using Ozawa as a special representative of the Kantei had again proved successful.

As deputy CCS, Ozawa demonstrated coordination skills in the domestic political scene and negotiation skills in bilateral sessions. Both had a very positive effect on his political career. Kunihiro, who supported Ozawa at the Kantei, emphasized Ozawa's political influence within the government: "In the domestic negotiations among the ministries, the Japanese high officials were persuaded because Mr. Ozawa was directly involved. Under the Nakasone cabinet, I took advantage of the 'lion's skin' of Mr. Gotoda. Under the

Takeshita cabinet, I used Mr. Ozawa's. As Mr. Ozawa was seen as a close associate of Prime Minister Takeshita at that time, I might have been indirectly using the 'lion's skin' of Mr. Takeshita."[81] Even Ozawa's political rival Hiromu Nonaka recognizes Ozawa's achievements in his memoir. "[Mr. Ozawa] emerged within the faction when he solved all the U.S.-Japan trade frictions as deputy CCS under the Takeshita cabinet."[82] As Nonaka confirmed, successful negotiations with the U.S. government were a turning point in Ozawa's political career. Ozawa was later appointed LDP secretary-general under the Kaifu administration with the strong support of Shin Kanemaru, who formally replaced Takeshita as faction leader in the aftermath of the Recruit Scandal. At age forty-seven, he matched Kakuei Tanaka as the youngest to assume this post.

More recently, under the Koizumi administration, Shinzo Abe also became the party's secretary-general immediately after serving as deputy CCS. That younger politicians who proved their ability at the Kantei were promoted to the number 2 position in the ruling party is proof that the Kantei has become highly regarded within the political community. Ozawa set a precedent, demonstrating that the Kantei can play a central role in coordinating conflicting interests among different ministries in the area of foreign affairs.

The Kaifu Cabinet and the SII Talks

While Ozawa enjoyed political influence as a rising star, Prime Minister Toshiki Kaifu's power base within the ruling party was very limited. Kaifu was not a faction leader but a member of the LDP's smallest faction, Komoto. His unlikely ascension came in the aftermath of the Recruit Scandal, in which an ambitious business owner secretly allocated unlisted stock in his company to many senior LDP leaders in return for favorable treatment for his corporate group. Former prime minister Takeshita handpicked Kaifu as the national leader because of his untainted image, which Takeshita saw as key to regaining the public's confidence. In return, however, Kaifu was dependent on the Takeshita faction's support throughout his term. Under these circumstances, Secretary-General Ozawa, representing the Takeshita faction in the LDP, was a very powerful political figure.

In the Kantei, however, there was a power vacuum in foreign affairs after Ozawa left. Kaifu, whose only cabinet experience was as education minister, had done little in the diplomatic area. During his two-year tenure in 1989–91, Kaifu appointed three CCSs (Norio Yamashita, Mayumi Moriyama, and Misoji Sakamoto) and three parliamentary deputy CCSs (Setsu Shiga, Takao Fujimoto, and Tadamori Oshima). Inexperienced and serving for only brief intervals, these six were not instrumental in foreign affairs. Administrative Deputy CCS Nobuo Ishihara, busy assisting the inexperienced prime minister, was not active in diplomacy.

During that period, another major diplomatic issue emerged between the United States and Japan. Referring to the "Super 301" section of the 1988 Omnibus Trade Act, the U.S. trade representative announced on May 25, 1989, that Japan was maintaining unfair trade practices in supercomputers, satellites, and wood products. The representative claimed that Japanese procurement practices presented the primary problem in supercomputers and satellites and that tariffs and misclassifications effectively reduced Japan's demand for U.S. wood and paper products. The trade representative proposed starting the Structural Impediments Initiative (SII) talks, and the Japanese government agreed.

Japanese and American officials held frequent meetings to discuss and improve existing structural problems. The U.S. government cited six problem areas as obstacles to Japan's market access: (1) saving and investment patterns, (2) land policy, (3) the distribution system, (4) exclusionary business practices, (5) *keiretsu* arrangements among a set of companies with interlocking business relationships and shareholdings, and (6) pricing mechanisms. The Japanese negotiators initially came from MOFA, MOF, and MITI. However, since these issues cut across the jurisdictions of virtually all the ministries, the government had to change the team's structure. Deputy CCS Ishihara said, "At the beginning, we thought that the representatives of the three ministries could handle this issue with some involvement of the director of the Cabinet Office on External Affairs. But at some point in the fall, the Kantei began playing a central role."[83] Basically, Ishihara became aware of the need to fill the power vacuum himself.

The ministries and the ruling party did not cooperate with Ishihara on the SII issue, however. Ishihara explained: "In Japan, the mood was overwhelmingly against dealing seriously with this issue. All the ministries and the ruling parties reacted that way."[84] It was LDP Secretary-General Ozawa who offered a helping hand to the desperate Ishihara. Ishihara recalled:

Mr. Ozawa was determined to reach an agreement in the SII talks. Since the Japanese government ministries were not serious about the talks at the earlier stage, he felt he had to do something. . . . For example, some issues required the revision of existing laws such as the Large-Scale Retail Store Law and the Antitrust Law. Difficult revisions in particular would require consultation with LDP policy subcommittees. In such a case, we needed the support of the party leadership. Mr. Ozawa gave the support needed to back up the Kantei.[85]

Ozawa succeeded in persuading MITI to accept the final negotiating position. The Japanese government and the ruling party agreed to revise the law so as to relax some regulations against the establishment of large-scale retail stores. This would allow American large-scale retailers, such as Toys 'R' Us, to enter the Japanese distribution market. As a result of Ozawa's assistance, Ishihara and the Kantei persuaded the related ministries to offer concessions, and the two governments reached an agreement by the end of June 1990.

Conclusion

This chapter examined the early stages of the Kantei's involvement in foreign affairs. Although still inefficient, the Kantei had established institutional support for the prime minister under the Nakasone administration. Under the Takeshita cabinet, the Kantei played a central role in coordinating the interests of different ministries in order to solve economic frictions between the United States and Japan.

However, there was no guarantee that the institutional arrangements in the Kantei would function as designed. Kunihiro, the first director of the Cabinet Office on External Affairs, stated: "Without solid support from the prime minister and the CCS, Kantei initiatives do not work."[86] At that time, the supporting institution at the Kantei was still limited in capacity, so personal factors had a dramatic impact on the Kantei's effectiveness. Under the Kaifu administration, for example, LDP Secretary-General Ozawa, not the prime minister, was the main backer of the Kantei's diplomatic initiatives for trade negotiations with the United States.

In short, the Kantei's position was not fully institutionalized in the early 1990s. A month after the SII agreement was reached, the Kantei faced a much bigger international crisis when Iraq invaded Kuwait. As the Cabinet Secretariat's operations had been limited to the trade arena until then, the situation presented the Kantei with its first serious national security challenge after its 1986 reorganization. The reactions of the prime minister and the Kantei are examined in the next chapter.

A TRAUMATIC EXPERIENCE

From the Gulf Crisis to the International Peace Cooperation Legislation

On August 2, 1990, Saddam Hussein invaded Kuwait, alarming the international community. Prime Minister Kaifu, however, did not identify the invasion as a major national security crisis, which would have allowed the Kantei's Cabinet Office on Security Affairs to take charge. Instead, Iraq's action was handled as a normal diplomatic matter by the Ministry of Foreign Affairs (MOFA), and its policy coordination was limited. The lack of interagency coordination delayed Japan's response to the crisis and provoked international criticism.

When the invasion began, Kaifu was on vacation in the mountain resort of Nagano. He received the news that afternoon but did not return to Tokyo until the following evening. Even then, he failed to convene the cabinet-level

Security Council of Japan to discuss important national security issues, highlighting the lack of urgency he assigned to the situation. That night, the Kaifu cabinet decided to freeze Iraqi and Kuwaiti assets in Japan but postponed a decision on further economic sanctions for Iraq, such as an oil embargo, until the United Nations Security Council agreed on a resolution.

On August 4, President George H. W. Bush called Kaifu to urge Japan to join the United States, European countries, and Canada in imposing economic sanctions on Iraq in order to protest the invasion. Then the Kaifu cabinet reacted, announcing the following day that Japan would embargo Iraqi and Kuwaiti oil, suspend all financial transactions with Iraq, and place a freeze on foreign aid to Iraq.

Financial Contribution: "Too Little, Too Late"

In mid-August, the U.S. government officially requested that the Kaifu government provide financial aid to the multinational forces operating in Iraq, economic aid to the Gulf region, and increased financial support to U.S. forces in Japan. More important, Washington asked for personnel contributions to the multinational forces.

The Japanese government responded positively to the first and second requests without much hesitation, but the prime minister and the Kantei did not take the initiative to make concrete decisions. MOFA officials felt pressure from the U.S. Congress and suggested giving a couple billion dollars of financial aid to the multinational forces. After examining the MOFA proposal, which lacked concrete supporting documentation for the amount, the Finance Ministry cut the aid to $1 billion.[1] When the Kaifu cabinet announced Japan's initial contribution plan on August 30, the international community criticized it as "too little, too late." Deputy CCS Nobuo Ishihara recalls Prime Minister Kaifu talking on the phone to President Bush about the contribution: "I was with the prime minister when he made the call. Mr. Bush usually expressed his appreciation loudly. At that time, however, his response was blunt. It was a disappointment for the United States. Later, I learned that Washington expected Japan to contribute about $3 billion."[2]

U.S. Treasury Secretary Nicholas Brady visited Tokyo on September 7 and met with Finance Minister Ryutaro Hashimoto. Brady requested an additional $1 billion contribution to the multinational forces and $2 billion in economic aid for the Gulf region. When Hashimoto said he could not make an immediate decision, Brady responded that he would not be able to go back to Washington with empty hands.[3]

The U.S. Congress was highly frustrated by Japan's passivity. Congressman David Bonier (D-Michigan) introduced a resolution demanding that Tokyo bear the entire cost of U.S. forces in Japan if the Japanese would not make additional contributions. The resolution passed the House of Representatives by an overwhelming majority (370 to 53) on September 12. Two days later, Japan announced it would contribute $2 billion dollars to the multinational forces and $1 billion in economic aid to the region. Unfortunately, Japan's generosity was viewed as a response to pressure from the U.S. government, leaving the international community unimpressed. Foreign Vice Minister Takakazu Kuriyama lamented in his memoir, "That result was a great disappointment to us."[4]

Battles over Personnel Contributions

More controversial, of course, was the U.S. government's request for personnel assistance. On August 15, 1990, the U.S. ambassador to Japan, Michael Armacost, had presented Kuriyama with a list that mentioned "medical volunteers, logistic support in transporting personnel and equipment to Saudi Arabia, Japanese help in managing the anticipated exodus of large numbers of refugees from Kuwait, and participation in the multinational naval force through the dispatch of minesweepers to help clear the Gulf and transport vessels to carry equipment from Egypt to Saudi Arabia." Armacost describes Kuriyama's response as "mixed." He reports: "[Kuriyama] readily acknowledged the importance of a substantial Japanese contribution. . . . He hinted at Japan's readiness to offer support beyond financial subventions. But he emphatically noted the political and constitutional difficulties that would attend any involvement of Japanese Self-Defense Forces (SDF) in the area of strife and clearly signaled that there was no likelihood that Japan would dispatch minesweepers."[5] According to Armacost, Washington was very eager to receive logistics support for the U.S. Navy. However, legal problems and opposition from the seamen's union prevented Tokyo from providing such support.[6]

On the matter of personnel, MOFA organized a task force with its United Nations Bureau and the Treaties Bureau. Since the legal basis of

Japan's personnel contribution was to cooperate with UN peacekeeping operations (PKO), the United Nations Bureau was instructed to play a central role. The Treaties Bureau, with its expertise in international law and treaties, took a traditional lead in drafting legislation.[7]

As the legislation was drafted and multinational forces deployed, not strictly under UN command, the task force came up with three options: (1) establish a separate organization excluding the SDF, (2) dispatch the SDF by revising the SDF law, or (3) reorganize the SDF into a different organization for supporting peacekeeping activities. On September 14, Vice Minister Kuriyama visited Kaifu to present these three options. Kuriyama argued that the first option would require a large budget and a long time and questioned the feasibility of recruiting enough members. The dovish prime minister was against dispatching the SDF itself. Kuriyama pushed for the third option, reorganizing the SDF to handle peacekeeping chores.

Prime Minister Kaifu had in mind something similar to the Japan Overseas Cooperation Volunteers, a Japanese version of the Peace Corps. He had helped establish this volunteer organization in 1964. Kaifu instructed Kuriyama to come up with a concrete plan for officially removing SDF members from the forces and sending them as officers of the Prime Minister's Office instead.[8] Kuriyama prepared the MOFA scheme that would place the unarmed PKO corps directly under the prime minister, not under the Japan Defense Agency (JDA).

JDA officials opposed Kuriyama's plan. They argued that SDF personnel were trained to act as units under their superior officers and would not be able to function effectively outside the SDF command structure. The Liberal Democratic Party (LDP) leadership, including Secretary-General Ozawa, sided with the JDA and pressed for the plan that would send the SDF as it was.[9] As the conflict between the JDA and MOFA intensified, Deputy CCS Ishihara and the rest of the Kantei team played the role of mediator. The resulting legislation would send the three (Ground, Maritime, and Air) SDF units to join in the Peace Cooperation Corps; this was closer to the vision of the JDA and Ozawa than to the original MOFA scheme.[10]

While the UN Peace Cooperation legislation followed the traditional path within the government as crafted by MOFA officials, the political approval process also adhered to the bottom-up pattern; the framework of the legislation was first introduced to the LDP policy subcommittees on October 11. At the joint meeting, the LDP subcommittees on Cabinet, Foreign Affairs, and National Defense accepted the government proposal on the condition that they reexamine the actual draft. On the same day, the LDP's full Policy Research Council and the General Council approved the framework. The draft proposal was presented to the LDP subcommittees on the morning of October 15, and the full Policy Research Council and the General Council discussed and approved it that evening.

On the following day, the Kaifu cabinet approved the UN Peace Cooperation legislation and sent it to the Diet. The legislation was flawed, however, reflecting severe disagreement within the government and the LDP. Deputy CCS Ishihara acknowledged, "The government submitted the bill to the Diet without fully considering it."[11] Prime Minister Kaifu publicly stated that he staked his political life on the bill's passage, but at Diet meetings, he emphasized only the idealistic aspects of the legislation since he didn't know the details. Kaifu even denied that the SDF could be dispatched to combat zones, although JDA and MOFA officials told opposition party members that the legislation would make deployment possible. The opposition parties attacked the government for its internal disarray and accused the prime minister of testifying falsely. LDP leadership tried to appease the opposition, but the latter would not relent and refused to settle the issue.

After failing to win cooperation from any opposition party, LDP Secretary-General Ozawa told Kaifu on November 5 that they had to let the legislation die. The prime minister said privately to a close associate, "See, I told you. It would have been different if they followed my opinion."[12] Ozawa later called on Ambassador Armacost and looked "genuinely pained" when he admitted that the votes were not there to pass the legislation.[13]

The Diet deliberations were so controversial that Japan's five major newspapers—*Asahi, Mainichi, Nihon Keizai, Sankei,* and *Yomiuri*—were divided in their opinions of the legislation. While the two conservative newspapers, *Sankei* and *Yomiuri,* were supportive of the Kaifu government's policy initiative, the other three were critical. *Yomiuri Shimbun,* on the one hand, ran an editorial endorsing Prime Minister Kaifu's statement in his policy speech that a "contribution to maintain peace is a necessary cost for Japan's position in the international community."[14] On the other hand, *Nihon Keizai Shimbun*'s editorial argued that Japan should only contribute financially and opposed hasty enactment of the legislation.[15] The two liberal newspapers, *Asahi* and *Mainichi,* strongly voiced their objections to dispatching the SDF.[16]

The public was generally hesitant about dispatching the SDF overseas for the first time. According to the *Asahi Shimbun* poll of October 1, 1990, 67 percent of respondents approved of the nonmilitary contribution while only 19 percent supported the SDF dispatch.[17] In another *Asahi* poll taken on November 6, 1990, 58 percent opposed the UN Peace Cooperation Bill and only 21 percent expressed support.[18]

Seeking another chance to enact the legislation, Ozawa approached Yuichi Ichikawa of Komeito and Takashi Yonezawa of the Democratic Socialist Party (DSP), two opposition parties, before the UN Peace Cooperation legislation died. He had built strong ties with both men under the Nakasone cabinet when he was the lower house's Rules and Administration Committee chairman. The two opposition parties agreed that the government would form an organization separate from the SDF that would participate in peacekeeping activities, strictly under UN command.[19]

A business leader was the first to express support for this movement. Chairman Takashi Ishihara of Keizai Doyukai (Japan Association of Corporate Executives) made a new year statement emphasizing the need to establish a system under which Japan could contribute to the international community. Even labor leaders were supportive of the three parties' policy initiative. They openly criticized the Socialist Party for not being involved in discussion of the new legislation.[20]

The United States began bombing Iraq on January 17, 1991. Three days later, Treasury Secretary Brady met with Finance Minister Hashimoto in New York to request an additional $9 billion for the multinational force. Hashimoto telephoned Prime Minister Kaifu to recommend that he accept this request. On January 24, the Kaifu cabinet announced that Tokyo would comply, making its total financial contribution $13 billion. Although the money was welcomed, Japan was criticized for refusing to commit personnel to the war, and its contribution was described as "checkbook diplomacy." The Gulf War was over on February 28. Two weeks later, the Kuwaiti government ran a full-page advertisement in the *Washington Post* and the *New York Times* to thank all the nations that had provided support, leaving Japan off the list. A MOFA report expresses Japanese sentiment at that time: "[T]he international community's lack of appreciation bewildered the Japanese people. This stinging criticism brought home to their minds the importance of sharing the burden with blood, sweat, and tears, and not just with money, as a responsible member of the international community striving for the common cause of maintaining peace with justice."[21]

Dispatching the Minesweepers

Reflecting this sentiment, the Kaifu cabinet began redrafting a new piece of draft legislation based on the three-party agreement that Ozawa managed to secure. The agreement to form a separate organization was an obstacle for the legislation. In early March 1991, MOFA officials and Parliamentary Deputy CCS Tadamori Oshima met with Ozawa and other LDP executives to explain the option based on the agreement: the separate organization would be organized with retired SDF personnel, and their mission would be limited to providing logistic support to military officials who would observe the cease-fire. Ozawa argued that the three-party agreement did not prohibit direct participation in peacekeeping activities that could go beyond a logistic nature. MOFA officials replied that the Japanese government needed to dispatch active SDF officials in order to directly participate in peacekeeping activities, but doing so would violate the agreement that only allowed Tokyo to send retired officials in a separate organization.[22]

Some LDP leaders began arguing that the government should send SDF units rather than form a separate organization. LDP Policy Research Council chairman Mutsuki Kato, for example, stated at a press conference that it was important for Japan to send armed officers to participate with peace-keeping forces and that he would persuade Komeito and the DSP to revise the three-party agreement. However, both Komeito and the DSP were hesitant to send SDF units abroad, highlighting the gap between themselves and the LDP.[23]

While the PKO issue was deadlocked, some officers in MOFA and many LDP politicians voiced their opinion that Japan should contribute manpower by dispatching minesweepers to the Persian Gulf. At the March 14 LDP National Defense subcommittee meeting, Michio Watanabe (leader of the Watanabe faction) expressed his support for deployment. On the same day, Foreign Minister Taro Nakayama, speaking at the lower house budget committee meeting, stated that the government would consider sending the minesweepers.[24]

The media again were split. While *Sankei* and *Yomiuri* encouraged the Kaifu government to dispatch minesweepers, *Nihon Keizai*, *Mainichi*, and *Asahi* were opposed. *Yomiuri Shimbun*'s editorial on April 11 urged the prime minister to make a political decision, as "minesweeping is necessary also for Japanese corporations to ship oil to Japan."[25] *Asahi* and *Mainichi*, in contrast, carried editorials against such a move, which could possibly be a step away from Japan's pacifism.[26] *Nihon Keizai Shimbun*'s editorial supported the general idea of sending the minesweepers but opposed the government action without new legislation to authorize it.[27]

Aware of the different opinions in the media, Prime Minister Kaifu was still hesitant about making a decision. At the March 15 meeting of the lower house foreign affairs committee, he said that it would be irresponsible to dispatch minesweepers without researching the current situation of the Persian Gulf. Komeito and the DSP were against sending the minesweepers as well, and Kaifu wanted to side with them to move forward on the PKO issue.

Intense pressure came from the business community. On April 8, Gaishi Hiraiwa, chairman of the Keidanren (Japan Federation of Economic Organizations), held a press conference and voiced his opinion that the Japanese government should dispatch minesweepers. It was quite unusual for the chairman of Japan's most powerful business organization to express his view on national security issues. His action reflected strong opinions among the business leaders in charge of worldwide business operations that Japan's contribution to the international community should go beyond financial aid.

In addition to Keidanren, organizations such as the Japanese Shipowners' Association, the All Japan Seamen's Union, and the Arabian Oil Company pressured the Japanese government to dispatch minesweepers in order to secure maritime safety in the Gulf. Responding to such demands, three defense-related policy subcommittees of the LDP passed a resolution urging the prime minister to send the minesweepers. Finally, Kaifu decided to support the dispatch.

Kaifu instructed LDP secretary-general Keizo Obuchi, who had succeeded Ozawa after the April 7 Tokyo gubernatorial election, to persuade Komeito and the DSP to back the minesweeper dispatch. While the DSP became supportive, Komeito did not change its stance on this issue. On April 24, Kaifu gave up on persuading Komeito leaders and decided to send the minesweepers without their support. The public overwhelmingly supported Kaifu's decision. According to an *Asahi Shimbun* poll, 56 percent of the respondents supported the dispatch of minesweepers while only 30 percent were opposed.

The SDF minesweepers successfully conducted operations and were greatly appreciated by the international community. Because of their success, public support for sending SDF units for peacekeeping activities increased. According to *Asahi Shimbun*'s June 1991 public opinion survey,

74 percent responded positively to an SDF dispatch overseas, and 50 percent supported SDF's participation in UN peacekeeping operations compared to 40 percent who were opposed. Compared with the public's earlier opposition to the UN Peace Cooperation legislation, these results represented a significant shift in public opinion.[28]

Redrafting the Legislation

The success of the minesweeping mission also changed Kaifu's view on PKO issues. According to Deputy CCS Ishihara, Kaifu finally realized that the government should send SDF units for effective peacekeeping operations.[29] The MOFA task force announced a new plan for dispatching SDF units, given these new conditions. They cited the following factors: (1) the success of the minesweeping mission had changed public opinion on SDF dispatch abroad; (2) Komeito had begun to reconsider its position on this issue; and (3) the United Nations was requesting personnel with military training and experience.[30]

In response to this plan, Komeito became more flexible on this issue. At the party's executive meeting on May 28, Chairman Yuichi Ichikawa stated, "Anti-war pacifism is still important. But should we stick with it forever?" Policy Council chairman Nobuaki Futami expressed a more concrete view on Japan's need to send active SDF personnel by saying, "At first, I thought that retired SDF officials would be capable of the mission. But all the other countries are sending military officers."[31] While consensus on the SDF dispatch was formed within the LDP and the DSP, Komeito showed its willingness to negotiate.

The new environment required a new piece of draft legislation, and Finance Minister Hashimoto suggested at a cabinet meeting that the Kantei handle the legislation. Deputy CCS Ishihara initially wanted to avoid a situation in which "the Kantei takes the task from MOFA's United Nations Bureau."[32] But he acquired Foreign Minister Taro Nakayama's approval and established an office in June to prepare the PKO legislation under the leadership of Tatsuo Arima, director of the Cabinet Office on External Affairs. Ishihara claimed success at bringing the task to the Kantei: "General issues of international cooperation are usually handled by MOFA. Since the peacekeeping activities involved the SDF, though, the JDA should have handled things. The JDA would not welcome the MOFA initiative. . . . Later, when we included the Japan Coast Guard [under the Ministry of Transportation], the Kantei needed to handle the legislation. MOFA officials would never be able to coordinate all these factors."[33]

As consensus on dispatching the SDF was built within the LDP, the next question arose: whether SDF participation with peacekeeping forces would go beyond logistic support. Kaifu instructed Ishihara to persuade LDP leadership to exclude participation in peacekeeping forces, but LDP secretary-general Obuchi strongly opposed this. MOFA vice minister Kuriyama proposed a compromise, suggesting that SDF would participate in peacekeeping forces under the following conditions: (1) a cease-fire must be in place, (2) the parties in the conflict must have consented to the operation, (3) the activities must be conducted in a strictly impartial manner, (4) participation may be suspended or terminated if any of the above conditions ceases to be satisfied, and (5) use of weapons shall be limited to the minimum necessary to protect the lives or bodies of personnel. These conditions were applied to general peacekeeping operations and were later known as "the five PKO principles."

On September 13, LDP secretary-general Obuchi met with the secretaries-general of Komeito and the DSP to finalize an agreement on the International Peace Cooperation legislation. Komeito accepted the government proposal, as it stipulated the five PKO principles. In contrast, the DSP demanded prior Diet approval of the dispatch. Although the demand was not refused, the DSP did not oppose introducing the legislation to the Diet. On September 19, the Kaifu cabinet approved the legislation, and it was introduced to the lower house.

On September 30, during deliberation of the International Peace Cooperation legislation, the lower house killed an important piece of legislation on political reform. Prime Minister Kaifu had staked his political life on this reform bill, implying that he would dissolve the lower house if the bill did not pass the Diet. The Takeshita faction, on which Kaifu had relied for support, withdrew its support. Powerless, Kaifu had to abandon dissolution. This incident underscored Kaifu's weakness, which led to his resignation.

New Legislation under the Miyazawa Cabinet

On November 5, a new cabinet led by Kiichi Miyazawa was formed. The new government's first task was to submit the PKO legislation to the Diet. Public reaction to the legislation was generally supportive. According to an *Asahi Shimbun* survey on November 10, 71 percent of the respondents supported the SDF dispatch abroad, while only 29 percent opposed it.[34]

Deliberations on the PKO legislation restarted in the lower house's Special Committee on International Peace Cooperation on November 18. Among the opposition camp, the Japan Socialist Party (JSP) and the Japan Communist Party (JCP) announced strong opposition to the legislation from the beginning. The Miyazawa cabinet sought cooperation from Komeito and the DSP as Kaifu had done. However, DSP chairman Keigo Ouchi demanded prior Diet approval before his party would support the legislation. This was not acceptable to the government side, as Diet approval would make it difficult for Japan to meet the UN request for personnel.[35] Prime Minister Miyazawa, LDP secretary-general Obuchi, and Deputy CCS Ishihara tried to persuade Ouchi, but the DSP leader refused any compromise on this point. Tadao Hirano of the lower house's secretariat analyzed Ouchi's stubbornness and found it was based on three factors. First, there was fierce competition within the DSP, and Chairman Ouchi was frustrated that he had not yet had a chance to demonstrate his political power in the policy process on the PKO legislation. Second, the DSP was negotiating electoral cooperation in the upcoming upper house election with the JSP, which was adamantly opposed to the bill. Third, one of the DSP's supporting organizations demanded prior Diet approval.[36]

On November 27, without support from the DSP, the LDP and Komeito passed the PKO legislation in the lower house special committee. Two days later, at the party conference, many party members accused the Komeito leadership of forcing the legislation through the committee. The party demanded another opportunity to deliberate the bill. The LDP agreed to send the legislation back to the committee for further questioning in order to help the Komeito leadership save face. After this unusual procedure, the bill passed the lower house on December 3.

Two days later, the upper house's special committee launched its deliberations. The opposition parties came up with many unexpected questions that had not been discussed in the lower house. Often, the committee chairman had to stop deliberations as government officials could not come up with appropriate answers. After Special Committee chairman Masao Goto resigned, taking responsibility for the rough deliberations in the committee, the Miyazawa cabinet gave up trying to pass the bill in the 1991 Diet session.

It was not until the end of April 1992 that deliberations over the PKO bill were restarted in the upper house. Meanwhile, in early February, Komeito secretary-general Ichikawa proposed a freeze on peacekeeping activities beyond those of a logistic nature in order to invite the DSP to join the supporting camp. In mid-March, Special Representative of the UN Transitional Authority in Cambodia (UNTAC) Yasushi Akashi arrived in Cambodia, making Japan's participation in peacekeeping operations in the country more urgent. At the April 21 party conference, DSP chairman Ouchi announced his intention to cooperate on the PKO bill.

On May 29, the secretaries-general of the LDP, Komeito, and the DSP agreed to freeze the provisions on dispatching the SDF for peacekeeping activities beyond a logistic nature until new legislation could be enacted. On June 5, the revised legislation passed the upper house special committee and was introduced on the floor, where the JSP and the JCP conducted many different kinds of filibusters to block voting on the legislation. They introduced no-confidence resolutions against Diet committee chairmen and cabinet members. For each vote, they used a traditional filibuster known as "cow walking" (walking extremely slowly during the voting) to use up the limited deliberation time allocated to the upper house. This filibuster had not been used since the 1988 deliberations on a tax reform bill. It took seventy-five hours to complete the voting process, but the PKO bill finally passed.

The revised bill was then reintroduced to the lower house special committee on the evening of June 9. Although the JSP and the JCP tried to block the legislation, it passed the committee in two days and was finally enacted on June 15.

The media's reaction was mixed. But this time, *Nihon Keizai Shimbun* joined *Sankei* and *Yomiuri* to express its support for the PKO legislation. The business newspaper praised the new law, as "it set up a framework for Japan to demonstrate how we would like to contribute to the world."[37] Two liberal newspapers, *Asahi* and *Mainichi*, remained critical because the government did not form units separate from the SDF as the newspapers had originally proposed in 1990.

After the legislation was enacted, the Headquarters of International Peace Cooperation was established in the cabinet. The International Peace Cooperation Law had taken a very unusual path among different ministries. It was originally initiated by MOFA and later crafted by the Kantei. MOFA handled the Diet operations, and after enactment, the Prime Minister's Office had jurisdiction. The Kantei played a central role for the first time by providing administrative assistance in the policy-making process that produced a major piece of national security legislation dispatching the SDF overseas.

Conclusion

This chapter examined Japan's reaction to the 1990 Gulf crisis and later the Gulf War. Prime Minister Kaifu's failure to recognize the incident as a crisis created delays in the government's response, drawing both domestic and international criticism. In order to make a personnel contribution to the multinational forces, MOFA organized a task force with its United Nations Bureau and the Treaties Bureau. When intense conflicts of opinion arose between MOFA and the JDA over the status of dispatched SDF officials, however, the task force could not reconcile the differences.[38]

As a result, the legislation introduced by the Kaifu cabinet was not well prepared. The media and the public did not actively support it. At the Diet debate, the dovish prime minister denied that the SDF might be placed in a combat situation, while government officials explained that the bill's wording would indeed allow the SDF to engage in combat areas. This forced the LDP to withdraw the bill.

After the successful dispatch of SDF minesweepers following the Gulf War, the political environment changed. With stronger support from the public and the business community, the Kaifu administration came up with new draft legislation to dispatch the SDF for UN peacekeeping activities overseas. In this policy process, the Kantei established a team to draft the bill, as the Kaifu administration needed interagency coordination among different ministries. The International Peace Cooperation legislation set the precedent of the Kantei drafting a major piece of legislation on national security.

Japan faced a series of other crises during the 1990s. When Hashimoto, who served as finance minister during the Gulf War, became prime minister in 1996, he started administrative reform efforts intended to improve the Kantei's crisis management capabilities. As a result, the supporting institution at the Kantei was significantly developed in January 2001. The following chapter examines the details of such improvements.

3

THE RISE OF THE KANTEI

During the 1990s, Japan's pronounced lack of effective leadership became a central issue in national politics. Crisis management was a particularly urgent concern, brought into sharp focus by disastrous handling of the Great Hanshin Earthquake and the Aum Shinrikyo sarin gas attacks in 1995, the embassy hostage crisis in Peru in 1995–96, and the 1997 oil spill in the Sea of Japan. In each instance, the national leader of the moment was heavily criticized for failing to take timely, decisive, and appropriate action.

When Prime Minister Ryutaro Hashimoto (1996–98) formed the Administrative Reform Council, one of its major goals was to reinforce the authority of the cabinet and the prime minister, provide them with more staff support, and give them firmer control in emergencies. One council mem-

ber stated: "Strengthening the cabinet function was a much more important achievement for the council than reorganizing the ministries, which
attracted the most media attention."[1]

The administrative reform–related bills passed in July 1999. They resulted
in significant institutional changes that strengthened the power and function of the Cabinet Secretariat, the prime minister's supporting body.

Considering Prime Minister Junichiro Koizumi's minimal diplomatic
experience and weak power base within the LDP, his adoption of a top-down
style of policy making rather than adherence to Japan's traditional consensus-
building style of politics made sense. Koizumi was fortunate that Hashimoto's
administrative reforms had strengthened the Kantei, which helped him exercise dramatically more effective policy-making leadership.[2]

Wielding its newfound authority also allows the Kantei to play an instrumental policy-making role as "core executive." According to Patrick Dunleavy and R. A. W. Rhodes, the core executive's role is to "primarily serve
to pull together and integrate central government policies, or act as final
arbiters within the executive of conflicts between different elements of the
government machine."[3] Since many major issues the government handles
involve the jurisdictions of two or more ministries, the Kantei must act as
the final authority when conflicting interests stall progress. This chapter analyzes how the new institutional changes have affected the Kantei's role and
altered its relationships with the central government agencies.[4]

The Rise of the Chief Cabinet Secretary

As actual head of the Kantei, the chief cabinet secretary (CCS) is of prime
importance to the Kantei as core executive; its statutory head, however, is
the prime minister. Confirming the definition Dunleavy and Rhodes established, former CCS Masaharu Gotoda summarized his old job as "to medi-
ate and settle disputes" between various government agencies participating
in the policy-making process.[5] Policy coordination requires political skill,
experience, and connections as well as knowledge of the content and an
understanding of the implications of specific policies. The CCS must work
with other members of the ruling party and the bureaucracy to coordinate
policy. According to Gotoda, the task depends "on the power balance
between the CCS and the relevant ministers of state. Thus it involves competition over their individual political power and character."[6]

Because the prime minister's time and energy are limited, many issues are handled without his involvement, even those that ostensibly should receive his attention. In the Japanese government's traditional bottom-up policy-making process, ministries attempt to deal with issues within their respective realms. Gotoda points out: "Although [officials from] the ministries are supposed to bring up important issues relating to other administrative agencies in the cabinet meeting, they may not do so because of jurisdictional conflicts. There are also occasions on which, by the time the issue reaches [the cabinet level], there is no room left for discussion."[7] One of the major tasks of the CCS and his support staff is to identify and present such issues to the prime minister.

As well as being a policy mediator, the CCS acts as spokesperson for the prime minister and his cabinet, holding official press conferences twice a day. Unofficial comments he makes outside of these conferences are also frequently quoted as statements by "the top official of the government" (*seifu shuno*). In a sense, the CCS position combines the duties of the U.S. chief of staff and the White House spokesperson. The CCS's role is probably much more influential, since he is also directly involved in the decision-making process for most of the government's important policy decisions. Even when the CCS is not directly involved, he must vet decisions. It is no exaggeration to say that the CCS is much more involved than the prime minister in the policy-making process. The increasingly elevated status of the CCS symbolizes the emergence of the Kantei.

The CCS's official title in Japanese, *kanbo chokan*, was first made known during the promulgation of the Cabinet Law in January 1947, but the original law did not define the job.[8] The 1949 revision of the law defined the role as "to control the administration of the Cabinet Secretariat" and allowed a cabinet minister to take the position.[9] It was not until 1966, however, that the CCS gained permanent status as a cabinet member.[10] In 1948, for example, under the second Shigeru Yoshida cabinet, Eisaku Sato was appointed CCS even though he lacked cabinet member status and was not even an elected Diet member.

Even after 1966, the CCS remained relatively low in the ministerial hierarchy. The prime minister often appointed a close associate from his own faction to support his administrative goals. In 1982, however, Prime Minister Yasuhiro Nakasone surprised many in political circles by appointing to the post Masaharu Gotoda, a former administrative deputy CCS and a member of the LDP's largest faction, led by Kakuei Tanaka. Nakasone needed Gotoda's skill and experience in controlling the bureaucracy in order to pursue his priority policy issue of administrative reform.

More recently, prime ministers have been appointing political heavyweights to the position of CCS. Prime Minister Ryutaro Hashimoto, for example, selected former LDP secretary-general Seiroku Kajiyama in 1996. The Hashimoto administration analyzed the lessons from the 1995 Hanshin earthquake and examined scenarios in which a prime minister is unable to perform his duties. The Hashimoto cabinet decided to designate the CCS as acting prime minister. This decision, however, applied only in the event of natural disasters.

That limitation caused a major legal and political debate in April 2000 when Prime Minister Keizo Obuchi fell into a coma and CCS Mikio Aoki was appointed acting prime minister. The selection was supposed to be based on Article 9 of the Cabinet Law, which stipulates that "if the prime minister is absent or has an accident, a state minister designated by him in advance shall assume the duties as prime minister as a tentative measure." The appointment did not require a cabinet decision. However, since Obuchi had not given Aoki clear and specific prior instructions, the latter's appointment sparked protests in the Diet, with Democratic Party of Japan (DPJ) Policy Committee chairman Naoto Kan strongly questioning its legality.

To avoid such confusion in the future, it became customary, after the first Mori cabinet was formed in April 2000, for every new cabinet to make a list of five cabinet officers in line for succession to the premiership.[11] The CCS is always at the top of the list and will continue to be so unless the position of deputy prime minister is officially introduced. In principle, when the prime minister is away from Tokyo, the CCS is expected to stay in town. The CCS in effect becomes a deputy prime minister in all but title.

Deputy Chief Cabinet Secretary: The Shadow Prime Minister?

As the status of the CCS rose, his deputies also began to play increasingly crucial roles. There are three deputy CCSs (*kanbo fukuchokan*), one administrative and two parliamentary; the latter two are appointed from among the Diet members, one from the lower house and the other from the upper house. The position of administrative deputy CCS is often considered the top post of Japan's entire bureaucracy. This individual serves as the liaison between the prime minister and the bureaucracy and frequently consults with the prime minister. Deputy CCS Teijiro Furukawa, for example, was the most frequent visitor to Prime Minister Hashimoto's office during 1997, according to an *Asahi Shimbun* survey.[12]

This post became a pivotal one during the lengthy tenures of two recent administrative deputy CCSs: Nobuo Ishihara, who held the job for seven years and three months (1987–95), and Teijiro Furukawa, who served for eight years and seven months (1995–2003). Before Ishihara was selected, prime ministers traditionally appointed someone new to the post when they took office. However, Ishihara and Furukawa served eleven prime ministers during their nearly sixteen years on the job. Their institutional memory proved invaluable to Japan's legion of short-tenured prime ministers, especially those with limited cabinet experience. For example, as described in chapter 2, Ishihara played a key role in the administration of Toshiki Kaifu, who was so unprepared to become the nation's leader that the media jokingly reported that the government was run by "Prime Minister Ishihara with assistance from Kaifu."[13]

Appointees for this position were usually officials from the prewar Ministry of Home Affairs (Naimusho), which, after World War II, was divided into several ministries—Construction, Home Affairs (Jichisho), Health and Welfare, and Labor—and the National Police Agency. Senior officials of these agencies were generally considered less partisan about ministry-related interests and more concerned about the interests of the nation as a whole.[14] Ishihara was a former vice minister of Home Affairs, and Furukawa was a former vice minister of Health and Welfare.

According to former administrative deputy CCS Furukawa, the holder of this post has five major functions: (1) policy coordination, (2) handling all issues brought to cabinet meetings, (3) chairing the sub-cabinet meeting, (4) screening the appointments of high officials, and (5) advising administrative vice ministers.

Furukawa explained that his most important task was handling policy coordination among different ministries and stressed how crucial impartiality is in this position: "The most important thing for the administrative deputy CCS is to be selfless. That is why I was able to serve in the position for more than eight years and gain the trust of the ministries. Justice was the keyword for decision making, and I thought that if my decision was made based on justice, it would be well accepted by the Japanese people."[15] Three assistant

CCSs and their staffs support the administrative deputy CCS in policy coordination. They are discussed in detail later in the chapter.

The second task performed by the administrative deputy CCS is to handle and prepare all the issues presented at cabinet meetings. He is the last person to check all the agenda items for the highest-level decision-making organ in Japan's executive branch.

The administrative deputy CCS's third critical role is to chair the administrative vice-ministerial meeting (*jimu jikan kaigi*), a sub-cabinet gathering attended by the top bureaucrats of all the administrative agencies. While the cabinet is the Japanese government's highest decision-making institution, decisions are rarely made in cabinet meetings. The agenda for a cabinet meeting is prepared at the sub-cabinet meeting, usually held the day before, and the agenda goes to the cabinet meeting along with a proposed decision. Although the sub-cabinet meeting has no legal authority or basis for its existence, the cabinet seldom repeals decisions made at this meeting.

Critics often describe this sub-cabinet meeting as evidence of Japan's bureaucratic supremacy. For example, Naoto Kan, president of the DPJ, forcefully criticized the meeting and included its abolition as a campaign promise in his party's manifesto for the November 2003 general election.[16] In an interview, Furukawa, who chaired the sub-cabinet meeting for more than eight years, countered Kan's criticism in this way:

> Mr. Kan totally misunderstands the purpose of the sub-cabinet meeting. The meeting is not the place to make final decisions, which are usually made beforehand in the process of policy coordination. Because decisions made by the cabinet, the highest decision-making organ of the government, must be flawless, the sub-cabinet meeting serves as the place for final checking by experts, including the officers of the Cabinet Legislation Bureau. Those at the meeting never oppose decisions initiated and decided by the cabinet and sometimes are not involved at all in cabinet decisions. For example, the Koizumi cabinet's economic reform policy, decided by the Council of Economic and Fiscal Policy, was not even brought to the sub-cabinet meeting.

Furukawa also stressed the other function of the sub-cabinet meeting:

The meeting is the last stage of the government's bottom-up decision making. At the same time, the meeting is where the administrative deputy CCS reveals the intentions of the prime minister, and it could be the first stage of the top-down decision-making process.[17]

The fourth important function of the administrative deputy CCS is to screen candidates for high positions (bureau chief and above) for all the ministries. As a result of Hashimoto's administrative reforms, the cabinet must now approve these appointments, and the administrative deputy CCS screens candidates prior to cabinet approval to confirm that appointees will help promote the prime minister's policy goals. In several cases, Furukawa rejected the ministries' choices, but quite often he was privy to early information from the ministries and removed some appointees from consideration. This meant he had de facto appointive power over high officials in all the ministries, giving him tremendous influence vis-à-vis the bureaucracy.

Advising the administrative vice ministers was another vital task. After the January 2001 reorganization, the vice ministers, especially those in the newly merged ministries, faced many difficulties in running their own institutions, primarily because they lacked relevant experience. In many cases, the administrative deputy CCS was the only one who could provide knowledgeable counsel. This also increased the Kantei's sway over the ministries.

The parliamentary deputy CCSs have also gained more influence.[18] Often recruited from the prime minister's faction, these two deputies serve a different function from the administrative deputy CCS. While the administrative deputy acts as a crucial link between the CCS and the entire bureaucracy, the primary role of the parliamentary deputy is to assist the CCS in matters relating to the ruling party or to work on issues assigned by the prime minister. However, parliamentary deputies are not directly in the line of command. A former officer of the Kantei bluntly stated: "However strongly a parliamentary deputy CCS opposes a certain policy, it does not matter too much for the bureaucrats if it is approved by the CCS."[19] The same officer observed:

The tasks of the parliamentary deputy CCSs vary depending on their respective interests and expertise. I closely observed three parliamentary deputy CCSs—Fukushiro Nukaga [1997–98, 1999–2000], Muneo Suzuki [1998–99], and Shinzo Abe [2000–2003].

Mr. Nukaga, for example, was involved in a wide variety of domestic policy issues since he was a well-known policy expert. Mr. Suzuki concentrated heavily on foreign policy and political affairs. Mr. Abe spent most of his time dealing with foreign affairs and national security issues.[20]

Although the post of parliamentary deputy CCS is a sub-cabinet position, it is often more important than some cabinet positions in terms of policy making. This is why senior LDP members with prior cabinet experience were sometimes selected.[21]

Restructuring the Kantei

The 2001 central government reforms changed the Kantei structurally as well. One refinement gave the prime minister more leeway in determining the number of personal assistants he could appoint. The prime minister can now exceed the previous limit of five private secretaries by issuing an executive order. In addition, he may now have up to five special advisers, two more than before 2001. Another significant change opened up important Kantei posts to individuals from both inside and outside the government in order to avoid "inflexible methods of assigning particular posts . . . to officials from particular ministries."[22]

The two prime ministers after the 2001 reforms, Yoshiro Mori and Junichiro Koizumi, did not take full advantage of these changes. For example, neither increased the number of private secretaries. Mori had only two special advisers, and Koizumi had appointed four at most as of March 2005 but retained only two of them after the fall of that year.[23] Bureaucrats from the same old ministries received most of the political appointments in the Kantei.

The formal abolition of the three policy offices created during the 1986 reorganization, carried out under the Nakasone administration, was a more significant institutional change in the Kantei. The Offices on Internal Affairs (headed by a MOF official), External Affairs (headed by a MOFA official), and Security Affairs (headed by a Japan Defense Agency [JDA] official and later called the Office on National Security and Crisis Management) were created to strengthen the Kantei. During Hashimoto's administrative reform efforts, however, these offices were strongly criticized for their lack

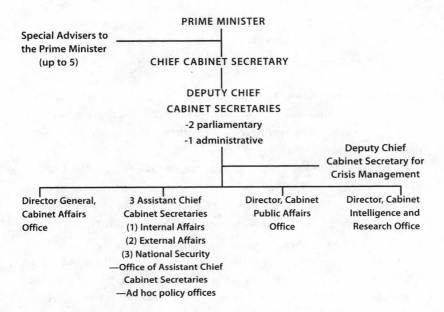

Fig. 3.1 Organization of the Kantei after 2001

of coordination and for problems caused by interagency rivalries.[24] All three offices and their director posts were formally abolished in January 2001. Three new assistant CCS (*kanbo fukuchokanho*) posts were created as political appointments to serve functions similar to those performed by the old directors.

Although more flexible appointments for the position of assistant CCS were expected in light of Hashimoto's reforms, Prime Minister Mori appointed three officers from the same ministries (MOF, MOFA, and the JDA) after the January 2001 reorganization. These appointees remained even after Koizumi took office in April 2001. Their boss, Deputy CCS Furukawa, defended this bow to the status quo:

> If national policies are divided into three major categories, they should be national security, foreign affairs, and domestic policies. If we have to choose the government officials in charge of the first two areas, it is natural to choose from the JDA and MOFA. For domestic affairs, we currently appoint a MOF official. But it is possible in the future to appoint somebody from the Ministry of Economics,

Trade, and Industry [METI]. We are hoping to see those positions held by officials who formerly served in the Kantei and have a strong concept of national interests rather than ministerial interests.[25]

According to Furukawa, although Hashimoto's administrative reforms changed these positions into political appointments, there is no intention to bring in people from outside the government unless the prime minister shows a strong will to do so.

At the same time, the organization of the Kantei's policy offices underwent a major change. Officially, all the policy offices were merged into one policy unit called the Office of Assistant Chief Cabinet Secretaries. This policy unit has about a hundred staffers to support the three assistant CCSs who handle policy coordination.

Despite the organizational reshuffle, elements of the three old offices remain. Although the Office on External Affairs was totally eliminated, a section of the old Office on National Security and Crisis Management still exists and operates autonomously, separate from the rest of the cabinet's policy unit; it is even located on a different floor of the Cabinet Office Building. The deputy CCS for crisis management (*kiki kanrikan*)—a post slightly above vice-minister level and held by a former National Police Agency official— heads this office with the help of the assistant CCS from the JDA. Some thirty staffers assist these two high officials.[26] The assistant CCS is in charge of national security and defense affairs, and the deputy CCS for crisis management handles all other crises including natural disasters and domestic security.

This division of labor and responsibility has become increasingly ambiguous, however. The January 1997 accident involving the Russian tanker *Nahotoka*, which sank about a hundred kilometers off the Shimane coast and spilled oil into the Japan Sea, for example, was handled as both a diplomatic issue with Russia under the assistant CCS from MOFA and a domestic pollution issue under the assistant CCS from MOF.

Another serious incident occurred in December 2001 when an unidentified ship was spotted inside Japan's exclusive economic zone. Initially handled by the Japan Coast Guard as a police action, the incursion was generally regarded as under the jurisdiction of the director for crisis management. After the Coast Guard vessel chased the unidentified ship, however, the vessel exploded and rapidly sank. It was later discovered to be a North Korean spy ship, so the incident became a diplomatic matter that fell under the juris-

Table 3.1 Policy Unit Staff under the Assistant Chief Cabinet Secretaries, as of December 2001

Assistant Chief Cabinet Secretary for Internal Affairs (from MOF)

Assistant Chief Cabinet Secretary for External Affairs (from MOFA)

Secretariat 1: General Affairs (4), Legislative Relations (2), Accounting (4), Personnel (3)

Secretariat 2: Research (3), Planning (2), Coordination (3)

Policy unit staffers by ministries of origin and expertise

Councillors (8) (*shingikan*, bureau chief level)

Cabinet Office, MOFA,[1] MPHP,[2] METI,[3] National Police Agency, Ministry of Justice, Public Prosecutors Office, Ministry of Finance Counselors (*sanjikan*, director level)

MPHP (2), MEXT[4] (2), MHLW[5] (2), METI (2), MLIT[6] (2), MOFA (2)

Group 1: MEXT (3), Ministry of Justice (2)

Group 2: MPHP (2), National Police Agency (2)

Group 3: Cabinet Office (3), Ministry of Finance (3)

Group 4: Indochina refugees (2), MOFA (2)

Group 5: METI (3), MLIT (3)

Group 6: MHLW (2), MAFF (3)

Assistant Chief Cabinet Secretary for National Security (from the JDA)

Group 1: 2 Counselors from the JDA

      JDA (3)

Group 2: Counselors from MPHP

National Fire Agency, Ministry of Agriculture, Forestry and Fishery, MPHP

Group 3: Counselor from MLIT

JDA, National Maritime Safety Agency, National Police Agency, MOF

Group 4: Counselor from the National Police Agency

National Police Agency, MOFA, MHLW

Group 5: Counselors from the JDA and MLIT

JDA, MPHP, MLIT (3)

[1] Ministry of Foreign Affairs

[2] Ministry of Public Management, Home Affairs, Posts, and Telecommunication

[3] Ministry of Economy, Trade, and Industry

[4] Ministry of Education, Culture, Sports, Science, and Technology

[5] Ministry of Health, Labor, and Wealth

[6] Ministry of Land, Infrastructure, and Transportation

diction of the assistant CCS from MOFA. "We need to figure out how we deal with these gray zone issues," Furukawa pointed out.[27]

The rest of the policy unit is located on the fifth floor and is divided into six groups. Three of the six groups formerly belonged to the Office on Internal Affairs, and their officers are from the domestic policy–oriented ministries. The other three groups were part of the Office on External Affairs and are foreign-policy oriented (see table 3.1). One or two counselors (at *kacho*, or division director, level) head each group.

To enhance coordination among the elements of the old offices, twelve counselors work in the same room while their subordinates work in separate rooms. The assistant CCSs assign tasks to these directors and their staffs. Often, more than one counselor is assigned the same task. Some counselors work for one assistant CCS in the morning and for another in the afternoon. The operation of the office is now much more flexible than it was before 2001.

Former Deputy CCS Furukawa explained the strategy he pursued: "What I pictured in my mind was my experience at the Anti-Pollution Headquarters under the Sato administration in 1970. As a young official from the Ministry of Health and Welfare who was sent to the headquarters, I observed that the organization changed its shape like an amoeba to deal with one pollution issue after another. I wanted that flexibility in the Kantei."[28]

In addition, Deputy CCS Furukawa created a new position, chief counselor (at director general, or *bucho*, level), between the three assistant CCSs and the cabinet counselors (see fig. 3.2), and appointed Hiroshi Ogawa from METI to this position to supervise the entire policy unit. Furukawa spoke highly of Ogawa's talents, stating, "Due to his work, we were able to eliminate the problem of sectionalism within the policy office."[29]

Some issues are supervised by more than one assistant CCS. For example, both the assistant CCS for internal affairs and the assistant CCS for external affairs handled the issue of human traffic from Southeast Asia to Japan. The assistant CCS for external affairs and the assistant CCS for national security handled the Iraq issue (examined in chapter 6). This dual assignment also helped the office work in a unified fashion. As one of the counselors stated, "The media often portray us as representing our home ministries and fighting turf battles in the office. In fact, we cooperate, and there is a sense of comradeship. Sectionalism no longer exists in our office."[30]

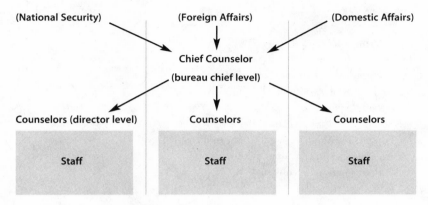

Fig. 3.2 Diagram of the Policy Unit Staff

Ad Hoc Policy Offices

In order to further coordinate policy among different ministries, Hashimoto's administrative reforms allowed the policy unit to create ad hoc offices for specific policy areas. This arrangement was meant to provide institutional flexibility by not designating policy issues to specific ministries, "thus enabling them to respond to situations in a timely manner," according to the government's official explanation.[31] As of May 2006, there were fifteen such ad hoc offices (see table 3.2). While some offices are established by laws or government orders, others exist without any legal basis. The procedures for forming and dissolving the ad hoc offices are very flexible. For example, the Office of Personal Information Protection, which was established in 2001, was dissolved after the Koizumi government passed personal information protection legislation in May 2003.

These ad hoc offices significantly expanded the size of the Kantei. According to the Cabinet Secretariat's official home page, the number of officials at the secretariat was 655, about three times more than before 2001.[32] The actual number may well be more than 700, since some officers, who are seconded from other ministries and remain on their payrolls, may not be counted as employed at the secretariat.

The quality of the officers in the Kantei has changed as well. A former

Table 3.2 Ad Hoc Policy Rooms under
the Assistant Chief Cabinet Secretaries,
as of May 2006

1. Information Security
2. Information and Technology
3. Administrative Reform Promotion
4. Treatment of Abandoned Chemical Weapons
5. Urban Renaissance
6. Special Zones for Structural Reform
7. Supporting Abductees and Their Families
8. Intellectual Property Strategy Promotion
9. Supporting Iraqi Reconstruction
10. Regional Renewal
11. Continental Shelf Research
12. Port and Airport Crisis Management
13. Privatization of Postal Service
14. Decentralization of Government Authority
15. Judicial Reform

assistant to the prime minister, Kenji Eda, who played an instrumental role in Hashimoto's administrative reform efforts, had this to say: "Before the Hashimoto reforms, the officers seconded from different ministries had very limited duties. Instead of initiating policy themselves, many just stapled the documents provided by their home ministries. Because their work was not substantial, the ministries were hesitant about sending their best men."[33]

This situation changed after Hashimoto's reforms. As Deputy CCS Furukawa explained, "Since the Kantei plays more of an instrumental role in policy making, the ministries now send more competent officers. For more senior positions, we even handpicked officers from other ministries."[34] The improved quality of officials has made the Kantei more effective at dealing with difficult issues.

Strengthened Institutions for Initiating Policy

In addition to organizational changes, the reforms enhanced the institutional authority of the prime minister and the Kantei. The revision of the Cabinet Law, meant to boost the power of the prime minister and the cabinet, was a central issue for Hashimoto's Administrative Reform Council. The national leader's authority at a cabinet meeting was ambiguous under the old law. Although it was possible for the prime minister to propose a policy, just like any other cabinet member, the prime minister and the rest of the cabinet rarely took that initiative. The revised Article 4 of the law clarifies the prime minister's authority to propose important, basic policies at such meetings. With this revision, institutional arrangements were clearly set for the national leader to initiate policies at the top.

The authority and function of the Kantei were also bolstered so that it could support the prime minister's policy initiatives. Under the old Cabinet Law, the Kantei's authority as policy coordinator was limited and passive. Article 12 of the law authorized the Kantei to coordinate "important policies of the cabinet" and policies "necessary for keeping integration" of the government. That was interpreted to mean that the office could act only on limited policy matters or only when other ministries requested policy coordination. The revised Cabinet Law allows the Kantei to initiate policies by clearly providing the authority to plan and draft concrete proposals under the direction of the cabinet and the prime minister.

Not surprisingly, the bureaucrats vehemently protested this change during the deliberations that took place in Hashimoto's Administrative Reform Council; the ministries clearly did not want the Kantei to plan and draft bills on matters under their jurisdiction. Further, the guideline on policy coordination (approved by the cabinet in May 2000) defines the Cabinet Secretariat's role as "to present policy direction for the government as a whole, and coordinate policy strategically and proactively." The guideline also instructs other ministries to recognize that "the Cabinet Secretariat is the highest and final organ for policy coordination under the cabinet."[35] This places the Kantei above other ministries and agencies. Statutorily, the prime minister and the cabinet can now initiate and execute policy independently of the relevant ministries, and the Kantei can finalize policy coordination with greater legal authority.

Interestingly, Hashimoto himself became the first minister to take advantage of this revision. In December 2000, he became the first state minister of administrative reform in the third Mori cabinet and directed the Kantei's administrative reform office. The following month, Hashimoto revealed the Kantei's reform plan for the civil service system in a speech at the Japan Press Club. The National Personnel Authority, which handles rules and reg-

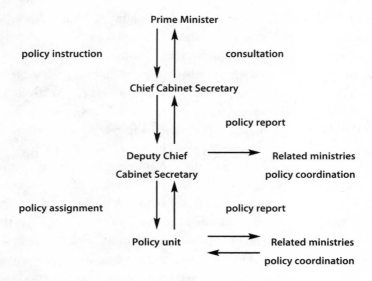

Fig. 3.3 Conceptual Lines of Decision Making (Figure presented by Teijiro Furukawa, October 30, 2003)

ulations of civil servants, subsequently filed complaints with the Kantei about the lack of prior consultation. However, Hashimoto rejected their complaints based on the Kantei's authority to initiate policy, which had been validated in the May 2000 cabinet decision.[36] In March 2001, the Kantei again exercised its authority on a policy initiative, submitting a reform plan for the civil service system to Prime Minister Mori.[37]

The Koizumi administration did not hesitate to exercise its policy initiative authority either. According to Deputy CCS Furukawa, Prime Minister Koizumi frequently instructed the Kantei on policy matters through CCS Yasuo Fukuda. Fukuda would order Furukawa to take action, and the latter would then assign officers in the policy unit to the task. The assigned officers consulted and coordinated with the related ministries and then reported back to Furukawa.

Furukawa explained the process: "The policy reports that I received from the Kantei officers were basically in final form. If necessary, I performed any further coordination needed and finalized them. I strongly felt that if I failed to catch a ball, it would go to the outfield without anyone running after it. Therefore, I tried to finalize the issue at my level. After doing so, I reported to CCS Fukuda."[38] (The process is illustrated in figure 3.3.)

Furukawa also described how final decisions were made:

> Sometimes we needed the prime minister's final decision, but more often than not, the CCS made the final call. On the most important policy decisions, however, I made sure the prime minister was involved. As deputy CCS, I was conscious of the different roles of the political leaders and the bureaucrats. I arranged all the decisions to be made by the CCS. CCS Fukuda and I had the same opinion in most of the issues we handled.[39]

Under the Koizumi administration, the Kantei handled many issues using the top-down decision-making process.

The IT Basic Law under the Mori Cabinet

Until recently, the Kantei rarely formulated policy. Before 2000, it was in charge of just two laws: the Cabinet Law and the Security Council Establishment Law (a minister-level council within the cabinet). These laws were not policy oriented, however, but were directly related to the cabinet's function and organization.

The Kantei has developed several important pieces of legislation since the Mori administration. In 2000, the Kantei initiated the first policy-oriented law under its new authority, the Basic Law on the Formation of an Advanced Information and Telecommunications Network Society (IT Basic Law). Although information technology was considered a "key to social economic development in the twenty-first century,"[40] policy coordination was difficult due to interagency conflicts between the Ministry of Posts and Telecommunications (which handled infrastructure) and the Ministry of International Trade and Industry (which supervised the electronics and computer industry). To formulate an effective "e-Japan" strategy, the Mori administration formed the IT Strategy Council under the Kantei in July 2000 to oversee policy coordination. The council, headed by Sony chairman Nobuyuki Idei, was composed of Idei and nineteen other members, mostly business leaders and academics. The council's deliberations resulted in the establishment of the IT Basic Law, which passed the Diet in December 2000.

Legislative Initiatives under the Koizumi Cabinet

Following this first success under the Mori government, the Kantei enacted seven major laws and three other measures under the Koizumi cabinet by the end of 2004. Four concern domestic and economic reform, and six are directly related to national security. The four domestic and economic reforms are the Special Public Corporations Reform Basic Law (21 June 2001), the Urban Renaissance Special Measures Law (6 April 2002), the Basic Law on Intellectual Property (4 December 2002), and the Law on Special Zones for Structural Reform (18 December 2002). The other six, which address national security and emergency-related issues, are the Anti-Terrorism Special Measures Law (29 October 2001), the Emergency Law (13 June 2003), and the Iraq Special Measures Law (1 August 2003) along with the Law to Protect People's Rights, the Law to Facilitate U.S. Military Actions, and the Law on the Use of Public Facilities (all 18 June 2004).

Among the domestic and economic reform laws mentioned above, the one dealing with special public corporations deserves close attention, since it was a major focus of the Koizumi administration throughout 2003. From the beginning of his administration, one of Koizumi's political slogans was "structural reform without sanctuaries." Reform of government-affiliated entities, also known as special public corporations, had been a political issue for a long time. Plans to reform these deficit-ridden organizations, however, had been pursued on a limited basis. During Hashimoto's administrative reform efforts, the special public corporations were heavily criticized for their inefficiency and lack of management transparency. However, the matter of their reform was separated from other issues and delegated to the LDP Headquarters for Promoting Administrative Reform, which did not produce any major concrete results.

With the January 2001 reorganization of the central government, the Mori administration established the Headquarters for Administrative Reform under the Kantei. As described earlier, Prime Minister Mori appointed former prime minister Hashimoto as the cabinet minister in charge of administrative reform. The secretariat operated under the assistant CCS for internal affairs to deal with three major areas: (1) special public corporations, (2) the public service system, and (3) administration-commissioned public service corporations. Having led major reform efforts as national leader, Hashimoto was well aware that reforming the special public corporations would require fundamental structural changes to Japan's political and economic system, as institutional complementarities had formed over many years. During his tenure as cabinet minister, Hashimoto focused on revamping the public servant system.[41]

A major policy shift took place at the headquarters when Koizumi became prime minister in April 2001. Koizumi had advocated reforming special public corporations and privatizing postal services for many years. He appointed Nobuteru Ishihara, a reform-minded, younger LDP Diet member, as minister for administrative reform and instructed him to focus on special public corporations. The headquarters' secretariat swiftly drafted a bill proposing establishment of the Special Public Institutions Reform Promotion Headquarters. This body would review all public corporations by March 2006 in order to determine which would be abolished, privatized, or allowed to continue. The cabinet approved the bill, which was then submitted to the Diet. After a short deliberation, the Diet enacted the measure in June 2001.

The political battles began after the law passed and the newly established headquarters began reviewing the corporations and deciding their fates. The seventy-seven special public corporations, originally established to rebuild Japan's infrastructure after World War II, were instrumental in facilitating Japan's economic growth by overseeing state loans and construction projects. Over the years, however, these quasi-governmental corporations grew increasingly inefficient and were costing Japanese taxpayers a collective 5.3 trillion yen a year. These funds were allocated to special public corporations as subsidies or government endowments. With fiscal pressure mounting, the media and the public had called for drastic reforms.

In August 2001, Prime Minister Koizumi publicly expressed his intention to cut 1 trillion of the 5.3 trillion yen allocated to special corporations in the fiscal 2002 budget. This statement led to the December 2002 cabinet decision to reform special public corporations, including the abolition or privatization of the Urban Development Corporation, the Japan National Oil Corporation, the Government Housing Loan Corporation, and the four highway-related corporations.

The highway-related corporations, particularly the Japan Highway Public Corporation, were among the public entities the media criticized most. By 1999, Japan Highway had accumulated a total debt of 24 trillion yen in the course of building 7,000 kilometers of highway. If Japan Highway were to fulfill the original government plan of building a total of 9,342 kilometers of highway, the corporation would require 300 billion yen of government funds annually, and its debt would swell to 44 trillion yen. As it sought to formulate a privatization policy for the controversial organizations, the Koizumi government formed the Promotion Committee for the Privatization of the Four Highway-Related Public Corporations directly under the cabinet in June 2002. Committee members engaged in a series of heated debates on whether to freeze plans for the remaining 2,342 kilometers of highway.

As road construction is highly integrated in local politics throughout the nation, this possibility attracted much media and public attention. In December 2003, based on the Promotion Committee's recommendation, the Ministry of Land, Infrastructure, and Transport announced its final plan to privatize the public corporation. Although the plan did not include freezing construction of the remaining 2,342 kilometers, as the Promotion Committee had strongly recommended, it would substantially cut construction costs by scaling down the original scheme. Throughout 2003, the cabinet committee led the debate on privatization and pressured the vested interest groups, highlighting the cabinet's initiative in the extremely political issue of road construction.

As it did in the case of special corporations reform, the Kantei often leads the way on politically difficult policy issues. The Kantei initiated the drafting of three pieces of domestic policy legislation—the Urban Renaissance Special Measures Law, the Basic Law on Intellectual Property, and the Law on Special Zones for Structural Reform—and established ad hoc policy offices to deal with these issues. The Office of Urban Renaissance plans drastic measures to advance urban redevelopment for future environmental needs, disaster prevention, and internationalization that will require deregulation in many policy areas. The Office of Intellectual Property Strategy Promotion develops measures for the creation, protection, and use of intellectual property by clarifying the responsibilities of the state, local governments, universities, and business enterprises. The Office of Special Zones for Structural Reform promotes the creation of specified deregulation zones based on plans submitted by municipal governments and private-sector enterprises. In each area, plans are advanced by the Kantei's initiative. Former Deputy CCS Furukawa proudly stated, "These plans require intensive policy coordination among several ministries. If this had not been handled by the Kantei, policy advancement would not have happened as swiftly."[42]

Power Shift in Foreign-Policy Making

In the areas of foreign and defense affairs, the Koizumi government successfully enacted six major pieces of legislation, three of which are discussed in detail in chapters 4–6. The Kantei, not MOFA, was central to the policy making for these laws.

In preparing the 1990 UN Peace Cooperation legislation (described in chapter 2), MOFA failed to reconcile the differences of opinion over the status of dispatched SDF personnel, so the Kantei took the initiative on drafting new legislation. MOFA officials saw this as a defeat. In an attempt to recover, they reorganized their ministry, and the result was the Foreign Policy Bureau, established in August 1993. By appointing a future vice minister as bureau chief, the bureau set itself up as the most important bureau in the ministry and expected to play a central role in drafting and planning foreign policy on behalf of the entire ministry. However, it had to handle an unexpectedly large number of daily tasks to coordinate operations within the ministry as well as negotiations with other ministries and was unable to fulfill its original role.

The September 11 terrorist attacks, occurring not long after the Koizumi cabinet was in place, brought dramatic changes to international politics. MOFA again had difficulty adjusting to a complex and rapidly developing situation. The Treaties Bureau's traditional approach would not work, and the new Foreign Policy Bureau was not yet fully functional. In addition, MOFA was tainted by highly publicized financial scandals. A manager in the ministry's Overseas Visit Support Division, which organizes trips by prime ministers and other high-ranking government officials, was arrested after it was discovered that he was routinely depositing ministry funds into his own bank accounts to buy condos, racehorses, and golf-club memberships. MOFA claimed that the official was a single bad apple. It later came to light, however, that many divisions of MOFA were embezzling ministry funds for entertainment. The media savaged the ministry on a daily basis.

In the midst of these scandals, the sharp-tongued daughter of the late Prime Minister Kakuei Tanaka, Makiko Tanaka, was named foreign minister under the new Koizumi cabinet in April 2001. Soon after assuming office, Tanaka called MOFA "the Pandemonium" (*fukumaden*) and began an open feud with MOFA officials. The fight severely impeded the daily diplomatic operations of the ministry as well as internal organizational reform efforts and personnel appointments.

Tanaka came under fire as well. Her qualifications for the position were already being questioned within weeks after she assumed the post. Her critics pointed to three specific incidents. The first, in May 2001, was Tanaka's cancellation of a meeting with U.S. deputy secretary of state Richard Armitage because she was reportedly too exhausted and busy reading up on her new responsibilities. In the second, in November 2001, Tanaka arrived late for a meeting with Iran's foreign minister because she was "looking for a lost ring." The most serious incident occurred in September 2001, when she revealed the U.S. State Department's evacuation location after the terrorist attacks. These are only a few examples of her misconduct. As a result of Tanaka's incompetence and battles with her own subordinates, MOFA was malfunctioning.

Tanaka also picked a fight with Muneo Suzuki, a powerful LDP politician who had held the posts of foreign vice minister and parliamentary deputy CCS. Suzuki maintained a great deal of influence with many MOFA officials as an experienced member of the LDP's subcommittee on foreign affairs. In January 2002, Tanaka claimed that Suzuki ordered MOFA officials to exclude two nongovernmental organizations from the International Conference on Reconstruction Assistance to Afghanistan.

As the fight between Tanaka and Suzuki escalated, the media uncovered multiple incidents of fraud that demonstrated Suzuki's undue influence on MOFA. Prime Minister Koizumi ended up dismissing Tanaka as foreign minister and forcing Suzuki to step down from his position as chairman of the lower house's Rules and Administration Committee. Later, Suzuki's unlawful influence on some MOFA projects led to the arrest of two MOFA officials. Suzuki himself was arrested for bribery in June 2002.

MOFA was in total chaos after Tanaka's dismissal, and the Kantei's grip on foreign affairs grew even stronger. At that time, the media portrayed the Kantei as having essentially three other "foreign ministers" in addition to the prime minister, who was the "first foreign minister": CCS Yasuo Fukuda, Parliamentary Deputy CCS Shinzo Abe, and Administrative Deputy CCS Teijiro Furukawa.[43] Although Environment Minister Yoriko Kawaguchi even-

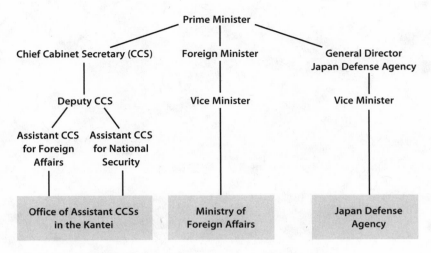

Fig. 3.4 Institutions of Foreign Policy

tually became foreign minister, as a non-politician, her political influence was very limited. Fukuda, Abe, and Furukawa at the Kantei were always involved in any foreign-affairs issue that required political judgment and coordination.

The CCS and the deputy CCS brought foreign-policy issues at the Kantei to the office of the assistant CCS. An assistant CCS from MOFA, Shotaro Yachi, regularly used his office on the fourth floor of the prime minister's official residence. Partly because of his close proximity, he began to act as a foreign-policy adviser to the prime minister. In the area of national security, the assistant CCS from the JDA, Keiji Ohmori, played a central role, with assistance from the old Office on National Security and Crisis Management. For foreign- and defense-policy making that requires coordination among different ministries, the Kantei is in a better position than MOFA to plan and draft policies.

In effect, there was a power shift from MOFA to the Kantei (see fig. 3.4) in the area of foreign and defense affairs, which is a desirable phenomenon. The emergence of the Kantei has created a strong core in the concentric circles model of Japan's policy making and has made it easier for the prime minister to exercise leadership. The following three chapters demonstrate how Prime Minister Koizumi and the Kantei played a central role in the policy-making process of three major pieces of national security legislation and effectively confirmed the essential role of Kantei diplomacy.

4

KOIZUMI'S RESPONSE TO TERRORISM

The 2001 Anti-Terrorism Legislation

On September 19, 2001, Prime Minister Junichiro Koizumi announced his intention to actively back American reprisals for the terrorist attacks in New York and Washington, D.C., referring to terrorism as "Japan's own security issue." On October 8, immediately after the first U.S. air attack against Afghanistan, he expressed full support for U.S. and British military action and said Japan would do everything possible within the framework of its Constitution to help.

Prime Minister Koizumi backed up his words with action. The Koizumi cabinet submitted anti-terrorism legislation to the Diet that would allow the overseas dispatch of Japan's Self-Defense Forces (SDF) under wartime conditions for the first time since World War II. The legislation was enacted in the Diet three weeks later—an incredibly quick passage for such a major bill.

The results of Koizumi's forceful top-down style of leadership were seen as a sharp break from Japan's prior pacifism and the slow, unclear response patterns of the past. This chapter first explores how Koizumi became prime minister despite a very limited power base within the Liberal Democratic Party (LDP) and then examines the Koizumi cabinet's policy process for the 2001 anti-terrorism legislation in terms of the concentric circles model.

Koizumi's Surprise Victory

Koizumi was elected the LDP president and thus the prime minister in April 2001, surprising many observers of and experts on Japanese politics who had predicted the victory of former prime minister Ryutaro Hashimoto because of his strong power base within the party. However, the 1994 electoral reform introduced a single-seat district system for the lower house and changed the power balance within the LDP. As younger members demanded a more democratic election process for selecting the LDP president, the rules were changed in 2001, and those changes had an unexpected impact on the election result.

During its long, single-majority rule of 1955–93, the LDP became highly decentralized. Powerful LDP members formed and maintained separate factions that competed for political influence. Leaders of large factions played decisive roles in LDP presidential elections because factional coalitions with a majority chose the party leader, who then became prime minister. In return for its support for the national leader, the largest faction could send its member to the powerful position of LDP secretary-general, effectively controlling party affairs. This often caused a dual power structure, as occurred under the Kaifu administration (described in chapters 1 and 2).

The old electoral system of the lower house, with three to five seats in each district, encouraged multiple candidates from the LDP. As LDP candidates relied more on their factions than on the party organization for financial and other campaign resources, their loyalties were aligned with their factions, not with the LDP leadership or the prime minister. This further decentralized the power structure of the LDP.

Under the non-LDP cabinet led by Morihiro Hosokawa (1993–94), new electoral rules were introduced with the major objective of weakening the power of factions. As the lower house's old "middle-size" electoral system encouraged multiple candidates from the LDP, the competition among candidates from different LDP factions was much fiercer than competition with opposition parties, due to their similar support bases. LDP candidates, therefore, had to rely not on the party organization but on their factions for financial and other campaign support. This strengthened the power of factions and decentralized the power of the LDP leadership and the prime minister. It was also considered a cause of political corruption, since LDP factions had to actively seek financial resources in order to compete among themselves.

This 1994 electoral change weakened some functions of the LDP factions, although it did not eliminate them. Factions still exist and remain an important factor in the stability of the government and the allocation of many positions, such as vice ministers and Diet committee chairmen. However, the new electoral system created a significant shift in the power balance within the LDP, which indirectly weakened factional influence over the prime minister. Under the old system, a district's constituents brought casework to more senior and politically powerful politicians when there were two or more representatives of the government party. Young LDP members in a single-seat electoral district now receive virtually all of their constituents' requests and have found themselves on a more equal footing politically vis-à-vis the party elders.

These politicians have become more vocal about criticizing the government and older LDP members. For example, Taro Kono openly criticized powerful LDP secretary-general Hiromu Nonaka for the LDP's "defeat" in the 2000 general election and called for his resignation. Under the old electoral system with its multi-member districts, a powerful faction could often suppress such criticism by threatening to send a rival candidate to compete in the younger Diet member's district. With a single-seat district system, however, no LDP candidate is allowed to challenge an incumbent, making such a threat invalid. Kono and about forty other younger LDP members from different factions, including Nobuteru Ishihara and Yoshimi Watanabe, formed the Group to Build a Japan for Tomorrow, calling for drastic reform of the LDP. Their Internet home page displays their laments: "The LDP is experiencing a melt-down. Without drastic reform, the LDP will collapse from a true national party into a party that represents special interests."[1]

For the LDP presidential race of April 2001, younger members demanded that the LDP president be chosen not only by LDP Diet members but also by local members of the LDP. At the March 2001 LDP meeting, Kono presented their plan, which would allocate 346 electoral votes to LDP members across the nation in addition to the votes held by the party's 346 lawmakers. The public and the media were highly critical of Prime Minister Yoshiro Mori's selection by LDP leaders in a closed-door session after the sudden death of Keizo Obuchi. Although LDP faction leaders did not want to allocate so many votes to non-elected LDP members, which would take the election out of their control, the faction leaders were forced to make the election more transparent and democratic. They compromised by giving each LDP prefectural chapter 3 votes instead of 1. With a total of 141 local votes, less than half the number of lawmakers' votes, faction leaders could introduce "reform" yet limit uncertainty.

The largest Hashimoto faction, with 101 LDP Diet members, who boasted of their connections with local chapters, looked upon the electoral change very optimistically. However, several younger members of the faction stated openly that they might vote against the faction's decision to support Hashimoto in the election. Younger members of the other factions also called for voting rights independent of factional lines. They called for an open forum at which to question the four LDP presidential candidates and held a two-day session with them before the election. Many went back to their districts and expressed their personal support for Koizumi. Outspoken female politician Makiko Tanaka accompanied Koizumi on the campaign trail and offered speeches in support. Koizumi and Tanaka were enthusiastically welcomed all over the nation.

In the preliminary election among the forty-seven local chapters, Koizumi won 123 out of 141 votes. Hashimoto received only 15 votes from five prefectures. Jumping on the bandwagon, Shizuka Kamei withdrew his candidacy and expressed his faction's support for Koizumi. In the end, Koizumi won a landslide victory, with 298 out of 487 votes. Hashimoto received only 155 votes with the support of his faction and the Horiuchi faction. Five younger members of the two factions voted for Koizumi against factional lines. This underlined the weakening power of the LDP factions.

Koizumi was the first party president and prime minister to be selected outside the traditional factional power struggles. He was elected by an overwhelming majority of LDP local branches, thus earning enough legitimacy to pick his own party leaders and cabinet. He named Taku Yamasaki, his close friend, to the powerful position of LDP secretary-general. He picked up the phone, without consulting faction leaders, and persuaded Taro Aso and Mitsuo Horiuchi to assume the party's two other top positions. These LDP top executive posts usually had been filled based on factional balance.

As evidence of his independence from the old party chieftains, Koizumi's new cabinet had an unprecedented number of women (five) and civilians (three). Koizumi appointed Makiko Tanaka, who assisted him during the LDP presidential race, to the prestigious post of foreign minister. In an effort to invigorate government reform, he chose a leader from among the young politicians, Nobuteru Ishihara, to be a cabinet minister in charge of administrative reform. In a press conference, Koizumi boasted, "LDP members finally understand what 'appointments without factional intervention' is. They realize that I am serious."[2] Polls taken by major newspapers immediately after the establishment of Koizumi's cabinet showed his initial support had rocketed to the highest in the history of collecting such data: 78 percent by *Asahi*, 85 percent by *Mainichi*, and 87 percent by *Yomiuri*. According to the *Asahi Shimbun* poll, the biggest reason for the public's support was Koizumi's rejection of factional influence.[3]

The new electoral rules for the lower house shifted the balance of power between junior and senior members of the LDP, which led to changes in the LDP presidential election rule. After Koizumi became LDP president, the rule was further revised to provide LDP local chapters with 300 votes, more than doubling the previous number of 141. The influence of LDP factions in the presidential election was further weakened as a result, as seen in Koizumi's reelection in September 2003. Under this new rule, a candidate with wider popular support, like Koizumi, has a better chance of winning the presidency and therefore the prime ministership. The prime minister, who was selected outside of factional influence, enjoys stronger control over his cabinet. This enabled him to achieve his national security goals, as shown in his response to the September 11 terrorist attacks on the World Trade Center and the Pentagon.

Initial Reaction

Five months after Koizumi became prime minister, he faced a serious national security challenge. Unlike Prime Minister Kaifu during the 1990 Gulf crisis, Koizumi responded quickly to the 9/11 incident. Forty-five minutes after the attacks occurred, he established a liaison office at the Situation Center of the Cabinet to gather information. An hour later, when the severity of the situation had been assessed, he upgraded the office to the Emergency Anti-Terrorism Headquarters, with himself in charge. Emergency teams were dispatched from all the related ministries and agencies, and Prime Minister Koizumi situated himself at the headquarters.[4]

By identifying this tragedy as a "significant emergency," he placed the incidents under the cabinet's jurisdiction. The next morning, he called a cabinet-level meeting of the Security Council of Japan for the first time since the 1998 Taepodong missile incident involving North Korea. At a press conference after the meeting, Koizumi announced the government's initial plan of action and described the terrorist attacks as "grave challenges, not only to the United States, but also to all democratic societies."

This swift response was inspired largely by lessons Japan learned during the 1990s. The Gulf crisis and a series of domestic incidents had led to the creation of new positions and institutions for crisis management. The reforms reinforced the idea that the Cabinet Secretariat would handle crisis management, fostering a quicker reaction and a stronger display of leadership.

Top officials in the Koizumi government also understood the importance of promptly labeling this situation as a crisis. Many remembered how Prime Minister Toshiki Kaifu had failed to identify the Gulf crisis as a significant emergency. MOFA had handled that issue through normal diplomatic channels; logically, the Cabinet Security Affairs Office of the Cabinet Secretariat, which was designed to handle interagency coordination in an emergency, should have been in charge. Japan's crisis response lagged as a result.[5] This time, with the crisis swiftly recognized, Koizumi took advantage of newly created institutions such as the Situation Center.

Not everything went smoothly, however. Foreign Minister Makiko Tanaka was constantly in conflict with her own ministry's officials, presenting Koizumi with a painful bureaucratic headache. On September 11, Tanaka revealed secret information to the media on the emergency relocation of top U.S. diplomatic officials. On September 19, when MOFA officials asked Tanaka to visit Pakistan to seek that country's cooperation, she flatly refused, reportedly saying that she was a woman and could not go to such a dangerous place. Senior Vice Minister Masatake Sugiura visited Pakistan on her behalf and acquired President Pervez Musharraf's understanding on Japan's assistance to the United States. After these incidents, Tanaka was left outside the decision-making loop, putting the prime minister and the Cabinet Secretariat firmly in control of the anti-terrorism campaign.

After the initial response, Deputy Chief Cabinet Secretary Teijiro Furukawa quickly formed a study group with the two assistant chief cabinet secretaries from the Japan Defense Agency (JDA) and the Ministry of Foreign Affairs (MOFA), Keiji Ohmori and Kazuyoshi Urabe, MOFA's Foreign Policy Bureau chief Shotaro Yachi and North American Bureau chief Ichiro Fujisaki, JDA vice minister Ken Sato and Defense Policy Bureau chief Shingo Shuto, and deputy director general of the Cabinet Legislation Bureau Osamu Akiyama. To save time, Furukawa included an official from the Cabinet Legislation Bureau who would be in charge of examining the legal aspects of proposals in the draft formulation process.

Furukawa took full advantage of the January 2001 Cabinet Secretariat reorganization. As described in chapter 3, although the old Cabinet Office on External Affairs was abolished, the old Cabinet Office on National Security and Crisis Management (CONSCM) still existed informally, separate from the office of the assistant chief cabinet secretary (CCS). In his first policy speech in May 2001, Prime Minister Koizumi declared, "I intend to move forward with consideration on emergency legislation."[6] Soon after this speech, the Koizumi cabinet formed the Task Force on Emergency Legislation under CONSCM. The task force was headed by Assistant CCS Ohmori and staffed by a dozen young officers, mostly from the JDA, MOFA, and the National Police Agency. Two months later, officers from the Ministry of Internal Affairs and Telecommunications and the Ministry of Land, Infrastructure, and Transport joined the task force to increase its members to fifteen.

After 9/11, Deputy CCS Furukawa assigned this task force to serve as the secretariat for his study group. MOFA officials played subordinate roles in the task force. MOFA's weaker presence under the new institutional arrangement of the Cabinet Secretariat actually minimized interagency conflicts between the JDA and MOFA, making the Cabinet Secretariat, at the core of the concentric circles model used in this book, more effective.

By September 19, Prime Minister Koizumi was able to announce his plan to actively support American reprisals for the terrorist attacks. His plan included the dispatch of SDF ships to help the United States collect intelligence, deliver supplies, and provide medical services and humanitarian relief. He also pledged to strengthen protective measures for U.S. bases in Japan. Koizumi announced non-military measures as well, including an offer of $10 million to help fund rescue and cleanup work in the United States, a plan to provide emergency economic aid to Pakistan and India to help solicit their cooperation, and measures designed to avoid upset in the international economic system.

In formulating these points, members of Furukawa's study group carefully examined lessons from the Gulf crisis. Although Japan had provided as much as $13 billion in financial aid during that conflict, its contribution was criticized as "too little, too late." The group recognized that the international community would not welcome financial donations alone. Furukawa proudly stated that the Kantei had served a core role in getting the decisions made. "If the Kantei had not handled this issue, we could not have done this quickly."[7]

On September 25, Koizumi visited the United States to meet President George W. Bush and pledged speedy implementation of his plan. Koizumi's actions were more far-reaching than many experts in Japan and the United States had expected and received wide praise. The White House even issued a press release specifically expressing its appreciation.[8]

Public support for strong leadership helped enable Koizumi's quick response. In a policy speech on September 27, Koizumi expressed his determination to implement his plan quickly. Making such an international commitment without the traditional discussion and consultation, however, drew loud criticism from the opposition parties and even some LDP members. Yet the criticism faltered in the face of increased public support of the Koizumi cabinet after the announcement. According to a poll conducted by *Nihon Keizai Shimbun* on September 21–22, 70 percent of the respondents supported Japan's rear-echelon support of U.S. military action.[9] The Koizumi cabinet's approval rating had risen to an impressive 79 percent, up 10 percent from July 2001.

The media generally responded positively as well. Among the five major newspapers, *Nihon Keizai*, *Mainichi*, *Sankei*, and *Yomiuri* supported the government's policy of legislating a new law for dispatching the SDF to support U.S. forces. Only *Asahi Shimbun* maintained its traditional position against the SDF's dispatch overseas.[10] The strong backing of the public and the media, representing two of the outermost rings in the concentric circles model, successfully pushed the core's initiative forward.

The Political Process Inside the Coalition

The popular support he enjoyed enabled Prime Minister Koizumi not only to make a swift initial response but also to shepherd the anti-terrorism legislation through some unusual shortcuts in the political process. He was very aware that timeliness in implementing policy could affect perceptions of

Japan's contribution to the campaign against terrorism. The normal political process might delay implementation and again invite international criticism for a slow and inadequate response.

As Hilsman's model assumes that each ring is not composed of a monolithic entity, the ruling party, in the first outer ring, is a very decentralized organization with different groups of policy experts. As explained in chapter 1, the relevant subcommittee of the LDP's Policy Research Council would usually be the first body consulted on a proposed government policy. After a policy gained approval in the committee, it was sent to the LDP's General Council to build party consensus and become the party's official policy. Under the coalition government, the LDP's coalition partners in the second outer ring—Komeito and the Conservative Party—must agree to the policy before cabinet approval is sought.

To save time, Koizumi reversed this political procedure and sought agreement on the anti-terrorism legislation from coalition partners in the second ring before consulting the LDP's policy subcommittees. The highly popular prime minister was well aware that once the three parties reached an agreement, it would be difficult for individual LDP members to oppose the decision, especially on such an urgent international issue. Direct pressure from the second outer ring and indirect pressure from the public in the outermost ring suppressed opposition from the first outer ring.

To secure agreement with the coalition partners, especially from Komeito, which was proud of its pacifist stance on national security issues, the Koizumi government decided not to provoke constitutional arguments. Although the anti-terrorism legislation was closely related to the argument of collective self-defense, which would require reinterpretation of the Constitution, Prime Minister Koizumi repeatedly stated that the measure would be kept within the constitutional framework.

On September 25, the three coalition parties agreed on the outline of a new law to allow provision of rear-echelon support for U.S. forces in the Indian Ocean area and humanitarian assistance to refugees. It was announced that the new legislation would be based on relevant United Nations resolutions in order to avoid constitutional arguments. Furthermore, dispatching the SDF would not require prior approval from the Diet, but a post-dispatch report would be made.

On the following day, the government went over the outline with representatives of the opposition parties. A day later, on September 27, LDP members at the General Council were finally briefed. Members of LDP policy subcommittees—which had been the first political forum in the traditional bottom-up process, part of the first outer ring in the concentric circles model—were the last to learn officially about the planned legislation at a joint meeting of the Cabinet, Defense, and Foreign Affairs subcommittees on September 28. The joint meeting was held to hasten the political process within the LDP, but it also served to limit the influence of powerful *zoku* members.

This legislation addressed a major issue that fell within the jurisdictions of all three subcommittees. One of the most powerful members of the Foreign Affairs Subcommittee, Muneo Suzuki, complained that this process downgraded the importance of discussions in his panel. Younger members of the defense panel demanded a more prominent role for the Diet, saying that prior approval should be required before dispatching the SDF. These dissenting voices were ignored, however, largely because the protesters did not form a majority at the joint meeting.

When the task force in charge of the policy-making process came up with the specifics of the legislation, Prime Minister Koizumi again sought agreement among the three coalition parties first. On October 1, the secretaries-general and the policy committee chairmen of the three parties basically approved the legislation and agreed to build a consensus within their respective parties. The following day, Koizumi government officials explained the details of the legislation to a joint meeting of the three LDP policy subcommittees.

The defense panel approved the government draft of the legislation but at the same time passed a resolution calling for prior Diet approval of any SDF dispatch. By doing so, panel members expressed their frustration at being excluded from the decision making but did not block the policy process. The panel members well knew that quick enactment of the legislation was needed and did not want to be blamed for any delay.

As a result, the LDP General Council approved the legislation on October 4, and the bill was approved by the cabinet and submitted to the Diet the next day. The initial agreement reached with the coalition partners in the second outer ring effectively suppressed LDP opposition coming from the first outer ring.

Interestingly, the ministry in charge of this legislation was not MOFA, which usually handled such bills in the Diet, as described in chapter 2. There was a significant change in the institutional arrangement, however. Bureaucratic assistance with responses in Diet meetings had been abolished in 1999, leaving the cabinet minister responsible for answering questions from the opposition parties. Leaders of the government and the ruling party had no confidence in Foreign Minister Makiko Tanaka's ability to perform this important task, however. Ongoing battles with MOFA officials were having an adverse effect on Tanaka's performance in the Diet. Other Tanaka missteps—including leaking private comments made by Emperor Akihito—were factors in the decision. Such slips of the tongue in the Diet could result in the delay or blockage of a bill. The legislation was therefore placed under the jurisdiction of the Cabinet Secretariat, making CCS Yasuo Fukuda responsible for introducing it and answering related questions in the Diet.

Diet Operations

The opposition parties, represented by the third ring in the concentric circles model, criticized the government draft. The Social Democratic Party (SDP), formerly the Japan Socialist Party, denounced the U.S. intention to retaliate and portrayed the Koizumi plan as a step toward Japan's remilitarization. On the rightist front, Ichiro Ozawa of the Liberal Party released a position paper that heavily criticized Koizumi's plan as "ad hoc, spur-of-the-moment half-measures." The Liberal Party maintained that the use of armed forces must be approved by the UN, as in the case of the Gulf War, before Japan could send its troops into an international conflict. Ozawa also criticized Koizumi for ducking discussions of collective self-defense and constitutional reinterpretation.

Wishing to avoid Diet passage by the ruling coalition alone, the Koizumi government sought cooperation from the largest opposition party, the Democratic Party of Japan (DPJ). Many within the DPJ supported Koizumi's initiative on this issue as well as on other reform efforts, weakening the unity of the opposition parties. The DPJ, for example, was the only opposition party to support a Diet resolution passed on September 27 that condemned the terrorist attacks in the United States. At the October 11 meeting of the lower house Special Committee on Anti-Terrorism Legislation, Koizumi stated, "We would like to show our attitude to fight against terrorism as a member of the international community by achieving wider support from different political parties and the Japanese people."

DPJ leader Yukio Hatoyama presented the conditions needed to gain his party's support, which included requiring prior Diet approval for "stronger civilian control" over the SDF and prohibiting the transportation of arms and ammunition. At an October 13 meeting between the ruling parties and the DPJ, a political compromise was offered that would prohibit land transportation of arms and ammunition but allow ocean transportation. The DPJ accepted this compromise. As for obtaining Diet approval before dispatching the SDF, which the LDP's defense panel had also called for, indications were that Koizumi might offer a compromise bill at a summit meeting with Hatoyama.[11]

Before the summit meeting, however, LDP's coalition partner, Komeito, firmly opposed such a compromise with the opposition party. Komeito members suspected Prime Minister Koizumi did not like having their party, with its Buddhist background, as an LDP coalition partner. Komeito's concern was that the popular prime minister might dissolve the current coalition and run the government with the DPJ instead. In order to avoid a possible coalition breakup, Komeito demanded that Prime Minister Koizumi offer no further compromises to the DPJ. On October 15, the leaders of the three coalition parties decided on the government's final proposal without securing prior Diet approval. It required only reporting of the basic dispatch plan and Diet approval within twenty days after the plan was implemented.

On the same day, a summit meeting between Koizumi and Hatoyama broke up, forcing the ruling parties to pass the bill through the Diet alone. The leaders of the ruling parties were confident that the public would support the legislation even without the DPJ's cooperation. They were right. According to an *Asahi Shimbun* poll conducted on October 13–14, 51 percent of the respondents supported the anti-terrorism legislation while just 29 percent were opposed.[12] On behalf of the business community, Keidanren chairman Takashi Imai praised the swift passage of the legislation, which would enable Japan to contribute to the war against terrorism.[13] In contrast, the largest labor union, Rengo, publicly announced its opposition, stating that the legislation might conflict with the Constitution, which prohibits Japan from exercising the right of collective self-defense.[14]

After the decision was made to push the legislation through without support from the opposition parties, Diet action was swift. On October 16, the revised government bill was introduced and the lower house special committee approved it. Two days later, the lower house passed the bill. DPJ leader

Hatoyama had a difficult time persuading some twenty Democratic lower house members, who were supportive of the bill, not to vote for it. The bill was enacted on October 29, after only twenty-four days of Diet deliberations. The committees of both houses spent a total of just 62 hours deliberating these bills, compared with 179 hours on the 1992 International Peace Cooperation legislation and 154 hours on the 1999 Regional Crisis legislation. Koizumi's top-down style of leadership, initiated and powered by the core of the model, enabled the quick passage of a major piece of legislation, aided by strong public support from the outermost ring, which overcame resistance from the opposition parties in the third outer ring and elements of the LDP as well.

5

PREPARING FOR A NATIONAL CONTINGENCY

The 2003 Emergency Legislation

While the anti-terrorism legislation of 2001 had a built-in, but extendable, expiration date, the emergency legislation passed in 2003 provided a permanent legal framework for allowing the Self-Defense Forces (SDF) to use force in the event of an armed attack against Japan.

Throughout the postwar era, leftist opposition parties such as the Japan Socialist Party (JSP) and the Japan Communist Party (JCP) strongly objected to enacting such legislation, arguing that it represented a step toward the nation's remilitarization. In a 1965 Diet session, a JSP member discovered and criticized the Mitsuya Study, a comprehensive contingency study, produced by officials at the Joint Staff Council of the Japan Defense Agency (JDA), that presented the case of a military crisis on the Korea Peninsula.

As this study was conducted without the explicit instruction of a political leader, it was seen as an illustration of eroding civilian control of the military. The revelation created excessive sensitivity toward such a study and made constructing an emergency plan a political taboo. In 1977, when the Fukuda cabinet instructed the JDA to study contingency plans related to the SDF, it attached a strict condition that the study would not serve as preparation for legislation.

A major breakthrough in the late 1990s, however, loosened up political debate on the topic. In October 1999, when the Liberal Democratic Party (LDP), the Liberal Party, and Komeito agreed to form a coalition government, they declared the enactment of emergency legislation to be a mutual goal. The three coalition parties formed the Government Parties National Security Project Team (hereafter referred to as the GP Project Team).

In May 2000, the Liberal Party broke up. Some of its members formed the Conservative Party, which replaced the Liberal Party as a coalition partner. The new three-party coalition decided to maintain the GP Project Team and its emergency legislation preparation and to strive for consensus among the coalition partners, which occupy the second outer ring of the concentric circles model.

In January 2001, Prime Minister Yoshiro Mori publicly stated that the government would "initiate consideration" of emergency legislation.[1] As an official at the Maritime Staff Office of the JDA explained, "This statement transformed a study within the JDA into a government-wide operation."[2] Three months later, when Junichiro Koizumi became prime minister, he instructed his defense minister to prepare legislation that would provide a legal framework for defending the nation. In May 2001, Koizumi directed that a task force be formed under the old Cabinet Office on National Security and Crisis Management. A prefabricated three-story building was constructed next to the Cabinet Office Building for the task force. The task force was given an emergency assignment to prepare anti-terrorism legislation in September 2001; after that legislation passed in late October of the same year, the task force went back to its original assignment.

The number of task force staffers increased from fifteen to twenty, including officials from the JDA, the Ministry of Foreign Affairs (MOFA), the National Police Agency, the Ministry of Land, Infrastructure and Transport, and the Ministry of Internal Affairs and Telecommunications. The Kantei, the core in the concentric circles model, again took the lead in preparing the legislation, with the JDA and MOFA assuming subordinate roles. The JDA formed a conference to consider emergency legislation, headed by the defense policy bureau chief, with twenty-six staffers from that bureau as well as from the Ground, Maritime, and Air Staff offices.[3] At MOFA, the National Security Division of the Foreign Policy Bureau took on the coordinating function. The bureau's Human Rights and Humanitarian Division was in charge of a study on international humanitarian issues related to dealing with hostages. The Japan-U.S. Security Treaty Division of the North American Bureau handled issues related to U.S. bases in Japan.[4]

The Kantei again became a central player in national security affairs after the anti-terrorism legislation. Deputy CCS Furukawa emphasized its importance: "The most important point in policy making was to establish a common view between the government and the public on national security. It was more appropriate for the Cabinet Secretariat, rather than the JDA, to achieve this goal."[5] The Kantei worked effectively at keeping all the above-mentioned issues moving along simultaneously.

The Policy Process in the Coalition

On December 22, 2001, against the backdrop of the 9/11 terrorist attacks and while the Kantei-led policy process of formulating emergency legislation was proceeding, a North Korean ship entered Japan's exclusive economic zone and was blown up by its crew while being chased by three Japan Coast Guard vessels. The ship was widely suspected to have been involved in a spying or smuggling operation. This incident convinced many in Japan that external threats to the nation existed and strengthened the public's sense that national security must be increased. This, in turn, boosted support for establishing a legal framework for national emergency responses. Three days later, Prime Minister Koizumi instructed the task force to prepare the emergency-related bills.

On January 23, 2002, the government parties established the Conference on National Emergency Legislation for Diet Deliberation (hereafter referred to as the GP Conference). LDP secretary-general Taku Yamasaki headed the GP Conference, and he, along with the secretaries-general of the other ruling parties, discussed the political process and the existing GP Project Team, which dealt mostly with policy aspects.

Koizumi employed the same strategy he had used with the anti-terrorism legislation. The Kantei, as the core in the concentric circles model, was in charge of preparing the legislation. In the political process, building a favorable consensus among the three coalition parties, in the second outer ring, represented a higher priority than doing so within the LDP, in the first ring.

In his February 2 policy speech, Prime Minister Koizumi stated: "The issues of terrorism and unidentified armed vessels have once again made clear that there exist forces capable of threatening the lives of our people. We should bear in mind the adage 'Be prepared and have no regrets.'"[6] In the same speech, he declared that his cabinet would introduce the emergency legislation in the current Diet session.

Although preparation of the legislation went smoothly, the Koizumi cabinet faced a serious political problem. The ongoing in-house battle between Foreign Minister Makiko Tanaka and MOFA officials escalated when Tanaka accused lawmaker Muneo Suzuki of pressuring MOFA to ban two nongovernmental organizations from the January 2002 International Conference on Reconstruction Assistance to Afghanistan. Claiming that the Suzuki-Tanaka scandal would dilute political support for his budget proposal and emergency bills, Prime Minister Koizumi fired Tanaka on January 29. The public, which saw Tanaka as a reformer, sent tens of thousands of e-mails a day to the Kantei to protest the sacking of the popular foreign minister. The Koizumi cabinet's public approval rating dropped from 72 percent to 49 percent immediately after Tanaka was fired.[7] For nearly half a year afterward, the public was about evenly divided between those who viewed the Koizumi government favorably and those who disapproved. At the same time, MOFA's power weakened further, boosting the Kantei's status.

Even with less public support, the Koizumi cabinet continued to prepare the emergency-related bills. On March 20, Assistant CCS Ohmori, who headed the task force, reported the outlines of the bills to the GP Project Team and the GP Conference, seeking initial agreement from the coalition partners occupying the second outer ring of the model. As Ohmori explained, the cabinet would introduce one bill that provided a legal framework for emergency legislation and three issue-based bills. The framework bill specified fundamental policies and processes to be followed if Japan suffered a direct attack. In such an event, the government would declare a "state of armed attack," and the cabinet would decide how to respond. The decision would eventually require Diet approval, but the law permitted ex post facto approval in an urgent situation.

The legislation revising the Self-Defense Forces Law would establish special measures to allow the SDF to operate smoothly. The special measures included exempting the SDF from the Road Law, which requires obtaining permission from the Japan Highway Authority before making any alterations to roads for the purpose of transporting troops. The legislation revising the Security Council Establishment Law would strengthen the minister-level Security Council of Japan and create an Emergency Response Special Committee, chaired by the chief cabinet secretary, to conduct investigation and analysis in the event of an emergency. Finally, the Legislation to Facilitate U.S. Military Actions would provide U.S. forces in Japan with the same degree of legal exemption as granted to the SDF in an emergency.

After studying Ohmori's explanations, some lawmakers in the GP Project Team and the GP Conference questioned why the four pieces of legislation would not cover responses to terrorist attacks in Japan or a situation similar to that of the unidentified ship entering Japan's exclusive economic zone. Assistant CCS Ohmori acknowledged the incompleteness of the bills but argued that they were only the initial step, for the current Diet session, and a more complete set would be proposed in the future. The chairman of the GP Project Team, former defense minister Akio Kyuma, expressed his understanding of the government's point.[8]

Two weeks later, the government decided not to submit the bill seeking a legal exemption for U.S. forces and informed the government parties on April 3 that it would introduce only the three bills. The GP Project Team accepted this change; however, the LDP joint subcommittees in Cabinet, National Defense, Foreign Affairs, and Land, Infrastructure, and Transport, part of the first outer ring of the model, voiced strong criticism of the remaining government proposals. For example, an influential member of the national defense subcommittee, Shigeru Ishiba, complained: "It is difficult to understand why we have to deal first with an armed attack by a foreign country, with low probability, and postpone preparing for a possible terrorist attack. In fact, an unidentified ship came close to Japan."[9]

The task force did not take this opinion into consideration when drafting the legislation and ignored the LDP experts. On April 8, it introduced more details of the bills to the GP Project Team and the GP Conference. Four days later, when the GP Conference officially approved the bills, the task force took it as the end of the policy process within the government parties. On April 16, the Koizumi cabinet approved the bills for submission to the Diet the next day.

Diet Operations

On April 26, deliberation on the emergency-related bills began. With its approval rating hovering around 40 percent, the Koizumi cabinet faced powerful resistance from the opposition parties. On the left, the Communist and Socialist parties, which for many years had argued that emergency legislation represented a step toward Japan's remilitarization, announced their displeasure with the bills. On the right, the Liberal Party and its leader, Ichiro Ozawa, roundly criticized the government proposal: "It is dated, and does not reflect the post–Cold War national security environment. It does not deserve the name of emergency legislation."[10] During the Cold War era, the most likely threat would have been an armed attack by the Soviet military. In the post–Cold War period, however, a terrorist-type attack was considered more probable than an armed attack by a foreign country. Ozawa pointed out that the government proposal was not designed to prepare the nation for such attacks.

That left the Koizumi cabinet only one potential ally, the Democratic Party of Japan. The DPJ, however, was sharply divided on the issue. On the one hand, the younger DPJ members, including Policy Research chairman Katsuya Okada, recognized the urgent need for emergency legislation. On the other hand, many former members of the Japan Socialist Party within the DPJ vehemently opposed the government proposal. To vent the heat of conflicting opinions within the party, the DPJ called for a long deliberation period on the legislation. Discussions on the anti-terrorism legislation took only sixty-two hours—perhaps understandable, since it was temporary legislation. Because any emergency legislation would be permanent, the DPJ representative asked the LDP for at least one hundred hours of deliberation in the lower house Special Committee on Emergency Legislation.[11]

LDP Diet Policy Committee chairman Tadamori Oshima responded coldly to the request, saying that fifty hours would be more than enough. Meanwhile, many members of the LDP coalition partner Komeito were still worried that Prime Minister Koizumi might seek to ally with the DPJ instead of their party. New Komeito pushed the LDP not to cooperate with the DPJ.[12] On May 21, Chairman Oshima decided to approve the schedule for the special committee's public hearing without the opposition parties in attendance. Flexibility in the public hearing schedule was regarded as an important part of the Diet legislation process and traditionally required a certain degree of cooperation with the opposition parties. The LDP, however, ignored this political tradition.

This decision hardened the DPJ position toward the proposal. The DPJ joined the other opposition parties in boycotting Diet operations until the ruling parties changed the public hearing schedule. The unity of the opposition parties boosted their influence significantly. During the Diet deliberations on the emergency legislation that took place between April and July 2002, more citizens disapproved of the cabinet than approved, with approval hovering around 40 percent. With lower public support and the media siding with the opposition parties, the ruling parties decided on May 27 to withdraw their proposed schedule. They then informed the DPJ representatives that they would be flexible on the hours of deliberation and possible amendments.

The Impact of Hawkish Statements

Although the DPJ agreed to restart Diet deliberations, more trouble hit the Koizumi cabinet. The May 28, 2002, issue of *Mainichi Shimbun* carried a scoop, revealing that a Maritime SDF lieutenant commander had compiled a list of individuals who had filed petitions to view government records. The DPJ severely criticized this action as a violation of basic human rights guaranteed by the Constitution and announced its determination to confront the government on this issue in the Diet.

Meanwhile, a weekly magazine reported that Parliamentary Deputy CCS Shinzo Abe had argued for the constitutionality of Japan's possession of nuclear weapons in a speech to college students.[13] On May 31, CCS Yasuo Fukuda commented: "We are discussing constitutional revisions, and we may change our three non-nuclear principles depending on the international situation."

These statements did not conflict with the previous government explanation. In 1960, Prime Minister Nobusuke Kishi stated in the Diet that it is not unconstitutional for Japan to possess nuclear weapons. But having two Kantei leaders make hawkish statements in the midst of Diet deliberations on the emergency legislation further hardened the attitudes of the DPJ and other opposition parties, which had already taken a rigid stance because of the JDA scandal. The opposition parties in the second outer ring maintained solid unity.

In deliberations in the special committee, a series of questions arose about both the JDA's compilation of personal data and the comments of Fukuda and Abe. When it was revealed that the JDA itself, not an individual SDF official, had made a systematic effort to gather personal data on information seekers, some members of the ruling parties requested that JDA director general Gen Nakatani resign. Younger LDP members were also critical of Fukuda's statement. For example, Shigeru Ishiba stated, "The government may not be serious about [the emergency] legislation"; his colleague Yasukazu Hamada said, "[Fukuda] should know what consequences such a statement would create."[14] The LDP, in the first outer ring of the model, was also reluctant to support Koizumi on the emergency legislation.

While the LDP was not providing solid support for Koizumi, at the core, the elements of the third ring were united in attacking the Koizumi government. The four opposition parties jointly submitted a request to dismiss CCS Fukuda and JDA director general Nakatani to the Diet. Although the ruling parties successfully rejected the request, they had to face rocky operations in the Diet.

The opposition parties maintained their unforgiving stance during the JDA scandal. On June 12, they agreed to boycott Diet deliberations on the legislation a second time after discovering that the government had not released all the research results they had requested. The umbrella organization of Japan's labor unions, Rengo, or the Japanese Trade Union Confederation, with a membership of 6.8 million, supported the opposition parties. On June 27, Rengo held a central committee meeting in Naha, Okinawa, and passed a special resolution calling for the blocking of the emergency legislation.

Faced with strong resistance from the opposition parties, the three ruling party secretaries-general and the Diet policy chairmen held a meeting on how to deal with Diet operations. At the meeting, LDP upper house secretary-general Mikio Aoki told the other members that he could not be responsible for deliberations in the upper house and voiced his opposition to the ruling parties' option of forceful passage. This effectively stalled passage of the emergency legislation during the current Diet session.[15]

On July 3, the three ruling parties officially decided to postpone the vote on the bills until the following extraordinary Diet session. The Koizumi cabinet did not see the same level of urgency for these bills as it had for the anti-terrorism legislation and decided that the public would not accept the emergency legislation being forced through.

At the July 24 meeting of the special committee, CCS Fukuda stated that the government's policy was to prepare the bill to protect citizens' rights in an emergency. Five days later, the Koizumi cabinet expanded the Task Force on Emergency Legislation from twenty to thirty staffers and organized five project teams for the revised emergency bills. Each team would work on one of the following five areas: (1) protection of people, (2) facilitation of SDF activities, (3) facilitation of U.S. forces in Japan, (4) treatment of hostages, and (5) punishment for inhumane behavior.

Abduction Issues and Koizumi's Rising Approval Rating

Although his cabinet's approval rating dropped after he fired Tanaka, Koizumi scored a major coup in September 2002. On September 17, he became the first Japanese prime minister to visit North Korea and meet with Kim Jong Il.

During this historic meeting, Koizumi brought up the issue of Japanese nationals who had reportedly been abducted by Korean agents. Kim divulged that thirteen Japanese nationals had in fact been taken during the 1970s and 1980s. Eight had died and five were still living in North Korea. Kim formally apologized, saying that it was regrettable that a group of special military forces took such actions. Koizumi and Kim signed the Japan–North Korea Pyongyang Declaration, which announced the commencement of normalization talks and included assurances from Japan of wide-ranging economic assistance in return for a moratorium on missile launches and compliance on the nuclear issues. At the same time, Koizumi demanded the return of the five known surviving abductees. On October 15, the five arrived in Japan to reunite with relatives, leaving their spouses and children in North Korea. The Japanese public reacted with overwhelming fury to the revelation of the kidnappings and realized that a criminal state existed in Japan's neighborhood.

On the following day, the U.S. State Department disclosed that North Korea had been secretly developing a nuclear program, violating the 1994 U.S.–North Korea Framework Agreement. In response to this announcement, the Koizumi government identified the nuclear program as a priority, along with the abductee issue, in its relations with North Korea and pressured Pyongyang to abolish the program.

On October 24, despite some opposition from MOFA, the Koizumi cabinet decided to allow the five abductees to remain in Japan. Further, the government demanded that North Korea allow other family members to join the returnees. Pyongyang denounced the Japanese government for betraying its trust and warned that it would postpone the Japan–North Korea security talks.

Some skeptics saw Koizumi's visit to Pyongyang as an attempt to recover his popularity. If so, he succeeded. According to an *Asahi Shimbun* poll taken immediately after the Pyongyang meeting, 81 percent of those polled appreciated the meeting, and the Koizumi cabinet's approval rating rose from 51 to 61 percent.[16]

In a November 2002 *Asahi Shimbun* poll, 78 percent of respondents supported the Koizumi government's call for North Korea to abolish its nuclear program and return the abductees' family members. The poll also showed that as many as 95 percent of those polled expressed their concern about North Korea's nuclear program.[17] Later in December, North Korea declared that it had resumed operation of its nuclear reprocessing facilities and expelled inspectors from the International Atomic Energy Agency. North Korea's desperate brinkmanship raised Japanese security concerns to a higher level, strengthening public support for the prime minister and the Kantei.

The Impact of the International Security Environment

On December 5, as many Japanese were focusing on developments in North Korea, Prime Minister Koizumi and CCS Fukuda met with LDP secretary-general Yamasaki and upper house secretary-general Aoki. At the meeting, the four reconfirmed that the emergency bills would be submitted at the next ordinary Diet session, which was to commence in January 2003. During the September 2002 cabinet reshuffling, Koizumi had removed JDA director general Gen Nakatani—whose resignation the opposition parties had demanded after the JDA scandal—and replaced him with Shigeru Ishiba, who was known as an expert on defense issues. Ishiba would manage Diet operations related to the emergency bills.

The Kantei task force made progress in preparing the legislation. The original government proposal was criticized for its vagueness with regard to protection of rights, so team members worked to devise more concrete proposals.

Meanwhile, North Korea further escalated its brinkmanship diplomacy. In January 2003, Pyongyang withdrew from the Nuclear Nonproliferation

Treaty, ended a freeze on plutonium production, and restarted its Yongbyon nuclear facility. In February, in response to the inauguration of South Korea's new president, Roh Moo Hyun, North Korea test-fired a missile into the Sea of Japan. Although the Japanese government responded calmly, stating that the anti-ship missile was not categorized as the type of ballistic missile banned by the Pyongyang Declaration, these events heightened the concerns of Japanese nationals.

The Japanese public and media also focused their attention on Iraq issues. The United Nations Security Council unanimously supported UN Resolution 1441, which pushed Iraq to unconditionally accept strict inspection of all possible facilities, including presidential palaces, that might be used to store weapons of mass destruction. The resolution stated that Iraq would face serious consequences if it did not comply.

The global community, however, was sharply divided on the effectiveness of such inspections. While France and Germany recognized that there were some positive results, the inspections did not meet the expectations of the Bush administration. In his State of the Union speech on January 28, President Bush emphasized the importance of disarming Iraq. In late February, the United States and Great Britain tried to obtain authorization from the UN Security Council for a strike against Iraq. The other permanent members of the Security Council—China, France, and Russia—strongly objected. France even threatened to use its veto power. As a result, the United States and Great Britain gave up trying to obtain authorization and decided to attack Iraq without UN backing.

When American and British forces invaded Iraq on March 20, Prime Minister Koizumi announced his support of their actions. At a press conference, Koizumi related Japan's support to the context of the threat from North Korea, arguing that the U.S.-Japan security alliance discouraged North Korea from attacking Japan: "Looking at the recent spate of provocative acts concerning nuclear issues, the perception of threat by many Japanese people is understandable, but it is my belief that the Japan-U.S. alliance is functioning effectively in regard to issues such as this."[18]

Since many in the three ruling parties shared Koizumi's view on the linkage between the Iraq and North Korea issues, the coalition government united to support Koizumi's decision. In a public opinion poll taken by *Asahi Shimbun*, however, only 39 percent approved of Koizumi's support for American actions in Iraq, while 50 percent disapproved. Among those who approved,

67 percent responded that they took the North Korean issue into consideration.[19] The conflict in Iraq, in addition to North Korea's brinkmanship, inevitably strengthened the country's awareness of national security issues.

Keizai Doyukai (Japan Association of Corporate Executives) announced its support for the government proposal. Its research group on the Constitution, chaired by Setsuzo Kosaka, published a policy proposal in April 2003. The proposal argued that it is an article of common sense among the international community that countries should protect themselves and encouraged swift passage of the emergency legislation.[20]

Enactment in the Diet

On April 4, the three ruling parties submitted the revised emergency bills to the lower house Special Committee on Security in Case of Armed Attack. In response to criticisms made during the previous Diet session, the revised proposal included anti-terrorism measures as well as a concrete plan for preparing a separate piece of legislation within two years to protect people's rights. On April 18, after official explanations of the legislation, the special committee began serious deliberations.

The opposition parties quickly focused on the details of protection for citizens during an emergency. CCS Fukuda explained that the new bill would call for citizen cooperation in voluntary evacuation and firefighting activities, give prefectural governors authority to decide when land and private property should be appropriated in time of need for medical facilities or other uses with the agreement of the owners, and appoint the national broadcaster, Nippon Hoso Kyokai (NHK), and private television and radio networks as designated broadcasters for government announcements. These answers demonstrated that the Kantei task force was prepared to meet requests from the ruling and opposition parties, in the first and third outer rings of the concentric circles model.

During this period, the DPJ leadership changed from Yukio Hatoyama to Naoto Kan. Kan, as new party president, wanted to demonstrate to the public that the DPJ was a viable opposition party capable of running the government by displaying its solid understanding of and policy for national security affairs. Kan intentionally disassociated his party from the other opposition parties, the Socialists and the Communists; the loss of unity weakened the third outer ring in contending with the government.

Kan appointed a well-known defense expert, Seiji Maehara, as the national security minister of the party's Next Cabinet, modeled after the British shadow cabinet. Kan asked Maehara to head a DPJ project team on emergency legislation. There was a precedent: the DPJ came up with financial reform legislation in 1998 and successfully enacted its proposal, demonstrating policy-making ability in economic matters. Kan wanted to do the same in defense affairs.

Maehara's project team produced a proposal, which was submitted to the Diet after it was approved by the Next Cabinet on April 24. It included two pieces of legislation, the basic bill on emergencies and the bill to revise the government proposal. The basic bill covered situations including not only armed attacks but also terrorist attacks and large-scale natural disasters. It also would clearly guarantee the basic human rights of citizens, give the Diet the authority to end SDF activities, require the government to keep the public informed, and establish a new Crisis Control Agency. The revision bill would exclude private television and radio networks from serving as designated broadcasters for government warnings. When Maehara explained the DPJ proposal at the May 6 lower house special committee meeting, the ruling parties expressed their willingness to hold a conference to amend their bills.

At the conference, GP Project Team chairman Akio Kyuma represented the three ruling parties, and Maehara represented the DPJ. Adapting some of the DPJ suggestions, the ruling parties quickly agreed on the Diet's role in ending SDF activities and on the government's obligation to provide information. Yet Kyuma told Maehara that it would be difficult to legislate the basic bill to protect citizens' rights during the current Diet session. After a week of meetings, the ruling parties and the DPJ agreed to postpone enactment of the basic bill and to issue a joint statement that they would work to enact it within a year. They also agreed that private television and radio networks would be included among the designated broadcasters of government warnings, but their freedom of broadcast would be guaranteed.[21]

The secretary-general-level meeting between the ruling parties and the DPJ approved the agreement on May 13, 2003. The second ring and part of the third ring of the concentric circles model agreed to support the core's initiative. Koizumi expressed his satisfaction to the media, saying, "It was epoch-making in the political history that the ruling parties and the largest opposition party came to agree" on the emergency legislation, which used to be regarded as a political taboo.[22]

The amended emergency bills passed the special committee on May 14 and the lower house on the following day with support from the ruling parties as well as the DPJ and the Liberal Party, which constituted 90 percent of members present. The upper house special committee began deliberations on May 20. At the committee meeting, Prime Minister Koizumi stated that he was happy that the ruling and opposition parties had the same views on the need for the emergency legislation and explained that North Korea's nuclear development and its abduction of Japanese citizens made "the sense of threat among the Japanese people greater than ever."[23]

Maehara expressed a similar opinion in his *Asahi Shimbun* interview: "The North Korean factor had great impact. An unidentified ship in fact came to Japan, and North Korea admitted to the kidnappings. In addition, there was the missile test-firing and the declaration of nuclear development. This international environment surrounding Japan would require a more realistic national security and foreign policy from not only the ruling parties but also the opposition parties."[24]

The public and the media generally agreed on the need to have a legal framework for dealing with emergencies. According to a *Yomiuri Shimbun* poll on April 5, 2003, 47.6 percent of the respondents supported the emergency legislation, compared with 21.1 percent who were opposed. All five newspapers concurred that the nation needed the legislation. Even the liberal *Asahi Shimbun* ran an editorial welcoming the bills' passage by stating "we need the minimum necessary preparation."[25]

On June 6, 2003, 202 of the 235 members at the upper house floor meeting voted for the emergency bills. A quarter century after the 1977 first government study, Japan was finally equipped with a legal framework to deal with a national emergency. In the end, the first, second, third (except for the Socialist and Communist parties), fourth (except for the labor union), and fifth rings of the model all came together to support the policy initiative of the core.

6

DISPATCHING THE SDF TO RECONSTRUCT IRAQ

The 2003 Iraq Special Measures Legislation

O n March 19, 2003, U.S. forces initiated hostilities against the Saddam Hussein regime. Immediately afterward, Prime Minister Koizumi declared Japan's support for the United States, seeking to maintain strong security relations between the two countries. Public opinion, however, was sharply split on whether the Japanese government should support the attack.

After President Bush declared the end of major combat operations on May 2 of the same year, the Koizumi government moved swiftly on a plan to dispatch Self-Defense Forces (SDF) to provide reconstruction assistance in Iraq. Within three months, Koizumi managed to pass the Iraq Special Measures Law (Law Concerning the Special Measures for Humanitarian and Reconstruction Assistance in Iraq) in the Diet.

Koizumi's Decision to Support Bush

In his January 2002 State of the Union address, President Bush used the phrase "the axis of evil" to condemn Iraq, Iran, and North Korea for "arming to threaten the peace of the world."[1] Two weeks later, the president visited Japan. In his speech to the Diet on February 18, he praised Japan's contribution to the war in Afghanistan but said nothing about his plans for Iraq. However, Bush had a private meeting that day with Prime Minister Koizumi, joined only by National Security Adviser Condoleezza Rice and Foreign Deputy Minister Toshiyuki Takano. According to a media report released four months after the meeting, the president told Koizumi that the United States was going to attack Iraq. Koizumi responded that Japan would always stand with the United States in the war against terrorism.[2] If this report is accurate, the American intention to attack Iraq and Japan's support for it were set as early as February 2002—more than a year before the campaign actually began.

As promised, Koizumi announced his support for the U.S. attack on Iraq after Bush's March 17, 2003, speech giving Saddam Hussein and his sons forty-eight hours to leave Iraq. Koizumi held a meeting of the Security Council, a ministerial-level cabinet meeting, on March 18, and discussed Japan's possible responses. At a press conference afterward, he stated, "Having listened to President Bush's speech, I felt that it must have been a painful decision. The president must have made various efforts to obtain international collaboration. Under such circumstances, President Bush was left with no other option, and I support this."[3] Yukio Okamoto, foreign policy adviser to the prime minister, reveals that Koizumi used his own script during the press conference, not the memorandum the bureaucrats prepared. Okamoto states in his article on *Gaiko Forum*:

> How would [Prime Minister Koizumi] explain to the people
> his support for America's use of force? The government officials
> in charge wrote out explanations and a preliminary meeting was
> held. The bureaucratic language of the drafts clearly irritated Koizumi. I don't remember exactly what he said in the meeting, but he
> declared he wouldn't just read from text prepared by the officials.
> He had thought about the matter himself and he would tell the
> people his conclusions in his words.[4]

Okamoto discloses the difficulty Koizumi had in making the final decision to support the United States. "[Koizumi's] hesitation was only natural, since supporting the war was certain to lower his popular support ratings. After a short time, he did decide to support the war in Iraq, and he did not waver thereafter."[5] Koizumi's concern was legitimate; his support did decline. According to a *Nihon Keizai Shimbun* poll taken immediately after the U.S. invasion, 49 percent of the respondents disapproved of Koizumi's stance, while only 40 percent approved.

The drop in his cabinet's approval rating was actually rather small—down four points to 42 percent—while the disapproval rating increased by six points to 41 percent. Although the Kantei, the core of the concentric circles model, was determined to take action, the public, in the outermost ring, initially was not supportive.

The Kantei Takes Charge Again

After Prime Minister Koizumi announced Japan's support for the U.S. attack, the government actively began the policy-making process to determine its contribution to Iraq's reconstruction. At a Security Council meeting on March 20, 2003, Koizumi and the council formulated a five-point action plan: (1) ensure the safety of Japanese nationals in Iraq and surrounding areas, (2) protect key facilities such as U.S. bases in Japan and diplomatic establishments, (3) ensure safe navigation for Japanese vessels, (4) prevent confusion in international economic systems, and (5) provide emergency humanitarian assistance.

Immediately after this session, Koizumi held an emergency cabinet meeting to establish the Policy Measures Headquarters on the Problem of Iraq in the cabinet. He then convened this new body, seeking to determine government policies on providing assistance to countries bordering Iraq, strengthening Japan's support in the fight against terrorism in Afghanistan and elsewhere, and preparing new legislation to enable Japan to contribute to the reconstruction effort in Iraq. These swift, coordinated reactions showed Japan's preparedness on this issue and clearly demonstrated Koizumi's determination.

The Kantei initiated the policy-making process in a manner similar to its initiation of the 2001 anti-terrorism and 2003 emergency legislation, as described in chapters 4 and 5. CCS Yasuo Fukuda again instructed Assistant

CCS Keiji Ohmori to form a team to prepare the legislation. Ohmori gathered a dozen officials from MOFA, the JDA, and other agencies in the prefabricated building next to the Cabinet Office building. Since the Cabinet Secretariat, MOFA, and the JDA had unofficially been planning Japan's contribution to the Iraq reconstruction for nearly half a year, the team was well prepared to work swiftly.

The National Security Division of the Foreign Policy Bureau was MOFA's headquarters on this policy matter. The United Nations Policy Division in the same bureau was responsible for negotiating with other nations through Japan's Permanent Mission to the United Nations. The Legal Affairs Division of the Treaties Bureau also provided legal assistance on legislation. These divisions supported the Kantei's Iraq team. The Iraq legislation was prepared in the framework of international collaboration, not the U.S.-Japan alliance. The U.S.-Japan Security Treaty Division of the North American Bureau therefore did not play a central role in the policy-making process.

On March 20, the JDA formed a task force headed by Director General Shigeru Ishiba. Ishiba instructed JDA officials to strengthen their information-gathering system and tighten the security patrols of SDF vessels and aircrafts. The Defense Policy Bureau and the Plans and Program Divisions of the Staff Offices of the SDF (Ground, Maritime, and Air) played a subordinate role to the Kantei's Iraq team.

In early April, the Iraq team announced its action plan for Iraq reconstruction. The plan called for economic assistance, on-the-ground reconstruction assistance, humanitarian assistance, the dismantling of weapons of mass destruction, and minesweeping. The Japanese government would need to dispatch the SDF for all activities except the economic assistance. If the United Nations started peacekeeping operations, however, the Japanese government would be able to send the SDF under the 1992 International Peace Cooperation Law, but that possibility was seen as slim. As the Japanese government developed possible activities under the current laws, the Kantei prepared the new bill.

Linkage with the North Korean Issue

The new Iraq legislation was spearheaded from the core of the concentric circles model, and the Koizumi cabinet followed its previous tactic of reaching agreement with coalition partners in the second outer ring, bypassing the Liberal Democratic Party (LDP), in the first ring. While the three coalition parties announced their support for the government stance on the American attack on Iraq, a significant number of their members did not and were against sending the SDF. Many legislators realized that the Middle East was important to Japan, but they were not confident that the public would support the dispatch. On March 10, 2003, LDP Policy Research Council chairman Taro Aso suggested that LDP secretary-general Taku Yamasaki form a council to deal with both the Iraq and North Korean issues under the theme of weapons of mass destruction.

Yamasaki liked Aso's idea. The coalition parties formed the Government Parties Council for Iraq and North Korea (hereafter referred to as the GP Council). After North Korea returned several Japanese abductees in October 2002, many Japanese recognized the threat the secretive nation posed.

The Japanese government needed to strengthen its alliance with the United States in order to gain American support on this issue. Party executives at the core found a way to appeal to many realists in the coalition parties in the second ring. On March 12, the secretaries-general of the three parties held the first meeting of the council to discuss their policy on the new Iraq legislation.

The government's official stance on the legislation remained undeclared, however, even after the fall of Baghdad on April 9 and President Bush's May 2 declaration that major combat operations had ended. Deliberations on the emergency legislation continued in the Diet. Since the bill would provide a legal framework for mobilizing the SDF if outside forces attacked Japan, the Koizumi government was unwilling to spark another controversy by disclosing information about it. Prime Minister Koizumi, Chief Cabinet Secretary Fukuda, and Foreign Minister Kawaguchi officially maintained that they would consider the possibility of new Iraq legislation in accordance with developments in world affairs.

Prime Minister Koizumi was actually the first government official to refer to the new legislation, making a brief statement from his jet on May 21 while en route to the United States. Some LDP defense experts claimed that a UN resolution was necessary before Japan could participate in Iraq's reconstruction.[6] Luckily for Koizumi, the UN Security Council passed Resolution 1483, which requested contributions for reconstruction from member countries. This resolution would allow Japan to send the SDF based on the UN request, clearing one hurdle to gaining support for the new legislation within the LDP.

On May 23, Koizumi visited President Bush's private residence in Crawford, Texas. In his conversation with the president, Koizumi said, "It was good that combat operations in Iraq ended early, and that the adoption of UN Security Council Resolution 1483 led to the rebuilding of international solidarity." Bush expressed his appreciation for Japan's support for military action in Iraq and requested Japan's "visible cooperation for the reconstruction of Iraq."[7] According to Foreign Deputy Minister Hitoshi Tanaka, who was present at the meeting, Koizumi stopped the president by saying, "There is no need for you to make further requests."[8] Koizumi also stated that "Japan would proactively consider what to do for the reconstruction of Iraq and play a positive role." On SDF contributions, the prime minister mentioned the possibility of using the force's C-130 aircraft to transport humanitarian supplies, based on the existing laws. In addition, he spoke of his intention to pursue a new law, saying that "the dispatch of the SDF and others to assist in the reconstruction of Iraq was something for Japan itself to decide, and Japan wished to make a contribution commensurate with its national power and standing."[9]

During the policy process surrounding the 2001 anti-terrorism legislation, the opposition parties had heavily criticized Koizumi because he made a pledge to the U.S. president before consulting with domestic political players. Again, Koizumi made a similar international commitment to President Bush before informing domestic political elements and the public.

The LDP against Top-down Decision Making

After Prime Minister Koizumi returned from his trip to the United States and the Middle East, the government and the ruling coalition parties began discussing the political schedule for submitting the Iraq legislation to the Diet. On June 4, the Kantei's Iraq team came up with the outlines of the legislation. The legal basis for activities under the new law would be a series of UN Security Council resolutions, and activities would be limited to non-combat areas. In order to obtain quick Diet approval, the team also proposed that the restriction standard on arms use for SDF officials remain unchanged.

On June 7, a day after the emergency legislation was enacted in the Diet, Prime Minister Koizumi and CCS Fukuda met with the secretaries-general of the three coalition parties and informed them that the government was going to submit the Iraq legislation during the current Diet session. At this meeting, the party leaders agreed that the law would be effective for just four years and that it would be submitted together with the revision extending the anti-terrorism legislation for another two years.

In addition, Koizumi and Fukuda requested approval for an official cabinet decision to submit the bill to the Diet by June 13. This left only six days to go through the first and second outer rings of the concentric circles model. Although unofficial consultation among the ruling parties must have been conducted beforehand, this required an unusually swift procedure, showing the strong determination of the Koizumi government in the core.

On June 9, Assistant CCS Ohmori, speaking to the GP Council on behalf of the Kantei, provided details of the Iraq legislation. The new law would allow the government to send both SDF personnel and civilians on missions that included providing humanitarian and reconstruction assistance, supporting U.S. and other forces to ensure security, and assisting in the dismantling of weapons of mass destruction. The council representatives approved the outlines of the legislation and agreed to seek approval from their respective parties in order to build consensus within the second outer ring.

On June 10, Ohmori gave the same briefing to the joint conference of the LDP's Cabinet, Defense, and Foreign Policy subcommittees. When he told the legislators that the SDF's activities would be limited to noncombat areas, however, one younger member, Taro Kono, questioned whether noncombat areas really existed in Iraq. Ohmori could not provide a direct answer but stated, "It is reported that Baghdad and the southern areas are safer. Before we dispatch the SDF, we will conduct more detailed research and consult with American forces."[10] There was other criticism of the government proposal, which did not relax the standard of arms use to international levels. The LDP joint conference postponed voting until the next day, showing the first outer ring's unwillingness to blindly support the government proposal.

The LDP General Council held an unofficial session after this conference. There was also strong opposition to the proposal from the LDP's anti-Koizumi camp, especially from members of the Hashimoto faction, which saw the decision-making process as hasty and autocratic, without sufficient consultation of LDP members. Former JDA director general Yoshinari Norota stressed that "it would be impossible to make a cabinet decision by June 13." Former LDP secretary-general Hiromu Nonaka wondered "how to draw the line between combat and noncombat areas."[11]

On June 11, the Kantei came up with an answer to Nonaka's question. The legislation would not differentiate between combat and noncombat areas; after the legislation was enacted, however, the action guideline would be submitted to the Diet specifying where the SDF could operate after research was conducted and current conditions were carefully examined. Although members of the LDP policy subcommittees were not totally satisfied with this solution, they decided to approve the government proposal on the final day of the three-day session. The subcommittees did issue a resolution calling for new permanent legislation to meet the international standard for arms use for the protection of SDF forces. In addition, the LDP lawmakers demanded exhaustive research in Iraq, sufficient prior consultation with the LDP, and sufficient explanations of SDF activities for the Japanese public.[12]

Approval by the policy subcommittees was not the end of the story, however. On the same day, the General Council, which usually blindly endorses the subcommittees' decisions, refused to approve the government proposal without amendment. In addition to policy-oriented factions within the LDP, the ruling party was sharply split between pro- and anti-Koizumi camps against the backdrop of the upcoming LDP presidential election in September. The pro-Koizumi camp wanted this legislation enacted in order to tighten Japan's alliance with the United States. The anti-Koizumi camp, however, wanted to take advantage of the public's antiwar sentiments to cripple Koizumi. Former LDP secretary-general Nonaka, a leading figure in the anti-Koizumi camp, opposed the proposal at the council meeting, saying, "We do not have to dispatch the SDF. Humanitarian and reconstruction activities can be conducted by civilians." He further criticized the policy process, noting: "We should not submit this important legislation at the chaotic end of the Diet session." Former JDA director general Norota said, "The inclusion of the 'weapons of mass destruction' clause in the legislation was too excessive," noting that such weapons had not been found in Iraq.[13]

Facing such powerful criticism, the General Council postponed approval. During deliberations within the LDP, Komeito and the Conservative Party—both LDP coalition partners in the second outer ring—had completed the approval process. Only Koizumi's own party in the first ring had not reached a decision.

A compromise of some kind was needed. The anti-Koizumi camp suggested to LDP Policy Research Council chairman Aso that the General Council would approve the government proposal if the "weapons of mass destruction" clause were removed. Aso asked Assistant CCS Ohmori to do so, but when Ohmori consulted with CCS Fukuda, Fukuda said no. Fukuda then asked Aso to negotiate with the anti-Koizumi camp to settle for removal of the clause from the action guideline but not from the legislation. When the anti-Koizumi group refused this offer, Aso agreed to remove the clause from the legislation so as to get the General Council's approval on June 13.[14]

The Koizumi government had received approval of the Iraq legislation from coalition partners in the second outer ring first. In the case of the anti-terrorism legislation, enacted when Koizumi's job approval rating was high, coalition approval pressured LDP lawmakers to fall in line. The public was ambivalent on Japan's contribution to the reconstruction of Iraq, however. As mentioned earlier, a late March *Nihon Keizai Shimbun* poll showed 42 percent of the public approved of the Koizumi cabinet but 41 percent did not. With this low level of support, early approval by the coalition did not create enough pressure to affect LDP members. The Koizumi cabinet also needed to make a significant political compromise on the legislation before it managed to gain approval from the LDP, in the first ring, as the party was highly factionalized along policy lines and between the pro- and anti-Koizumi camps.

Diet Operations

Despite major policy battles within the LDP, the Iraq legislation was still on track. Immediately after receiving the General Council's approval, the Koizumi government made a cabinet decision to submit the legislation on June 13. Three days later, Prime Minister Koizumi met with leaders of the two other coalition parties. They mutually agreed to extend the ordinary Diet session for forty more days. When the three parties asked the speakers of both houses of the Diet for the extension, however, the opposition parties were united in opposing it. They argued that such an extension for major legislation submitted at the end of the session was against the general operating rules of the Diet. The ruling parties, however, forced the extension through both houses.

Deliberations on the Iraq legislation got off to a predictably turbulent start. However, the forced passage did not lower public support for the Koizumi cabinet. According to a *Nihon Keizai Shimbun* poll announced on June 23, the job approval rating of the cabinet was 49 percent, 7 percent higher than in late March when the U.S.-led war began. Public approval for the Iraq legislation stood at 43 percent, a little higher than the 41 percent disapproval rating.[15] This heightened support from the outermost ring allowed the core to aggressively pursue its passage vis-à-vis the opposition parties in the third ring.

Deliberations in the lower house started on June 24. The Koizumi government planned to pass the legislation in the lower house within two weeks and to enact it by July 28, the last day of the Diet session. Such swift approval usually requires an agreement from the largest opposition party, the Democratic Party of Japan (DPJ).

In order to gain DPJ support, the legislation allowed room for several political compromises. First, it would require Diet approval of the action guideline for dispatching the SDF but did not require prior approval. In the process of the 2001 anti-terrorism legislation, the DPJ demanded prior approval as a way of strengthening the role of the Diet and was expected to do the same for this legislation. Second, the life span of the legislation was four years, but the Koizumi government signaled that it was willing to cut this to two years. Third, the legislation would allow ground transportation for munitions to the SDF, which was prohibited under the 2001 anti-terrorism legislation. The DPJ was expected to demand that the government prohibit ground transportation. Fourth, the legislation was legally based on UN Security Council Resolutions 678, 687, 1441, and 1483. Having the first three resolutions as a legal base, the new legislation would recognize the legitimacy of the American attack on Iraq. The DPJ would have liked to dispatch the SDF based solely on Resolution 1483, in which the UN requested its member states to contribute to Iraq's reconstruction without recognizing such legitimacy. These changes were also demanded in discussions within the LDP. But the deputy chairman of the LDP's Policy Research Council, Akio Kyuma, a former JDA chief, persuaded LDP members to leave room for political compromise during negotiations with the opposition parties.

With compromise in mind, the government sought an early conference with the DPJ, but the DPJ refused. On June 19, the DPJ's Next Cabinet approved a report on the Iraq issue by its project team, which had visited Iraq earlier that month. Titled "Our Position on Reconstruction Assistance to Iraq," the report rejected the proposal to dispatch the SDF. The team reached the following conclusions: (1) that they could not identify any immediate need for the SDF troops, (2) that it was difficult to draw the line between combat and noncombat areas, (3) that SDF units might be targeted by anti-American groups in Iraq, and (4) that it would be difficult to predict how long SDF troops would be needed.[16] By approving this report, the DPJ formalized its opposition to the proposed legislation.

The LDP again attempted to negotiate with the DPJ, but the DPJ declined the request to hold an official conference. Instead, it submitted its own legislation for the reconstruction of Iraq, which excluded the SDF dispatch. The DPJ argued that as long as there was no clear difference between combat and noncombat areas, sending the SDF might violate Article 9 of the Constitution, which prohibits Japan's belligerency. DPJ leader Naoto Kan wanted to prove the DPJ's status as a responsible party by showing its willingness to contribute to the reconstruction of Iraq even though it opposed the government's proposal to dispatch the SDF. The ruling parties, however, regarded this bill as a refusal to negotiate.

The DPJ's refusal made it impossible for the Kantei to win an overwhelming majority to pass the legislation. However, submitting a bill of its own committed the DPJ to attending the Diet session. This meant the ruling parties could avoid the worst possible scenario—a boycott of deliberations by all the opposition parties. The legislation passed the lower house on July 4. By submitting its own bill, the DPJ also disassociated itself from the other opposition parties, weakening the solidarity of the opposition in the third outer ring of the concentric circles model.

Meanwhile, another obstacle surfaced, revealing another split within the LDP. The government wanted to jointly pass both the Iraq legislation and the revised anti-terrorism legislation. LDP upper house members, however, preferred to hold back the revised anti-terrorism legislation and deliberate it during the fall Diet session. This course of action would significantly reduce the chance that Prime Minister Koizumi would dissolve the lower house during the session. That in turn would mean a better chance for a so-called double election—simultaneous elections for both the lower and upper houses in July 2004. A double election would fully activate the LDP's election machine across the nation, to the benefit of LDP upper house candidates. Cooperation from LDP upper house members was essential to the Koizumi government's smooth enactment of the Iraq legislation during the current Diet session. The government was finally forced to separate deliberations on the two pieces of legislation. Nevertheless, there was no chance that negotiations between the government and the opposition parties were going to take place in the upper house. The opposition parties sought to attack the government in order to put themselves in a better position for the upcoming general election.

During the upper house deliberations, Prime Minister Koizumi gave a couple of baffling answers. On July 9, for example, when an opposition leader criticized Koizumi for suggesting that Saddam Hussein's Iraq had weapons of mass destruction although none had yet been found, Koizumi's response was, "You cannot say President Hussein did not exist because he cannot be found now, and it is the same [with weapons of mass destruction]."[17] Another example is Koizumi's answer when DPJ leader Kan demanded on July 23 that Koizumi specifically name any noncombat area in Iraq. Koizumi retorted, "Of course, I do not have an answer right now." Kan had to state, "It is an appalling response."[18]

Despite these problematic responses in the Diet, deliberations in the upper house moved ahead as scheduled. The opposition parties introduced a no-confidence motion against the Koizumi cabinet on July 25 in a bid to delay passage. On the following day, however, the ruling parties voted for and enacted the legislation to dispatch Japanese troops to Iraq.

Public opinion was split on the Iraq legislation. According to an *Asahi Shimbun* poll of July 1, 2003, 46 percent of the respondents supported the legislation while 43 percent opposed it. Among the five major newspapers, *Nihon Keizai*, *Sankei*, and *Yomiuri* expressed support for the legislation. *Mainichi Shimbun* published an editorial supporting dispatch of the SDF to Iraq on the condition of a UN resolution requesting member nations to contribute personnel.[19] Only *Asahi Shimbun* clearly opposed the legislation by questioning the legitimacy of the Iraq War since weapons of mass destruction had not been found. Among major interest groups, the business community was generally supportive, while the labor union was against the war but did not act against the legislation.[20] The lack of strong opposition from the two outermost rings allowed the core, with the compromise it had made to placate the first ring, to successfully enact the Iraq legislation.

The Impact of the Iraq Situation on the General Election

On August 1, 2003, the day the Iraq Special Measures Law was promulgated, the government established the Office to Promote Reconstruction Assistance to Iraq within the Kantei. A JDA official, Kohei Masuda, was named to head the office, and seven other officials from the JDA and MOFA joined him as staff members.

Despite President Bush's May declaration that major combat operations had ended, terrorist activities kept Iraq volatile. On August 20, terrorists bombed the UN headquarters in Baghdad, killing 23 people, including top UN envoy Sergio Vieira de Mello, and injuring more than 120. This changed the atmosphere at the United Nations. Secretary-General Kofi Annan agreed that a multinational force would be established under U.S. command to deal with the unstable situation. The U.S. government began drafting a UN Security Council resolution to establish such a force.

The Japanese government supported the American proposal. The passage of such a resolution would provide legitimacy for American and British forces to stay in Iraq. In the future, Japan would be able to join the multinational force under UN auspices, which would coincide with the interests of the Japanese government.

The Japanese government lobbied member countries of the UN Security Council in support of the proposal. Japan's lobbying of Syria was especially critical. The United States had identified Syria as a state that continued to aid Palestinian terrorists, and Washington's embargo of U.S. exports and economic assistance to Syria left it without an effective diplomatic channel to the country. Japan, however, had provided Syria with 200 billion yen of official development assistance. Tokyo persuaded Syrian representatives at the United Nations to vote for the proposal. As a result, UN Security Council Resolution 1511 was adopted unanimously on October 16. When President Bush met with Prime Minister Koizumi the next day, he expressed his appreciation for Japan's diplomatic efforts, stating that "the role Japan played in realizing a unanimous adoption of United Nations Security Council Resolution 1511 was commendable."[21]

Meanwhile, Prime Minister Koizumi successfully dealt with the domestic political challenge. He won the September 22 LDP presidential election with 339 votes, more than twice as many as received by the second candidate, Shizuka Kamei, who had 139. On October 10, the Koizumi government managed to pass the revised anti-terrorism legislation, which included an extension of more than two years. On the same day, Koizumi dissolved the lower house and called a general election.

During the November 9 general election campaign, the opposition parties—the DPJ, the Japan Communist Party, and the Socialist Democratic Party—pledged to fight the SDF dispatch to Iraq. All the ruling parties—the LDP, Komeito, and the Conservative Party—avoided discussion of the issue. The LDP eventually dropped 10 seats in the election, going from 247 to 237. The Conservative Party lost 5, lowering its total to just 4 seats and forcing the party to merge with the LDP. The DPJ emerged as an effective opposition party, gaining 40 seats for a total lower house membership of 177. The incumbent coalition parties managed to maintain an absolute majority of 275 seats in the 480-seat lower house, however, with Komeito going from 31 to 34 seats. On November 19, the ruling bloc reappointed Koizumi as national leader.

The emergence of the DPJ and its opposition to deployment of the SDF changed the political climate within the ruling coalition parties. Many LDP members began to express hesitation about an immediate dispatch. At the same time, the situation in Iraq remained very unstable. American casualties after President Bush's May 2 declaration that major combat was over totaled 116, surpassing the 115 casualties sustained during combat. Moreover, Italian troops were attacked in Nasiriyah on November 19, only one hundred kilometers away from Samawah, the SDF's planned destination. The action guideline for dispatching the SDF was originally planned for cabinet approval on November 14. The domestic political climate and the Iraq situation, however, forced the Koizumi cabinet to postpone approval.

In the extraordinary Diet session that began on November 19, the SDF dispatch was a focal issue. DPJ leader Naoto Kan argued that Iraq had returned to a state of war and asked Prime Minister Koizumi whether he intended to dispatch the SDF by the year's end and whether he would label Samawah a noncombat area. In response, Koizumi repeatedly stated that he would make a judgment based on future developments.

Slain Diplomats and Approval of the Action Guideline

During the extraordinary session, shocking news swept through Japan. On November 29, two Japanese diplomats, Katsuhiko Oku and Masamori Inoue, were killed on their way to Tikrit to attend a U.S.-led conference on reconstruction efforts. The attack proved that even the noncombat zone was not safe.

The opposition parties, in the third outer ring of the model, declared that the government assessment of Iraq's situation was not accurate and demanded that the SDF be held back. On December 1, Prime Minister Koizumi expressed his anger about the attack but also affirmed his determination to move forward: "We have a responsibility to provide humanitarian and reconstruction aid in Iraq. There is no change to our policy of not giving in to terrorism."[22] On the following day, at the joint session of the LDP's policy subcommittees on foreign policy and defense, LDP lawmakers stated that the nation should not give in to terrorism. With this support from the first ring of the model, the Kantei formed its action guideline.

To avoid opposition from both the ruling and the opposition parties, the action guideline was formulated in private. "It is not always good to discuss sensitive issues openly. Some kinds of information are better kept secret," Prime Minister Koizumi told journalists, revealing that he had ordered government officials to remain silent on this matter.[23] But elements within the ruling parties, in both the first and the second rings, vigorously protested this secrecy. At the December 4 session of the LDP's defense panel, LDP lawmakers criticized the director of the Office of Iraq Reconstruction Assistance at the Kantei, Kohei Masuda, because the government mission that visited Iraq in late November had submitted no report.[24] At a Komeito executive meeting, party leader Takenori Kanzaki also complained about the lack of official explanation. Despite these complaints, CCS Fukuda maintained that the secrecy would continue: "It is difficult to explain before making a decision. I cannot explain the process leading to the decision as it relates to what kind of decision will be made."[25]

The Kantei's secrecy policy also extended to other government agencies. A MOFA official testified, "The policy process of the Iraq legislation and the action guideline was not open as in the case of the anti-terrorism legislation. This frustrated me. The dispatch of Ground Self-Defense Forces is more politically sensitive than that of maritime forces. But a more important factor in the secrecy was CCS Fukuda, whose power significantly increased behind the closed doors of the policy process."[26]

On December 8, the Koizumi cabinet finally disclosed the outline of the action guideline. The SDF would be sent for one year, beginning December 15, and up to six hundred Ground SDF troops would be going. The troops would carry out humanitarian and reconstruction activities in the southeastern part of Iraq, mainly in the province of al Muthanna.

Prime Minister Koizumi invited Foreign Minister Yoriko Kawaguchi and

JDA director general Shigeru Ishiba to his office that morning and instructed them to consult with the ruling parties, again to build consensus within the second outer ring. At the Government–Ruling Parties Conference held that afternoon, the two cabinet members requested the two top leaders of Komeito, President Takenori Kanzaki and Secretary-General Tetsuzo Fuyushiba, to cooperate by swiftly approving the guideline.

Later that afternoon, the GP Council on Iraq and North Korea and the joint session of the LDP's policy subcommittees for cabinet, defense, and foreign policy were held. The government officials explained the outline of the guideline. SDF activities would be limited to noncombat areas, which were defined as "areas where combat is not taking place at present and where it can be confirmed that combat will not take place for the duration of the time activities are conducted." LDP lawmaker Taro Kono strongly opposed the guideline, arguing, "You stated that major combat operations were over. But there are new developments that violate the conditions of the Iraq Special Measures Law." Despite his statement, an overwhelming majority of lawmakers present approved the guideline, forming a consensus within the first outer ring of the model.[27]

Many members of Komeito, which had boasted of its pacifist stance, were unwilling to support the SDF dispatch. The party, however, held a policy committee meeting on December 9 and approved the guideline. Later that day, party leader Kanzaki met with Koizumi to announce its approval. But Kanzaki attached one condition, demanding that the government conduct careful research before the SDF dispatch. With Komeito's agreement, the cabinet approved the action guideline. Again, agreement from the coalition partner mattered more than LDP approval.

At the press conference following this cabinet decision, Koizumi responded to criticism that the dispatch of the SDF was unconstitutional, quoting from the preamble to the Constitution: "We believe that no nation is responsible to itself alone. . . . We, the Japanese people, pledge our national honor to accomplish these high ideals and purposes with all our resources." Koizumi then stated, "Indeed, I believe that the international community is calling upon Japan, and the people of Japan, to act in accordance with the ideals of our Constitution."[28]

Critics quickly attacked Koizumi for ignoring another part of the preamble, which stated Japan's desire for "peace for all time." Lawmakers within the ruling parties criticized Koizumi's brief, limited efforts to persuade their fellow members as well as the public. An *Asahi Shimbun* poll taken immediately after the cabinet decision revealed Koizumi's approval rating dropped significantly, from 47 to 41 percent. Only 23 percent responded that his explanation was persuasive, while 64 percent said it wasn't. Although only 34 percent of the respondents supported the SDF dispatch (55 percent opposed it), up to 64 percent supported a Japanese contribution to the reconstruction of Iraq. The poll results clearly showed public frustration at Koizumi's lack of effort to persuade them.[29]

The SDF Dispatch and Diet Approval

The opposition parties in the third outer ring derided the cabinet decision. Communist Party chairman Kazuo Shii claimed the action guideline would "deploy military force to assist in the lawless war of aggression and occupation of Iraq" and called it "the worst kind of option which lacks any justification."[30] Socialist Democratic Party chairwoman Mizuho Fukushima argued that "participation in the Iraq war would increase terrorism and hatred, and would delay the reconstruction of Iraq."[31] DPJ president Naoto Kan also criticized the decision, saying, "It is difficult to establish the parameters of the noncombat zone in Iraq. A dispatch of SDF troops under present conditions would exceed the provisions of the Iraq Special Measures Law. Furthermore, depending on the circumstances, there is a risk that it might infringe upon the Constitution."[32]

The DPJ, however, was clearly attempting to show its competence to run the government and to prove its viability as a responsible party, looking ahead to the upcoming July 2004 upper house election. The party said it would support the SDF dispatch if the United Nations led the reconstruction efforts. The DPJ was again disassociating itself from the other two opposition parties, weakening the opposition's solidarity and ability to attack the Koizumi government. As a result, the opposition parties within the third ring could not stop the approval process.

After the cabinet decision, JDA officials compiled an implementation guideline to define SDF activities in Iraq in detail and presented it to Prime Minister Koizumi on December 18. Although the guideline did not state an exact date for dispatching each force, it showed that an air force contingent would be sent first. Koizumi approved the guideline. JDA director general Ishiba issued an order the following day to deploy the contingent, which would undertake liaison and coordination duties, and the contingent was eventually dispatched on December 26.

The dispatch of Ground SDF units was more controversial, as they would face a higher risk of attack. Komeito's supporting body, Soka Gakkai, had an influential women's bureau with strong pacifist inclinations. Komeito president Kanzaki was torn between the pacifist element within the party and the party's responsibilities as one of the government's coalition partners. He repeatedly stressed to Koizumi that the government should act cautiously. To learn about the situation and gain support from within the party, Kanzaki decided to visit Iraq himself. He went to Samawah, where Ground SDF units would be sent, returned to Japan, and reported to party officials that the area was relatively safe. Kanzaki later met with Prime Minister Koizumi on December 22 and told him he would approve the dispatch of Ground SDF units to Iraq. He did demand that the ruling parties consult before every dispatch of SDF units, and the prime minister agreed.

On January 6, 2004, as Kanzaki had requested, the government held a consultation meeting with the ruling parties, in the second outer ring. At the meeting, Assistant CCS Ohmori and Defense Vice Minister Takemasa Moriya met with LDP secretary-general Shinzo Abe and Komeito secretary-general Tetsuzo Fuyushiba and informed them that the government was sending an advance ground unit of some thirty troops to Samawah. Fuyushiba had to consult with his party and so could not offer immediate approval, but he expressed his satisfaction with the promised consultation. Two days later, Komeito executives approved the dispatch, and Fuyushiba informed Abe and Ohmori that his party was in favor. The next day, January 9, Defense Agency chief Ishiba ordered the advance ground unit dispatched.

The advance Ground SDF unit left Japan on January 16. According to an *Asahi Shimbun* poll taken immediately afterward, 40 percent approved of the deployment, but 48 percent were against it. But the approval rating was higher than that for the cabinet decision on the activity guideline (34 percent approved, 55 percent disapproved). Commenting on this poll, parliamentary deputy CCS Hiroyuki Hosoda said, "public understanding of the activities of the SDF is increasing." Koizumi's job approval also increased to 43 percent, five points higher than the disapproval rating. The improved support from the public in the outermost ring was good news for the Koizumi government.[33]

In his policy speech on January 19, Koizumi described his commitment in Iraq: "Like a pair of wheels, we will provide both financial assistance and a personnel contribution through the Self-Defense Forces." Explaining the need to send the SDF, he stated, "In personnel terms, given that the situation in Iraq is one that cannot always be described as being safe, I have decided to dispatch the SDF, which has had a daily training regiment and is capable of operating efficiently and avoiding danger in hostile environments. They will not use force."

Toward the end of his speech, Koizumi stressed the importance of the personnel contribution, saying, "Merely arguing is not enough to realize peace. Peace is something that can only be built by the combined capabilities of the international community. Understanding that Japan's security and prosperity is [sic] intertwined with world peace and stability, we must fulfill our responsibilities as a member of the international community through action."[34]

This speech sparked heated debate in the Diet. DPJ leader Kan said: "Whatever reasoning you provide, [the dispatch] violates the principles of the Constitution that prohibit dispatching the SDF into combat situations." He asked the prime minister whether defense against a terrorist attack would constitute "use of force." Koizumi answered that it would not constitute "a use of force that infringes the Constitution."[35] The Japanese government defines combat as "organized and planned attack by a state or actor equivalent to a state." According to this definition, a small-scale terrorist attack would not constitute combat but rather would be a deterioration in public order against which Japanese peacekeepers could act without violating the Constitution.

On January 23, 2004, during Diet deliberations on the SDF dispatch, some members of the advance ground unit came home from Samawah. They reported to JDA director general Ishiba that the situation around their base was stable. Assistant CCS Ohmori passed the report to the two secretaries-general of the LDP and Komeito, and they agreed to approve the dispatch of main Ground SDF units, nearly six hundred troops, by January 26, showing solid support from the second outer ring. At a January 26 meeting, Komeito's Executive Council decided to delegate authority for the final decision to party leader Kanzaki. Kanzaki informed Prime Minister Koizumi that afternoon that his party would approve the dispatch of the main Ground SDF unit to Samawah. Soon afterward, Ishiba issued the order to send the troops.

In the Diet, deliberations on the action guideline were somewhat rough due to miscommunication between SDF troops and the government. JDA director general Ishiba had to withdraw his previous statements on the Iraq situation several times. On January 30, although the opposition parties felt there had not been enough discussion of the proposal, the ruling parties forced the legislation through the lower house Special Committee on Iraq Reconstruction Assistance and then passed it on the floor, despite opposition from the third outer ring.

When deliberations moved to the upper house on February 2, the opposition parties boycotted the proceedings in protest against the forced passages in the lower house. The opposition parties in the third ring apparently felt that the public would not support a long boycott, however, and eventually took part in the deliberations. Although the boycott delayed the final passage for three days, the bill was approved with a majority in the upper house on February 9. All the legal processes for the SDF dispatch were finally complete. The day before, the main ground unit had joined the advance unit in Samawah. They jointly began reconstruction and humanitarian assistance activities in Iraq.

7

EVALUATING KANTEI DIPLOMACY

The analytical framework of the concentric circles model was very helpful in illustrating the top-down policy process the Koizumi cabinet used in formulating and passing the anti-terrorism, military emergency, and Iraq laws. Occupying the core of the model were the Kantei (with the prime minister and the Cabinet Secretariat) and the Liberal Democratic Party (LDP) executives, specifically Secretary-General Taku Yamasaki, who was instrumental to persuading the coalition partners. As discussed in chapter 3, Prime Minister Hashimoto's administrative reform efforts in 1997–98 strengthened the Kantei's authority, enabling it to initiate policy and helping the core function much more effectively.

Koizumi Diplomacy in the Concentric Circles Model

The three examples examined here—the 2001 anti-terrorism legislation, the 2003 emergency legislation, and the 2003 Iraq legislation—were all in the area of national security affairs, so it was very appropriate for the Kantei to play a central role. Although most of the policy issues were under the jurisdiction of the Japan Defense Agency (JDA) and the Ministry of Foreign Affairs (MOFA), these three cases, especially the emergency legislation, required government-wide involvement. MOFA, which had dominated national security issues in the post–World War II era, has lost a great deal of influence under the Koizumi cabinet. Hashimoto's reform had already abolished the Cabinet Office on External Affairs, formerly headed by a MOFA official. The conflict between Foreign Minister Makiko Tanaka and MOFA officials and a series of financial scandals involving its officials further lowered MOFA's power within the government. MOFA therefore accepted a subordinate policy-making role under the Kantei in developing the 2001 anti-terrorism legislation.

The lessons from the 1990 Gulf crisis also moved the Cabinet Secretariat to the forefront. The top officials of the Koizumi government and the leaders of the ruling parties shared the conviction that it was important to treat the attacks in New York and Washington, D.C., as a crisis immediately. Many remembered that Prime Minister Kaifu had failed to identify the Gulf crisis as a significant emergency, leaving MOFA to respond through normal diplomatic channels and significantly delaying Japan's response. As a result, the Kaifu government was criticized as offering "too little, too late" despite its financial contribution of $13 billion. With the 9/11 incidents, the Koizumi cabinet decided to seize the initiative. Deputy CCS Furukawa quickly formed a study group with high officials from the related ministries in the Cabinet Secretariat. The existing task force on emergency legislation in the former Cabinet Office on National Security and Crisis Management was asked to provide administrative assistance to this group.

The Cabinet Secretariat's centralized policy process enabled swift decisions and actions. The study group discussed the details of the anti-terrorism legislation, and its members coordinated with their own ministries. Based on directions provided by the study group, the task force managed to finalize the draft of the law within three weeks. After the legislation passed, the task force went back to its original job of preparing the emergency-related bills. The task force convened again to play a central policy-making role with the 2003 emergency

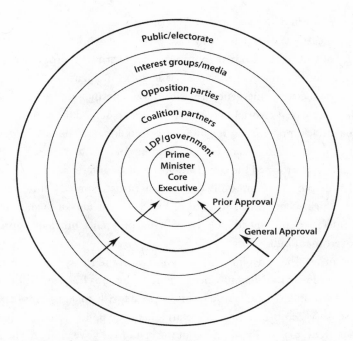

Fig. 7.1 Political Process for the Three Bills

legislation and the 2003 Iraq legislation. In the three examples studied, the Kantei successfully initiated and followed through with its policy processes as the core of the concentric circles model shown in figure 7.1.

Located in the first outer ring were the ministries and the LDP, both of which had enjoyed strong, direct influence in Japan's traditional policy-making process and often served as the first forum for political consultation. The policy process examined in this book, however, does not follow this traditional route. While there were significant amounts of unofficial consultation between the LDP and the Cabinet Secretariat, the Koizumi cabinet did not officially approach the LDP first. Instead, the cabinet sought general approval from the coalition partners Komeito and the Conservative Party, which constitute the second outer ring in the decision-making model.

The Koizumi cabinet tried to secure swift agreement from the coalition partners. Especially in the case of the 2001 anti-terrorism legislation, speed was very important so as to avoid criticism for a belated response. Since Komeito was proud of its pacifist stance on national security issues, the

Koizumi government tried to avoid constitutional controversy by keeping Japan's measures within the constitutional framework. Recognizing the urgency of enactment, Komeito approved the government proposal on September 25, only two weeks after the 9/11 terrorist incidents.

Because the 2003 emergency legislation was a permanent law that would provide a legal framework for allowing the SDF to defend the nation against external attack, preparation for those bills took longer. The task force regularly contacted members of the LDP and its coalition partners. The three coalition parties formed the Government Parties Conference on Emergency Legislation in order to smoothly build a consensus among the three parties. In early April 2002, the task force introduced more details of the bills to the GP Conference, and four days later, the GP Conference officially approved the government bills.

In contrast, the consultation process between the ruling parties and the Kantei was not so transparent when it came to the 2003 Iraq legislation. Dispatching Ground SDF units would involve greater risk, making it more politically sensitive, so the Cabinet Secretariat kept the policy process behind a veil of secrecy, essentially shutting out the rest of the government. The process was first revealed at the end of May. On June 9, Prime Minister Koizumi requested swift approval from the secretaries-general of the three coalition parties, and the parties did so just four days later.

For all three pieces of legislation, the government presented its proposals to the LDP, in the first outer ring, only *after* sharing them with the coalition parties. The *zoku* members in the LDP's policy subcommittees, usually the first to be consulted in the traditional policy process, complained that their panels had been left out. However, once the three coalition parties reached an agreement, it was very difficult for individual LDP members to oppose the decision, especially when, as was the case with the anti-terrorism legislation, the Koizumi cabinet enjoyed such high approval ratings.

After public support for the Koizumi government declined with the dismissal of the popular foreign minister Makiko Tanaka, however, it was relatively easy for LDP experts to openly criticize the government's emergency legislation. When the government-sponsored bills were deliberated in the Diet, LDP experts on defense affairs opposed the government proposal, which did not deal with possible terrorist attacks, helping the opposition parties block the bills.

With the Iraq legislation, LDP approval was more difficult to acquire because the longtime ruling party was highly factionalized along policy lines and between the pro- and anti-Koizumi camps. The LDP held unusual three-day conferences of the Policy Research Council and the General Council simultaneously. In the process of approving the government proposal, the anti-Koizumi camp demanded that the clause on weapons of mass destruction be removed. Although CCS Fukuda opposed this demand, the LDP's executives decided to yield for the purpose of building consensus for the proposal. This political compromise saved face for the leaders of the anti-Koizumi camp. While there was strong resistance within the first outer ring of the LDP, its members chose not to kill the proposal on which coalition partners composing the second outer ring had already agreed.

Among the opposition parties in the third outer ring, the largest, the Democratic Party of Japan (DPJ), served an important role as the LDP's negotiating partner for the three pieces of legislation. In order to avoid Diet passage by the ruling parties alone, the Koizumi government constantly sought cooperation from the DPJ. In the case of the anti-terrorism legislation, however, Koizumi's efforts were not successful because the LDP and Komeito did not agree on making political concessions to the DPJ in exchange for its support. The high level of public support for the Koizumi cabinet allowed the ruling parties to enact this important piece of legislation on their own.

In contrast, the DPJ played a decisive role in the policy-making process for the 2003 emergency legislation. The DPJ played a major part in blocking the vote on the original government bills in the 2002 ordinary Diet session. In the 2003 session, the DPJ involved itself directly in the policy process. The largest opposition party submitted its version of emergency legislation and showed its willingness to negotiate with the government. The DPJ agreed to hold a conference to negotiate over differences between the two proposals. After a weeklong conference, the two parties reached an agreement, leading enactment with an overwhelming majority in both houses of the Diet.

The Koizumi government also preferred to pass the Iraq legislation with support from the DPJ. The government intentionally left room for negotiations in its proposal. Before the upcoming general election, however, the DPJ wanted to showcase its difference from the LDP by opposing the SDF dispatch. The largest opposition party submitted its own bill on Iraq and ended up dissociating itself from the other opposition parties. This weakened the unity of the third inner ring, which helped the ruling coalition pass the legislation in the Diet in late July 2003.

After enactment, the SDF action guideline required Diet approval. However, the situation in Iraq worsened, and in late November 2003, two Japanese diplomats were killed on Iraqi soil. Members of the ruling and opposition parties became more cautious in their stance on dispatching the SDF. In light of this and to minimize political opposition, the policy-making process at the core became even more secretive than with the Iraq legislation. The Kantei unveiled the proposal to the ruling parties one day before the December 9 cabinet decision.

Again, approval from the coalition partners, in the second ring, became vital in the political process. Komeito, torn between its pacifist label and its responsibilities as a government coalition party, complained about the secrecy. While the party's leader went to Iraq and eventually supported the government proposal, Komeito requested closer consultation with the government. The Koizumi government kept this commitment in order to secure support from the second ring and successfully sent Air Force and Ground SDF units to Iraq by maintaining solidarity within the ruling coalition.

With regard to the three pieces of legislation detailed in this book, all of Koizumi's decisions carried high political risks: to send the SDF for the first time into active combat, through the 2001 anti-terrorism legislation; to overcome the political taboo against the SDF's use of force by enacting the 2003 emergency legislation; and to support the U.S.-led invasion of Iraq and dispatch Ground SDF units for the country's reconstruction with the 2003 Iraq legislation. Prime Minister Koizumi was willing to take these risks in order to maintain a close security relationship with the United States and was determined enough to enact these laws despite opposition within his own party. The support of Komeito, in the second ring, significantly helped the policy process within the government. Also, the DPJ's ambition to become a responsible party weakened solidarity among the opposition parties within the third ring.

In the fourth ring, the business community generally supported the three pieces of legislation advancing Japan's national security policy. Labor unions, in contrast, were against these laws, especially the 2003 emergency law.

The level of public and media support from two of the outermost rings determined the Koizumi government's actions vis-à-vis both the opposition parties and the LDP. With high public support for the anti-terrorism legislation, Koizumi could completely ignore the influence of LDP *zoku* members and passed the legislation in the Diet without any support from the

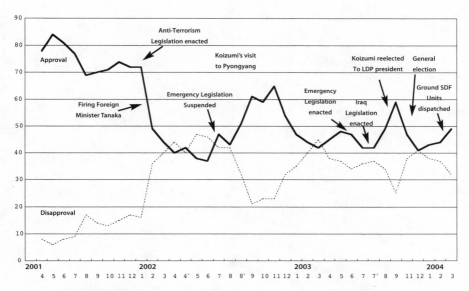

Fig. 7.2 Approval Ratings for the Koizumi Cabinet (based on *Asahi Shimbun* polls)

opposition parties. With lower public support for the emergency legislation, the Koizumi cabinet had to withdraw its original bills and modify them in accordance with the opinions of LDP and DPJ experts. The revised legislation received support from the public as well as the media.

The Koizumi cabinet chose to pass the Iraq legislation without any support from the opposition parties in late July 2003. Public opinion and the media were split on this issue. Koizumi took a great political risk with two major political events just around the corner: the September LDP presidential election and the November lower house election. Koizumi was reelected as LDP president and went through the general election without a major loss. The electorate in the outermost ring of the model seemed to generally approve of Koizumi's major decision on national security policy. Survival in these political events helped Koizumi rebuild his confidence so he could make a cabinet decision approving the action guideline dispatching the SDF and push it through the Diet (see fig. 7.2).

Throughout the legislative processes for the three laws, the Kantei, at the core of the model, played a central role, which was possible only because of

Table 7.1 Summary of National Security Legislation

Legislation	Central Bureau to Prepare Legislation	Organ for Initial Consultation	Media Support (among five major papers)	Support from Opposition Parties	Business Support	Labor Union	Public Opinion	Cabinet Approval Rating (percent)*
UN Peace Cooperation legislation 1990 (Kaifu)	MOFA UN Bureau	LDP policy subcommittees	*Sankei, Yomiuri*	No	Pro	Pro	Mixed	High (50s)
Minesweeper dispatch 1991 (Kaifu)	—	Urged by LDP	*Sankei, Yomiuri*	DSP	Pro	Pro	Pro	High (around 50)
International Peace Cooperation legislation 1992 (Miyazawa)	Kantei	LDP policy subcommittees	*Sankei, Yomiuri, Nihon Keizai*	Komei, DSP	Pro	Pro	Pro	Low (around 30)
Anti-terrorism legislation 2001 (Koizumi)	Kantei	Coalition partners	*Sankei, Yomiuri, Nihon Keizai, Mainichi*	No	Pro	Con	Pro	Very high (over 70)
Emergency legislation 2003 (Koizumi)	Kantei	Coalition partners	All	DPJ, Liberal	Pro	Con	Pro	Medium (40s)
Iraq legislation 2003 (Koizumi)	Kantei	Coalition partners	*Sankei, Yomiuri, Nihon Keizai*	No	Pro	Con	Mixed	Medium (40s)

*Ratings per *Asahi*

Prime Minister Koizumi's steadfast determination and the public's support for the government. The concentric circles model presents a clear explanation of how the prime minister succeeded in achieving these politically risky policy goals in a short time.

The Drawbacks of Kantei Diplomacy

As analysis with the concentric circles model suggests, the Kantei is the most appropriate Japanese government agency to handle major international issues and related legislation. The office is designed and authorized to coordinate the various interests of the ministries and agencies. Given its central position within the government infrastructure, it can directly support the prime minister and process policies more quickly than any other agency. However, Kantei diplomacy does have certain drawbacks.

Conflicts with MOFA

One of the negative aspects of Kantei diplomacy is the potential for conflict with MOFA, which once dominated diplomatic affairs. This is not an issue unique to Japan, of course. In the United States, for example, the National Security Council (NSC) and the State Department have often engaged in fierce turf battles. The head of the NSC, the national security adviser, has an office in the West Wing of the White House. This physical proximity to the president gives the adviser a significant advantage over State Department officials. In Henry Kissinger's words, "Propinquity counts for much; the opportunity to confer with the President several times a day is often of decisive importance, much more so than the chairmanship of committees or the right to present options."[1]

In their book *Our Own Worst Enemy*, I. M. Destler, Leslie H. Gelb, and Anthony Lake vividly describe how the national security advisers under the Nixon and Carter administrations, Henry Kissinger and Zbigniew Brzezinski, ignored the State Department when developing foreign policy.[2] If the Kantei intentionally excluded MOFA and its minister in this way, a major conflict would develop and make it difficult to obtain bureaucratic support.

In the case of the 1990 UN Peace Cooperation legislation under the Kaifu administration (discussed in chapter 2), members of the government strongly disagreed on the status of the SDF personnel dispatched. On the one hand,

Foreign Vice Minister Takakazu Kuriyama planned to send personnel separately from the SDF. On the other hand, Deputy CCS Nobuo Ishihara joined with LDP secretary-general Ichiro Ozawa on sending personnel as SDF units.

Although there have been occasional disagreements between the Kantei and MOFA, serious conflicts such as those between the NSC and the State Department are unlikely. Senior NSC officers are political appointees and operate autonomously, separate from other executive offices such as the departments of state or defense. Conversely, most Kantei officers involved in foreign and defense affairs are seconded from the ministries, such as MOFA and the JDA. They still maintain some degree of loyalty to their home ministries, which lowers the possibility of real conflict.

The Political Ambitions of Kantei Staff

The turf battles between the NSC and the State Department were sparked in part by the aggressive nature of the national security advisers. Kissinger and Brzezinski never hid their political ambitions or shied away from involvement in foreign affairs. After leaving office, both published memoirs boasting about their respective diplomatic records. To fulfill their political ambitions, they tried to gain the president's backing and exclude the State Department from diplomatic affairs.

In the Kantei, a similar risk may arise if a political appointee with big political ambitions is put in charge of foreign affairs. One rare example is Muneo Suzuki, who was a parliamentary deputy CCS under the Obuchi administration. As is widely known, the Northern Territories issue had been an obstacle to a bilateral peace treaty between Japan and Russia. The Japanese government had steadfastly demanded return of all the territories, but Suzuki was pushing for a more realistic approach. He proposed demanding half the territories, the Habomai group and Shikotan Island, first. Although Prime Minister Keizo Obuchi was interested in foreign affairs, he delegated relations with Russia to Suzuki.[3] CCS Hiromu Nonaka, Suzuki's political mentor, also allowed Suzuki to operate autonomously. This suggests that the indifference of the prime minister and the acquiescence of the CCS could allow a Kantei staffer to act independently from the intentions of the government.

As discussed in chapter 3, Hashimoto's administrative reforms significantly strengthened the Kantei, especially the power of an administrative deputy

CCS vis-à-vis other ministries. Although Hashimoto's reform plan recommended placing non-bureaucratic political appointees in key positions, such as administrative deputy CCS and assistant CCS, as of June 2006, bureaucrats had always occupied these posts. Some critics would argue that the bureaucrats still control the Japanese government, while the Kantei plays a more important part in policy making.

However, there is a clear hierarchy between the prime minister (or the CCS) and the administrative deputy CCS. The prime minister has true appointive power over the administrative deputy CCS position, while other ministers have nominal, mostly statutory control over their subordinates, such as vice ministers and bureau chiefs. Bureaucrats in a given ministry, therefore, may not be totally loyal to their minister. If a minister tries to dismiss his vice minister, for example, most officials in the ministry may oppose the action.

At the same time, the administrative deputy CCS is expected to act on behalf of the prime minister and the CCS. If a deputy does act against the will of the prime minister, dismissal is likely. Even if an ambitious Kantei staff member pursued his or her own political agenda, it would be difficult to directly oppose the prime minister. Risk only exists when the prime minister and the CCS do not pay enough attention to such activities.

Politically Motivated Foreign Policy

The Kantei's initiative allows the prime minister to conduct the country's foreign affairs according to his own views. When a power shift occurs and a new national leader arises, however, this centralized policy process may create incoherence in Japan's foreign affairs. Prime Minister Koizumi has, for example, constantly promoted policies stressing the importance of the U.S.-Japan alliance. His successors may not have the same degree of commitment toward the bilateral relationship, which would no doubt disturb Washington.

The prime minister may also use foreign affairs achievements for political purposes. Prime Minister Koizumi took advantage of his September 2002 visit to Pyongyang to boost his sagging job approval rating (see chapter 4), creating the momentum necessary to reintroduce the emergency legislation. Critics point out that Koizumi's second visit to Pyongyang in May 2004 was basically intended to boost his popularity for the upcoming July 2004 upper house election. The political schedule—such as elections, Diet deliberations, and voting on major legislation—is an important element in foreign-policy decision making. However, domestic politics may narrow political windows for serious diplomacy.

Political Isolation

The Kantei's initiative in foreign affairs enables swift policy making. At the same time, the centralized policy process means ignoring traditional consensus building within the government and the ruling parties. In the three examples studied here, LDP policy subcommittees that had once been instrumental in policy making did not play a key role. In the anti-terrorism legislation process, the Koizumi administration made agreement among the coalition parties its first priority and forced LDP subcommittees to accept the agreement. Koizumi's solid public support and the lack of a powerful successor allowed this strong-arm method of policy making. Despite intense dissatisfaction within the LDP, the party was unable to find another leader under whom it was willing to run an electoral campaign.

Strong public support also enabled smooth Diet operations. In the case of the anti-terrorism legislation, high cabinet approval ratings and victory in the July 2001 upper house election allowed the Koizumi cabinet to end negotiations with the DPJ and vote on the legislation by the ruling parties alone. A low cabinet approval rating once froze voting on the emergency legislation, but rising approval after Koizumi's September 2002 Pyongyang visit enabled his cabinet to resubmit the legislation to the Diet. Meanwhile, the DPJ, anxious to become a viable opposition party, actively participated in negotiations with the ruling parties on reaching a political agreement on the legislation. Throughout the time of the 2003 deliberations, most LDP members wanted to run an electoral campaign under Koizumi's leadership. Such political consensus made it possible for the Koizumi cabinet to finish the approval process for the Iraq legislation within the ruling parties in seven days without isolating the national leader.

The top-down, centralized policy process was bound to create intense dissatisfaction within the ruling parties and the government. The prime minister needs public support in order to overcome political opposition. On the one hand, when the public is supportive of the prime minister's policies, it is more difficult for ruling party members to openly oppose him. On the other hand, top-down policy making by an unpopular national leader ends up isolating him. An effective policy initiative by the prime minister requires effort on his part to earn the public's understanding.

The Merits of Kantei Diplomacy

Kantei diplomacy does have several advantages. As the examples in this book clearly show, centralized policy making is essential to foreign-policy issues that require interagency coordination, such as the 2003 emergency legislation and trade friction, or an urgent response to an international crisis like the 9/11 terrorist attacks. The Kantei can take advantage of the political influence of the prime minister and the CCS, can provide these political leaders with the necessary administrative support, and is in a better position to pursue national interests compared to MOFA, which may put a higher priority on friendly relations with foreign countries. Most important, as the Constitution gives authority to manage foreign affairs to the Cabinet, and not to MOFA, it is more legitimate for the prime minister and his supporting organ, the Cabinet Secretariat, to play the central role. These advantages far outweigh the drawbacks.

Interagency Coordination Capability

Kantei diplomacy under the Nakasone and Takeshita cabinets focused on economic issues, especially trade matters, as MOFA argued assertively against the Kantei's involvement in the political aspects of diplomacy. Economic matters, in contrast, would involve the other economic ministries, and it was more appropriate for the Kantei to coordinate such policies among the ministries. For MOFA, it was more desirable for the Cabinet Office on External Affairs, headed by a MOFA official, to handle trade issues than for the other ministries to take the initiative.

As Ichiro Ozawa showed while serving as a deputy CCS and government representative, solving complicated trade friction issues requires political leadership. Most trade issues are not really "international" or "economic" in nature; instead, their causes are rooted in domestic and political matters. Trade issues are often extraordinarily complicated and go beyond the jurisdiction of one ministry, as in the case of the U.S.-Japan construction negotiations described in chapter 1. In such cases, it would be more appropriate for the Kantei than MOFA to handle them.

National security is also an appropriate area for the Kantei's initiative. Here, a legal framework has been slowly but surely established and strengthened since the 1990s, with the 1992 International Peace Cooperation Law, the 1999 Regional Crisis Law, the 2001 anti-terrorism law, the 2003 emergency law, and the 2003 Iraq law. Since all these laws define the role of the SDF in action, they require the JDA's involvement, especially that of uniformed officers who know the reality of their activities. The emergency law also requires participation by other ministries: the former Ministry of Transport with the Japan Coast Guard, for example, would be in charge of guarding Japan's coastline, and the former Ministry of Home Affairs would be handling the division of roles between the national and local governments. The Kantei was in a better position than MOFA to handle coordination among these ministries.

A MOFA official stated his view on the Kantei's initiative in national security affairs: "Japan used to be like a utopian nation where people were allowed to consider foreign affairs independent from national security affairs. The September 11 attacks forced the nation to more seriously consider the two together. The Kantei would be more appropriate to take the lead than MOFA or the JDA alone."[4]

Responsiveness

The 2001 anti-terrorism legislation and the 2003 Iraq legislation required speed because the SDF had to be dispatched in a timely manner. During the policy-making process, the Kantei functioned with extraordinary effectiveness. As shown in chapter 3, the anti-terrorism law took less than two months from the 9/11 incidents to enactment, an unusually quick process for such important legislation. Although the Iraq law had a longer gestation period, it took only a week for the ruling parties to complete the political approval process and less than six weeks to pass the legislation in the Diet. Without the Kantei driving the process, such swiftness would never have been possible.

The Political Influence of the Prime Minister and the CCS

In chapter 1, a former director of the Cabinet Office on External Affairs related how he frequently took advantage of the "lion's skin" of the prime minister or the CCS to advance policy. Bureaucrats do acknowledge the prime minister's authority even if he has limited political influence. Any bills and important government policies require cabinet approval, and since the prime minister heads the cabinet, it would be impossible to make cabinet decisions by totally ignoring his intentions. The opposition may force the prime minister to accept political compromise; however, if the prime minister openly opposes a certain policy, it would be difficult for the government to ignore his position.

When the prime minister has a clear stance on a certain policy, his direct involvement in the policy process is not necessarily essential. Often, the CCS acts in the prime minister's stead. Prime Minister Nakasone provided political vision, for example, and CCS Gotoda used his extensive experience as a career bureaucrat to achieve the desired policy goals. More recently, Prime Minister Koizumi and CCS Yasuo Fukuda proved a great combination: Koizumi had a strong political will but very limited administrative skills; Fukuda, who had years of business experience and had served as assistant to the prime minister, made up for Koizumi's shortcomings. Both Gotoda and Fukuda became very influential vis-à-vis the bureaucrats. Kantei staffers serving under a strong CCS have a distinct advantage in their relations with other ministries.

A popular prime minister also boosts the Kantei's influence over members of the ruling parties and the other ministries. Criticism of Prime Minister Koizumi, who began his tenure with a historically high cabinet approval rating, was very limited at first. Members of the ruling parties who chose to openly oppose him put their own popularity at risk. If members of the ruling parties support the prime minister, it is difficult for bureaucrats to gain political support against his policy.

Here, it is important to note that popularity may not match the individual's professional reputation in the political world. Prime Minister Toshiki Kaifu enjoyed a relatively high level of public support throughout his tenure, but he was never able to translate it into support within the ruling party. Kaifu repeatedly stated that he would stake the life of his cabinet on reforming the electoral and campaign finance systems. However, he failed to pass the reform plan.[5] A poor reputation in the political community can limit the political influence of a highly popular national leader.

Alternatively, popular support can help the prime minister maintain his political influence even when the professional experts do not necessarily support him. The immediate result of Koizumi's second visit to Pyongyang in May 2004 was the release of only five of the eight family members of the Japanese abductees. The DPJ's new party leader, Katsuya Okada, publicly described the visit as a "diplomatic disaster."[6] However, according to an *Asahi Shimbun* poll taken immediately after this visit, 67 percent of respondents supported Koizumi's visit, and the cabinet's approval rating improved from 45 percent to 54 percent.[7] Koizumi's decision to visit Pyongyang a second time improved his public standing, helping him maintain political influence.

Pursuing National Interests

Diplomats are expected to represent their nation and act in its best interests while maintaining friendly relations with their counterparts from other countries. Sustaining that delicate balance is notoriously difficult, however, as an international incident in May 2002 demonstrated to MOFA officials.

The incident, which sparked harsh criticism of MOFA for harming national interests, involved five North Korean refugees who entered the Japanese consulate in Shenyang, China, seeking asylum. The five made it into the compound but were dragged out by armed Chinese police. An amateur video clearly showed that a Japanese official at the consulate made no attempt to prevent the police from invading the compound, which, as Japan's sovereign territory, is protected by international law. The Chinese government argued that the police entered with the permission of the Japanese vice-consul and were acting under the auspices of the Vienna Convention to prevent asylum attempts.

Although the Japanese government officially filed a complaint against Beijing for violating Japan's sovereignty and demanded an apology, critics argued that the initial reaction of the Japanese official, to allow the police intrusion, caused this blunder. One of those critics was former MOFA vice minister and ambassador to the United States Ryohei Murata. In his book, Murata argues that such developments occurred because many Japanese diplomats tried to resolve conflicts without causing problems with their counterparts.[8]

After entering the ministry, MOFA officials are divided according to their expertise in foreign language. Those specializing in the Chinese language are regarded as members of the so-called China School, which has been often a target of criticism within MOFA itself. Since assignments for these Chinese experts are limited, their career development path is rather inflexible. Their best option is to occupy China-related posts both at MOFA and at overseas facilities, and the ultimate goal is to serve as ambassador to China.

If they are to remain on this elite track, China School diplomats must maintain good personal relationships with Chinese government officials. Otherwise, their chances of promotion are dim. A former MOFA official, Hisahiko Okazaki, points out that the Chinese government applies a certain type of political pressure on individual MOFA officials and argues that MOFA needs to separate officials who make policy decisions on China from those who are engaged in maintaining friendly relations between the two countries.[9]

It is not unusual for diplomats with regional expertise to be accused of having an overly chummy relationship with their counterparts and of not always pursuing national interests. In the late 1980s, for example, James Fallows criticized America's Tokyo-based diplomats as having constantly sacrificed U.S. economic interests for the sake of the bilateral relationship.[10] Because MOFA and the U.S. State Department consist of regional departments covering the entire world, the diplomatic authority is expected to conduct a more balanced policy toward each region. In actuality, however, regional experts who are exposed to abundant information are very influential in the policy-making process. As these regional experts in the diplomatic authority tend to be sympathetic to the region, the Kantei or the U.S. White House is in a better position to pursue national interests.

Meeting the Needs of the National Leader

National leaders are often shielded from raw information about the true state of their country. Officials in any large bureaucracy regularly, even systematically, filter out vital data that they do not want the national leader to receive. Immediately after entering the office, Prime Minister Noboru Takeshita reportedly complained that all the information he received became "rounded." Former prime minister Yasuhiro Nakasone stated frankly that he did not believe the official information bureaucrats brought to him. CCS Masaharu Gotoda was well aware of this bureaucratic tendency to hide bad information from the Kantei. Gotoda specifically instructed his staff at the Kantei to bring "bad information" to him.[11] Kantei staffers often ask businesspeople in the private sector to provide foreign information different from what MOFA provides to the prime minister. To Kantei staffers, the MOFA information tends to emphasize Japan's good relations with other countries and is rarely negative or inflammatory.

In addition, the information MOFA supplies is often considered "too long, with too many details." Because the prime minister's time and energy are limited, he prefers concise briefings with policy options. Prime Minister Koizumi, for example, is known for his short attention span and his preference for policy briefings of fifteen minutes or less. He also preferred memos no longer than a single sheet of paper.

Furthermore, briefings by MOFA officials often lack a political point of view. A MOFA official who was seconded to the Kantei described the change in his thinking: "At the Kantei, when we plan foreign policy, we always have to consider the intention of the prime minister and the chief cabinet secretary as well as the political schedule, including the Diet deliberation. At MOFA, my policy planning was based largely on the logic within the ministry. But at the Kantei, it was essential for me to know the political considerations of the policy, such as reaction from the ruling parties and the related industries."[12] The Kantei staffers are in a better position to provide the prime minister with policy options that take political considerations into account.

Political Legitimacy and Accountability

As a country with a parliamentary democracy, Japan is expected to pursue a policy of "democratic diplomacy." In his classic book *Diplomacy*, British diplomat Sir Harold Nicolson defines "democratic diplomacy" as follows: "The diplomatist, being a civil servant, is subject to the Foreign Secretary [or Minister]; the Foreign Secretary, being a member of the cabinet, is subject to the majority in Parliament; and Parliament, being but a representative Assembly, is subject to the will of the sovereign people."[13] Professional foreign service officers are responsible and loyal to the cabinet, which is entrusted with executive power by the voters. In the context of democratic diplomacy, it is both desirable and politically legitimate for the prime minister and his cabinet, with assistance from MOFA, to take the lead in foreign affairs.

Since democratic diplomacy is conducted on behalf of the sovereign people, it is expected to reflect their collective will. By definition, democratic diplomacy must therefore be supported by public opinion. As Nicolson points out, however, ordinary people are not necessarily educated in the ways of foreign and defense affairs. He laments, "even educated electors are almost totally unaware what are the treaties by which their countries are bound. These treaties have been published, debated in Parliament and discussed in the press. Yet the vast majority of the people have no conception of their existence, have forgotten all about them."[14] Nicolson's concern should be shared by the diplomatic authority of Japan and all the nations of the world.

Even if the people are well informed, there is no guarantee that public opinion will express good judgment in foreign policy. A prominent American diplomat, George Kennan, offers a very pessimistic view of public opinion. In *American Diplomacy 1900–1950*, he describes the public reaction to foreign-policy questions as "erratic and undependable in the long term" and argues that "in the short term our public opinion, or what passes for our public opinion in the thinking of official Washington, can be easily led astray into areas of emotionalism and subjectivity which make it a poor and inadequate guide for national action."[15]

In order to achieve better judgment, Kennan firmly believes "that we could make much more effective use of the principle of professionalism in the conduct of foreign policy; that we could, if we wished, develop a corps of professional officers superior to anything that exists or ever has existed in this field; and that, by treating these men with respect and drawing on their insight and experience, we could help ourselves considerably."[16] What Kennan argues for is strong professionalism and elitism; diplomacy is too complicated for the ordinary citizen to understand and should be delegated to professional experts. This elitism, however, conflicts with the principle of democratic diplomacy.

Furthermore, it is difficult even for an educated citizen to produce a good judgment on foreign and defense affairs in a timely manner. The time lag can have a detrimental effect, according to Nicolson: "A democratic government has to wait until public opinion has digested its own conclusions. True it is that these conclusions, when reached, are generally more sensible and more stable than the somnambulist certainties of a dictator. Yet the months which must elapse before any definite public opinion can be ascertained is often fatal to efficient policy or negotiation."[17]

That time lag may be a span of years instead of months in Japan, where pacifism has been strong and the people have intentionally avoided serious discussion on national security for much of the postwar period. Public opinion on Japan's participation in United Nations peacekeeping operations in 1992 was sharply divided, for example, with many Japanese wary about dispatching the SDF overseas. Ten years later, however, very few Japanese opposed sending the SDF for peacekeeping activities. Even the Socialist Democratic Party, which strongly opposed the 1992 International Peace Cooperation legislation, expressed its support for participation in peacekeeping operations in the party's manifesto for the 2003 general election campaign. Similarly, although public opinion on the dispatch of Ground SDF units to Iraq was sharply divided in 2003, as discussed in chapter 6, it might be totally different in another ten years.

When the government tries to persuade the public to accept its stance on foreign and defense affairs, it may not be realistic to expect full understanding in a timely manner. But a democratic government must not neglect the persuasion process. If one asks whether MOFA has tried hard to persuade the public, the answer would be negative. Many MOFA officials acknowledge this problem and try to change MOFA's nature. After a series of scandals rocked the ministry, young MOFA officials came up with a report in July 2002 that includes a reform plan. The report points out that accountability and transparency were required in the foreign-policy-making process and argues that it is essential to develop a dialogue with people outside the ministry in order to conduct effective diplomacy with support from the public.[18]

The prime minister is in a much more appropriate position than any MOFA official to explain important foreign-policy decisions to the public. He is not only the nation's most visible political actor but also the head of the cabinet to which the people entrust executive power, including over foreign affairs. The prime minister is held accountable and is responsible for persuading the public. If he fails to do so, he would bear political responsibility as the voters would not support his party in the next general election.

The Japanese public has developed an awareness of the prime minister's accountability over major national issues. In March 2003, when Prime Minister Koizumi announced his support for the U.S. attack on Iraq, he tried to explain his position to the public in his own words, as described in chapter 6. Although the explanation was criticized as inadequate, the drop in the cabinet approval rating was marginal (four points).

In contrast, when the government decided in June 2004 that SDF units would join the multinational forces in Iraq, the prime minister did not make any special effort to persuade the public. The result was a sharp drop in the cabinet approval rating, from 54 percent to 40 percent. Respondents who disapproved of including the SDF in the multinational forces totaled 58 percent, while only 31 percent approved.[19]

The pacifism that has existed throughout the postwar period has become a substantial obstacle to any realistic understanding of national security and foreign affairs on the part of the public. However, because the world situation changes so rapidly and the international environment surrounding Japan requires realistic reaction, we can no longer separate national security from foreign affairs. It is the obligation of the sovereign people to seriously consider both. At the same time, the government is obligated to educate and persuade the public with regard to its policies.

From the viewpoint of democratic diplomacy, it is more desirable for the Kantei to take the lead in major foreign policies. To effectively pursue Kantei diplomacy, it is essential that the prime minister and the CCS take advantage of their political resources.

In the national security issues examined in this book, Prime Minister Koizumi demonstrated his political leadership. However, in domestic reform, he was frequently criticized for passing the buck to somebody else. As a result of this practice, his domestic reform plans, such as for the road construction business, ended up as political compromises, intended to avoid destroying vested interests. Unless the prime minister devotes his time and energy to attaining his politically difficult goals, he will not accomplish any of them. The prime minister is not allowed to thrust responsibility for important foreign and national security issues onto somebody else. The success of Kantei diplomacy depends on his political will and determination and on the political resources he can devote to achieving his policy goals.

Introduction

1. "Koizumi seiken de nani ga kawattaka" [What changed under the Koizumi administration], *Nihon Keizai Shimbun*, no. 4, August 8, 2003.

2. Ibid.

3. The author thanks Ellis Krause for his wisdom and assistance with the argument in this section. See also Robert Pekkanen and Ellis Krause, "Japan's 'Coalition of the Willing' on Security Policies," *Orbis*, Summer 2005.

4. Thomas Berger, "From Sword to Chrysanthemum: Japan's Culture of Anti-Militarism," *International Security*, Spring 1993.

5. Ichiro Ozawa, *Blueprint for a New Japan: The Rethinking of a Nation* (Tokyo: Kodansha International, 1994).

6. Cabinet Office, "Gaiko ni taisuru seron chosa" [Public opinion on foreign pol-

icy], October 2004. Available at http://www8.cao.go.jp/survey/h16/h16-gaikou/index.html (accessed December 20, 2005).

7. Christopher Hughes stresses the influence of public opinion on the Japanese government in pressuring it to become a "normal" nation. According to him, public opinion forced Japanese policy makers to pursue a "containment" policy toward North Korea after the 1998 Taepodong incident. Christopher Hughes, *Japan's Re-emergence as a "Normal" Military Power* (Oxford: Oxford University Press, 2004).

8. Paul Milford, "Japan's Response to Terror: Dispatching the SDF to the Arabian Sea," *Asian Survey*, March/April 2003, pp. 329–51.

9. See Michael Green, *Japan's Reluctant Realism: Foreign Policy Challenges in an Era of Uncertain Power* (New York: Council on Foreign Relations, 2001).

10. Tomohiko Taniguchi, "A Cold Peace: The Changing Security Equation in Northeast Asia," *Orbis*, Summer 2005: pp. 445–57.

11. Pekkanen and Krause, "Japan's 'Coalition of the Willing' on Security Policies."

12. Ozawa, *Blueprint for a New Japan*, pp. 23–25.

13. Among the important works on the subject of the ruling party and the bureaucracy are Robert Scalapino, ed., *The Foreign Policy of Modern Japan* (Berkeley and Los Angeles: University of California Press, 1977); and Gerald L. Curtis, ed., *Japan's Foreign Policy After the Cold War: Coping with Change* (Armonk, N.Y.: M. E. Sharpe, 1993). As far as I am aware, however, no academic had focused on the Kantei's function in foreign-policy making until my Japanese-language book *Kantei gaiko* was published in October 2004. This volume expands on the earlier work.

14. For the details of the policy process, see Soichiro Tahara's interview with Hitoshi Tanaka. Tanaka Hitoshi and Tahara Soichiro, *Kokka to gaiko* [The nation and diplomacy] (Tokyo: Kodansha, 2005).

15. Richard Neustadt, *Presidential Power and the Modern Presidents: The Politics of Leadership from Roosevelt to Reagan*, rev. ed. (New York: The Free Press, 1990), p. 10.

16. Graham Allison, *Essence of Decision: Explaining the Cuban Missile Crisis* (Boston: Little, Brown and Company, 1971).

17. Robert J. Art, "Bureaucratic Politics and American Foreign Policy: A Critique," *Policy Sciences* 4, no. 4 (December 1973): pp. 467–90; and Stephen D. Krasner, "Are Bureaucracies Important? (or Allison Wonderland)," *Foreign Policy*, no. 7 (Summer 1972): p. 167.

18. Roger Hilsman, *To Move a Nation* (New York: Doubleday and Company, 1967).

19. Allison, *Essence of Decision*, p. 157.

20. Roger Hilsman, *The Politics of Policy Making in Defense and Foreign Affairs: Conceptual Models and Bureaucratic Politics* (Englewood Cliffs, N.J.: Prentice-Hall, 1987).

21. For more detailed arguments on the role of Japan's core executive in foreign policy, see Tomohito Shinoda with Ian Holliday, "Governing from the Centre: Core Executive Capacity in Britain and Japan," *Japanese Journal of Political Science* 3, part 1 (May 2002): pp. 91–111.

22. Hilsman, *Politics of Policy Making in Defense and Foreign Affairs*, p. 220.

23. Ikuo Kabashima and Jeffrey Broadbent, "Preference Pluralism: Mass Media and Politics in Japan," *Journal of Japanese Studies* 12, no. 2 (Summer 1986): pp. 329–61.

24. John Creighton Campbell, "Media and Policy Change in Japan," in *Media and Politics in Japan*, ed. Susan J. Pharr and Ellis S. Krauss (Honolulu: University of Hawai'i Press, 1996), pp. 187, 190.

1   The Roots of Kantei Diplomacy

1. Gotoda Masaharu, *Seiji towa nanika?* [What is politics?] (Tokyo: Kodansha, 1988), pp. 147–48.

2. For the prime ministers' leadership in foreign policy, see Tomohito Shinoda, *Leading Japan: The Role of the Prime Minister* (Westport, Conn.: Praeger, 2000), pp. 53–57.

3. See Bradley M. Richardson and Scott C. Flanagan, *Politics in Japan* (Boston: Little, Brown and Company, 1984), p. 344.

4. In early 1994, for example, MITI minister Hiroshi Kumagai forced a bureau director to resign, and this became big news because political intervention in bureaucratic placement is extremely unusual.

5. Ishihara Nobuo, *Kengen no daiido* [The major transfer of authority] (Tokyo: Kanki Shuppan, 2001), p. 82.

6. Ibid., p. 90.

7. Ibid., p. 91.

8. Ibid., p. 85.

9. Ibid.

10. Aurelia George Mulgan, "Japan's 'Un-Westminster' System: Impediments to Reform in a Crisis Economy," *Government and Opposition* 38, no. 1 (Winter 2003): p. 80.

11. Nakasone Yasuhiro, *Tenchi ujo: Gojunen no sengo seiji wo kataru* [Affection in heaven and on earth: Talk on fifty years of postwar politics] (Tokyo: Bungei Shunju, 1996), p. 418.

12. Article 66 reads "The Cabinet, in the exercise of executive power, shall be collectively responsible to the Diet."

13. Nakasone, *Tenchi ujo*, p. 422.

14. Selected from Nakasone's list. Ibid.

15. About Nakasone's use of the advisory councils, see Shumpei Kumon, "Japan Faces Its Future: The Political-Economics and Administrative Reform," *Journal of Japanese Studies* 10, no. 1 (Winter 1984): pp. 143–65.

16. Yasuhiro Nakasone, interview by author, March 15, 2004.

17. Junzo Matoba, interview by author, December 16, 1992. I retold this story to former CCS Gotoda, who listened with a nod and a smile.

18. Nakasone, *Tenchi ujo*, p. 372.

19. Ibid., p. 388.

20. Takahama Tatoo, *Nakasone gaiseiron: Sori wa nani o mezashite irunoka?* [On

Nakasone's diplomacy: What is the prime minister trying to achieve?] (Tokyo: PHP, 1984), p. 70.

21. Nakasone, *Tenchi ujo*, pp. 445–46.

22. Yasuhiro Nakasone, interview by author, March 15, 2004.

23. Sejima Ryuzo, *Iku sanga* [So many mountains and rivers] (Tokyo: Sankei Shimbun, 1995), p. 428.

24. Ibid.

25. Hasegawa Kazutoshi, "Nakasone gaiko" [Nakasone diplomacy], in *Nakasone naikakushi: Rinen to seisaku* [The history of the Nakasone cabinet: Ideal and policy], ed. Sekai Heiwa Kenkyusho (Tokyo: Chuo Koron-sha, 1995), p. 178.

26. Nakasone, *Tenchi ujo*, p. 446.

27. Yasuhiro Nakasone, interview by author, March 15, 2004.

28. Nakasone, *Tenchi ujo*, p. 448.

29. Yasuhiro Nakasone, interview by author, March 15, 2004.

30. Ibid.

31. Nathaniel Thayer, "Japanese Foreign Policy in the Nakasone Years," in *Japan's Foreign Policy After the Cold War: Coping with Change*, ed. Gerald Curtis (Armonk, N.Y.: M. E. Sharpe, 1993), p. 101.

32. Hasegawa, "Nakasone gaiko," p. 182, and Nakasone, *Tenchi ujo*, pp. 440–41.

33. Yasuhiro Nakasone, interview by author, March 15, 2004.

34. "Statement at Williamsburg," May 29, 1983.

35. Yasuhiro Nakasone, interview by author, March 15, 2004.

36. *Mainichi Shimbun*, June 9, 1983.

37. Gotoda Masaharu, *Naikaku kanbo chokan* [The chief cabinet secretary] (Tokyo: Kodansha, 1989), pp. 30–35. See also Gotoda, *Seiji towa nanika?* pp. 143–48.

38. Masaharu Gotoda, interview by author, December 18, 1992.

39. Ibid.

40. Gotoda, *Naikaku kanbo chokan*, pp. 105–8.

41. Sassa Atsuyuki, "Nakasone naikaku to kuni no kanri [The Nakasone cabinet and the management of the nation]," in *Nakasone naikakushi*, p. 307.

42. Ibid.

43. Ibid.

44. Ibid., p. 308.

45. Junzo Matoba, interview by author, December 16, 1992.

46. Yasuhiro Nakasone, interview by author, March 15, 2004.

47. Gotoda Masaharu, *Jo to ri* [Emotion and logic] (Tokyo: Kodansha, 1998), p. 170.

48. Raisuke Miyawaki, interview by author, March 10, 1993.

49. Michihiko Kunihiro, interview by author, March 15, 2004.

50. Yasuhiro Nakasone, interview by author, March 15, 2004.

51. Michihiko Kunihiro, interview by author, March 15, 2004.

52. Gotoda, *Jo to ri*, pp. 170–72.

53. Sassa Atsuyuki, *Kiki kanri saisho ron* [On leadership in crisis management] (Tokyo: Bungei Shunju, 1995), pp. 229–30.

54. Michihiko Kunihiro, interview by author, March 15, 2004.

55. Ibid.

56. Ibid.

57. Ibid.

58. There were only two prior examples of such appointments: Toshio Kimura under the Sato administration and Takao Fujinami under the Nakasone cabinet.

59. Takeshita Noboru, *Shogen hoshu seiken* [Testimony on conservative administrations] (Tokyo: Yomiuri Shimbun-sha, 1991), p. 191.

60. Ishihara Nobuo, *Kantei 2668 nichi: Seisaku kettei no butaiura* [2,668 days at the prime minister's official residence: Behind the scenes of decision making] (Tokyo: NHK Shuppan, 1995), p. 91.

61. See Tomohito Shinoda, "Ozawa Ichiro as an Actor in Foreign Policy Making," *Japan Forum* 16, no. 1 (2004), pp. 37–62.

62. Michihiko Kunihiro, interview by author, March 15, 2004.

63. Ibid.

64. Yabunaka Mitoji, *Taibei keizai kosho* [Economic negotiations with the United States] (Tokyo: Saimaru Shuppankai, 1991), p. 59.

65. Michihiko Kunihiro, interview by author, March 15, 2004.

66. Ibid.

67. Yabunaka, *Taibei keizai kosho*, pp. 64–65.

68. Watanabe Kensuke, *Anohito: Hitotsu no Ozawa Ichiro ron* [That man: One theory on Ozawa Ichiro] (Tokyo: Asuka Shinsha, 1992), p. 226.

69. Jacob M. Schlesinger, *Shadow Shoguns: The Rise and Fall of Japan's Postwar Political Machine* (New York: Simon & Schuster, 1997), p. 255.

70. Ibid.

71. Yabunaka, *Taibei keizai kosho*, p. 65.

72. Ibid.

73. Schlesinger, *Shadow Shoguns*, p. 255.

74. For the details of this negotiation, see James Auer, "FSX kosho wa koshite kecchakushita" [How the FSX negotiation was settled], *Chuo Koron*, June 1990, pp. 156–71.

75. *Washington Post*, January 29, 1989.

76. According to Glen S. Fukushima, the Department of Commerce requested a copy of the MOU from the National Security Council in December 1988, but the request was denied. It was not until January 1989 that the department finally received a copy. Glen S. Fukushima, *Nichibei keizai masatsu no seijigaku* [Politics of U.S.-Japan economic friction] (Tokyo: Asahi Shimbun-sha, 1992), p. 266.

77. Statement made at the Domestic Determinants of Japan's Foreign Policy conference, Tokyo, July 14, 1998.

78. Yabunaka, *Taibei keizai kosho*, p. 115.

79. Ibid., p. 116

80. Ibid., p. 119.

81. Michihiko Kunihiro, interview by author, March 15, 2004.

82. Nonaka Hiromu, *Watashi wa tatakau* [I fight] (Tokyo: Bungei Shunju, 1996), p. 96.

83. Ishihara Nobuo, *Shusho Kantei no ketsudan* [The decisions of the prime minister's office] (Chuo Koron-sha, 1997), p. 60.

84. Ishihara, *Shusho kantei no ketsudan*, p. 61.

85. Ibid.

86. Michihiko Kunihiro, interview by author, March 15, 2004.

2   A Traumatic Experience

1. Deputy CCS Ishihara recalls, "The Ministry of Finance began examining the spending as usual. At the time of the war, there were not enough supporting documents. With the lack of sufficient documentation, the MOF budgeted $1 billion." Ishihara Nobuo, *Shusho Kantei no ketsudan* [The decisions of the prime minister's office] (Tokyo: Chuo Koron-sha, 1997), p. 68.

2. Ibid., pp. 68–69.

3. Asahi Shimbun Wangan Kiki Shuzaihan, *Wangan Senso to Nihon* [The Gulf War and Japan] (Tokyo: Asahi Shimbun-sha, 1991), pp. 68–70.

4. Kuriyama Takakazu, *Nichibei domei: Hyoryu kara no dakkyaku* [The Japan-U.S. alliance: From drift to revitalization] (Tokyo: Nihon Keizai Shimbun-sha, 1997), p. 28.

5. Michael H. Armacost, *Friends or Rivals?: The Insider's Account of U.S.-Japan Relations* (New York: Columbia University Press, 1996), p. 102.

6. Ibid., p. 105. For more on Japan's inability to contribute personnel, also see Kuriyama, *Nichibei domei*, pp. 36–37, and Tejima Ryuichi, *1991 nen Nihon no haiboku* [Japan's defeat of 1991] (Tokyo: Shincho Bunko, 1996), pp. 140–61.

7. Haruhiro Fukui describes the Treaties Bureau's role: "Acting as the central reservoir of knowledge and wisdom on all legal aspects of the nation's foreign relations, the Treaties Bureau officials—especially the bureau director and the head of its Treaties Division—assist and advise not only their colleagues and superiors in the ministry itself, but, even more importantly, the foreign minister and the prime minister. During the Diet sessions, the Treaty [*sic*] Bureau officials make themselves continuously available to cabinet leaders. In fact, without the bureau officials' help, cabinet leaders would be unable to answer most of the sharp questions opposition members ask on details of the government's transactions with foreign governments." See Haruhiro Fukui, "Policy Making in the Japanese Foreign Ministry," in *The Foreign Policy of Modern Japan*, ed. Robert Scalapino (Berkeley and Los Angeles: University of California Press, 1977), p. 17.

8. Ishihara, *Shusho Kantei no ketsudan*, pp. 73–74.

9. Kuriyama met with Kaifu and Ozawa and tried to convince Ozawa that the LDP's plan would change the nature of the Peace Cooperation unit. When Kuriyama told

Ozawa, "Please do not forget that the SDF is essentially a military force," Ozawa bluntly replied, "Of course, I understand," but remained opposed. Prime Minister Kaifu did not state his opinion at the meeting. Ishihara, *Shusho Kantei no ketsudan*, pp. 74–75.

10. Tejima, *1991 nen Nihon no haiboku*, p. 187.

11. Ishihara, *Shusho Kantei no ketsudan*, p. 76.

12. Tejima, *1991 nen Nihon no haiboku*, p. 196.

13. Armacost, *Friends or Rivals?* p. 118.

14. "Jieitai kaigai haken nado Kaifu shusho wa kenpo rongi ni dodo to idome" [Prime Minister Kaifu should confront the constitutional debate over dispatching the SDF], *Yomiuri Shimbun*, October 13, 1990.

15. "Shin jidai no kokuren no Yakuwari to Nihon no koken" [The UN's role in the new era and Japan's contribution], *Nihon Keizai Shimbun*, September 22, 1990; and "Kokuren heiwa kyoryokuho seitei wa sessoku wo sakeyo" [Avoid hasty enactment of the UN Peace Cooperation legislation], *Nihon Keizai Shimbun*, October 11, 1990.

16. "Nattoku dekinai Jieitai no sanka" [Unpersuasive argument for SDF's participation], *Asahi Shimbun*, 28 September 1990; and "Kyoryokuho wo tekkaishi denaose" [Withdraw the cooperation legislation and start over], *Mainichi Shimbun*, October 30, 1990.

17. "Jieitai haken sezu 67%" [67 percent against the SDF dispatch], *Asahi Shimbun*, October 1, 1990.

18. "Funso kanyo ni teikokan" [Reluctance to be involved in conflict], *Asahi Shimbun*, November 6, 1990.

19. Hirano Sadao, *Ozawa Ichiro tono nijunen* [Twenty years with Ozawa Ichiro] (Tokyo: President-sha, 1996), pp. 34–39.

20. Five major labor unions delivered a message to the Socialist Party in which they criticized the party for "not performing the role of the responsible, largest opposition party." *Yomiuri Shimbun*, January 29, 1991.

21. "Current Issues Surrounding UN Peace-keeping Operations and Japanese Perspective," January 1997. Available at http://www.mofa.go.jp/policy/un/pko/issues.html (August 24, 2005).

22. "PKO shin soshiki, taishoku jieikan ga shutai" [The new PKO organization, composed of retired SDF officials], *Asahi Shimbun*, March 9, 1991.

23. "Heiwa ijigun sanka mo?" [Possible participation in PKF?], *Asahi Shimbun*, March 12, 1991.

24. "Jinteki koken no akashi hoshisa?" [Wanting proof of personnel contribution?], *Asahi Shimbun*, March 15, 1991.

25. "Kaifu shusho wa Persiawan heno sokaitei haken wo ketsudan seyo" [Prime Minister Kaifu should decide on dispatching minesweepers to the Persian Gulf], *Yomiuri Shimbun*, April 11, 1991.

26. "Shomen kitta Jieitai rongi wo" [Need to discuss the SDF], *Mainichi Shimbun*, April 6, 1991; and "Sokaitei haken no tame no joken" [Conditions for dispatching minesweepers], *Asahi Shimbun*, April 13, 1991.

27. "Sokaitei no Wangan haken ni hitsuyona zentei joken" [Prerequisite for dispatching minesweepers to the Gulf], *Nihon Keizai Shimbun*, April 13, 1991.

28. "Jieitai no kaigai haken 74% yonin" [74% approved SDF dispatch abroad], *Asahi Shimbun*, June 19, 1991.

29. Ishihara testifies: "What changed Prime Minister Kaifu's view was obviously the success of the minesweepers' dispatch." Ishihara, *Kantei 2668 nichi*, p. 65.

30. "Heiwaijigun sanka ni michi" [Possibility of participating with PKF], *Asahi Shimbun*, May 24, 1991.

31. "PKO eno Jieitai katsuyo, tonai gatame e uyoku" [Willing to persuade the party on dispatching the SDF for PKO], *Asahi Shimbun*, May 29, 1991.

32. Ishihara, *Shusho Kantei no ketsudan*, pp. 73–74.

33. Ibid., pp. 77–78.

34. Among the 71 percent, 50 percent supported only nonmilitary activities and the remaining 21 percent supported the SDF's participation in military activities under the UN flag. "Heiwa ijigun eno Jieitai sanka, 58% ga hantai" [58 percent oppose the SDF's participation with PKF], *Asahi Shimbun*, November 10, 1991.

35. Deputy CCS Ishihara explains, "In actuality, it would be impossible to meet UN requests with prior Diet approval, which requires political debates with each request." Ishihara, *Shusho Kantei no ketsudan*, p. 91.

36. Hirano Sadao, *Komeito Sokagakkai to Nihon* [Komeito Sokagakkai and Japan] (Tokyo: Kodan-sha, 2005), pp. 289–90.

37. "PKO wo kumikomi sogo seisaku no tenkai wo" [Develop a comprehensive policy including PKO], *Nihon Keizai Shimbun*, June 16, 1992.

38. Katsuyuki Yakushiji, a journalist with *Asahi Shimbun*, explains the limitation of the Treaties Bureau: "The Treaties Bureau, with its expertise in interpreting and explaining treaties, is basically static and defensive. Therefore, it is not a dynamic section for actively drafting and planning new policies adjusted to the new environments or for promoting the given policy within the government and the political parties. Its officials are simply not good at it." Yakushiji concludes, "MOFA did not have the power to handle such a dramatic change in the international situation [as the Gulf crisis presented]." Yakushiji Katsuyuki, *Gaimusho: Gaikoryoku kyoka eno michi* [MOFA: The road to strengthening diplomatic power] (Tokyo: Iwanami Shinsho, 2003), p. 81.

3   The Rise of the Kantei

1. Ken Moroi, interview by author, Tokyo, October 22, 1998.

2. Although significant additions and revisions were made, this chapter largely relies on my earlier study "Japan's Cabinet Secretariat and Its Emergence As Core Executive," *Asian Survey* 45, no. 5 (September/October 2005), pp. 800–21. © 2005 by the Regents of the University of California, reprinted by permission of the Regents.

3. Patrick Dunleavy and R. A. W. Rhodes, "Core Executive Studies in Britain," *Public Administration* 68, no. 1 (1990), p. 4.

4. Although the role of the Cabinet Secretariat has become very important in Japan's central government, there is only a limited number of academic works covering this subject, especially in the English language. In addition to the work cited in note 2, other academic works are Kataoka Hiromitsu, *Naikaku no kino to hosa kiko* [The function of the cabinet and supporting organizations] (Tokyo: Seibundo, 1982), and Ian Neary, "Serving the Japanese Prime Minister," in *Administering the Summit: Administration of the Core Executive in Developed Countries*, ed. B. Guy Peters, R. A. W. Rhodes, and Vincent Wright (New York: St. Martin's Press, 2000), pp. 196–222. Two books on Japan's prime minister have sections on the Cabinet Secretariat: Kenji Hayao, *The Japanese Prime Minister and Public Policy* (Pittsburgh, Pa.: University of Pittsburgh Press, 1993), and Tomohito Shinoda, *Leading Japan: The Role of the Prime Minister* (Westport, Conn.: Praeger, 2000).

5. Gotoda Masaharu, *Naikaku kanbo chokan* [The chief cabinet secretary] (Tokyo: Kodansha, 1989), p. 3.

6. Ibid., p. 4.

7. Gotoda Masaharu, *Seiji towa nanika?* [What is politics?] (Tokyo: Kodansha, 1988), p. 90.

8. Before the establishment of this law, the position was called *shokikancho*.

9. Article 13 of the Cabinet Law.

10. The position gained cabinet-level status under the Sato administration, and the first CCS with ministerial status was Kiichi Aichi.

11. For example, the order of succession under the second Koizumi cabinet was (1) CCS Yasuo Fukuda, (2) Finance Minister Sadakazu Tanigaki, (3) Agriculture, Forestry, and Fisheries Minister Yoshiyuki Kamei, (4) Internal Affairs and Communications Minister Taro Aso, and (5) Economy, Trade, and Industry Minister Ichiro Nakagawa.

12. *Asahi Shimbun*, April 15, 1998.

13. For more details, see Shinoda, *Leading Japan*, p. 73.

14. According to former deputy CCS Masaharu Gotoda, "[The administrative deputy CCS needs] to conduct operations on the budget, personnel placement, and planning impartially, without any personal interest involved. Therefore, officials of the Finance Ministry, which has the budget bureau, or officials at the ministries of International Trade and Industry, Transportation, and Foreign Affairs are inappropriate." Quoted in Kawaguchi Hiroyuki, *Kanryo shihai no kozo* [The mechanism of bureaucratic control] (Tokyo: Kodansha, 1987), p. 45.

15. Teijiro Furukawa, interview by author, October 30, 2003.

16. The manifesto of the Democratic Party of Japan stipulates: "We will abolish the mechanism, symbolized by meetings of administrative vice-ministers, of advance manipulation of the Cabinet's agenda, and change it to a politically led mechanism of top-down decision-making centered on Cabinet meetings and meetings of senior vice ministers." The English version of the manifesto is available at http://www.dpj.or.jp/english/manifesto_eng/index.html (December 8, 2003).

17. Teijiro Furukawa, interview by author, October 30, 2003.

18. There was only one parliamentary deputy until 1998.

19. A former officer at the Cabinet Secretariat, interview by author, May 19, 2003.

20. Ibid.

21. Prime Minister Eisaku Sato appointed former CCS Toshio Kimura to this position. Also, Prime Minister Yasuhiro Nakasone appointed a former labor minister, Takao Fujinami, and Prime Minister Takeshita chose a former minister of home affairs, Ichiro Ozawa—both powerful members of their given factions—to this post. Prime Minister Kiichi Miyazawa appointed Motoji Kondo to the deputy CCS position directly from his post as minister of agriculture, forestry, and fisheries. More recently, Prime Minister Ryutaro Hashimoto selected a former education minister, Kaoru Yosano, for the same post.

22. See "Central Government Reform of Japan," http://www.kantei.go.jp/foreign/central_government/01_estaglishing.html (December 9, 2003).

23. The four advisers were (1) former foreign minister Yoriko Kawaguchi for foreign affairs, (2) former LDP secretary-general Taku Yamasaki for special missions, (3) former agriculture vice minister Yoshiaki Watanabe for the privatization of postal services, and (4) former construction vice minister Toru Makino for urban renaissance. Kawaguchi and Yamasaki resigned when they were elected to the Diet in fall 2005.

24. An assistant to Prime Minister Hashimoto, Kenji Eda, criticized the interagency rivalry in his book: "The old offices on internal affairs and on external affairs were working separately as if there were a high wall between them. The ministries provided information only to the officials they seconded to the Secretariat. As the director of the two offices were always from MOFA (on external affairs) and from the Ministry of Finance (on internal affairs), the subordinates in the office regarded them as representatives of their ministries instead of as their bosses. It was far from the situation in which both offices could play a role in policy coordination in important matters of internal and external affairs." Eda Kenji and Ryuzaki Takashi, *Shusho Kantei* [The prime minister's official residence] (Tokyo: Bunshun Shinsho, 2002), p. 98.

25. Teijiro Furukawa, interview by author, October 30, 2003.

26. Twenty-one officials are listed in table 3.1. This figure does not include temporary officials on loan from the other ministries.

27. Teijiro Furukawa, interview by author, October 30, 2003.

28. Ibid.

29. Ibid.

30. Counselor at the Cabinet Secretariat, interview by author, June 11, 2004.

31. Ibid.

32. The Web page is listed at http://www.cas.go.jp/jp/gaiyou/sosiki/index.html (March 31, 2006). The number under the Obuchi cabinet was 180, according to a newspaper article. *Nihon Keizai Shimbun*, July 29, 2004.

33. Kenji Eda, interview by author, July 30, 2001.

34. Teijiro Furukawa, interview by author, October 30, 2003.

35. "The Guideline for the Policy Coordination System," cabinet decision, on May 30, 2000.

36. Officer at the Cabinet Secretariat, interview by author, September 18, 2001.

37. For details of the proposal, see http://gyokaku/koumuin/ohwaku (December 4, 2003).

38. Teijiro Furukawa, interview by author, October 30, 2003.

39. Ibid.

40. Prime Minister Yoshiro Mori's address announcing the general resignation of the cabinet, http://www.kantei.go.jp/foreign/souri/mori/2001/0426kisyakaiken_e.html (December 4, 2003).

41. Official at the secretariat of the Headquarters for Administrative Reform, interview by author, October 20, 2003.

42. Teijiro Furukawa, interview by author, October 30, 2003.

43. "Koizumi seiken de nani ga kawattaka" [What changed under the Koizumi administration], *Nihon Keizai Shimbun*, no. 4, August 8, 2003.

4 Koizumi's Response to Terrorism

This case study was introduced in Tomohito Shinoda, "Koizumi's Top-Down Leadership in the Anti-Terrorism Legislation: The Impact of Institutional Changes," *SAIS Review* (Winter/Spring 2003): pp. 19–34.

1. See their home page at http://www.wakate.net/ (Japanese language only, February 25, 2006).

2. "Denwa ippon no Koizumi-ryu" [Koizumi style with a phone call], *Asahi Shimbun*, April 26, 2001.

3. This reason was cited by 72 percent of the respondents. Poll taken by *Asahi Shimbun*, April 27–28, 2001. "Koizumi naikaku, shiji saiko 78%" [The Koizumi cabinet's approval rate, 78%], *Asahi Shimbun*, April 30, 2001.

4. "Beikoku doji tahatsu tero hasseigo no seifu no taio" [The government's reactions after the 9/11 terrorism incident], *Toki no ugoki* (January 2002): pp. 6–8.

5. A former director of the Cabinet Security Affairs Office makes this point. Sassa Atsuyuki, *Shin kiki kanri no nouhau* [New know-how for crisis management] (Tokyo: Bungei Shunju, 1991), pp. 17–72.

6. "Policy Speech by Prime Minister Junichiro Koizumi to the 151 Diet Session," May 7, 2001, http://www.kantei.go.jp/foreign/koizumispeech/2001/0507policyspeech_e .html (March 9, 2005).

7. Teijiro Furukawa, interview by author, October 30, 2003.

8. "U.S. Welcomes Japan's Anti-Terrorism Assistance Package," White House press release, September 20, 2001, http://usinfo.state.gov/topical/pol/terror/01092018.htm (March 12, 2005).

9. "Koho shien 'sansei' ga 70%" [70% support rear-echelon assistance], *Nihon Keizai Shimbun*, September 25, 2001.

10. "Nihon no tero taisaku, yuji sokuou no taisei wo isoge" [Japan's anti-terrorism approach immediately needs an institution to deal with contingencies], *Sankei Shim-*

bun, September 14, 2001; "Tero taisaku tokusoho hoimo, jikko aru jieitai haken taisei wo isoge" [Surrounding anti-terrorism legislation, rush to establish an effective system for dispatching the SDF], *Yomiuri Shimbun*, September 21, 2001; "Takokusekigun koho shienho wo teian suru" [Proposal of law to provide rear-echelon support to the multinational forces], *Nihon Keizai Shimbun*, September 20, 2001; "Jieitai haken, kokusai shakai no soi niyoru kodo wo" [The SDF dispatch must be conducted based on the consensus of the international community], *Mainichi Shimbun*, September 21, 2001; and "Taibei kyoryoku, maenomeri wa yokunai" [We should not bend over backward to support the U.S.], *Asahi Shimbun*, September 14, 2001.

11. A compromise suggested at that time was that normal cases would require prior approval, but retroactive approval would be allowed in an emergency.

12. "Hoan sansei 51%, hantai 29%" [51% support the legislation with 29% opposed], *Asahi Shimbun*, October 16, 2001.

13. For example, see Imai's speech at the Foreign Correspondents' Club of Japan, November 7, 2001, http://www.keidanren.or.jp/japanese/speech/20011107.html (February 25, 2006).

14. "Tero taisaku tokubetsu sochi hoan to no seiritsu ni taisuru jimukyokucho danwa" [Statement by the secretary-general on enactment of the anti-terrorism legislation], *Rengo*, November 6, 2001.

5   Preparing for a National Contingency

1. Mori's statement reads: "Emergency legislation is necessary in order to ensure the security of the state and the people by the Self-Defense Forces under civilian control. Bearing fully in mind the views expressed by the ruling parties last year, I intend to initiate considerations in this regard." Policy speech by Prime Minister Yoshiro Mori to the 151st session of the Diet, January 31, 2001.

2. Official, Maritime Staff Office of the JDA, interview by author, March 4, 2002.

3. Among the twenty-six staffers, seven were full-time and nineteen were part-time. Ibid.

4. MOFA officer, interview by author, August 23, 2002.

5. Teijiro Furukawa, interview by author, October 30, 2003.

6. Policy speech by Prime Minister Junichiro Koizumi to the 154th session of the Diet, February 4, 2002.

7. *Asahi Shimbun*, February 4, 2002.

8. See Tanaka Shigenobu, "Yuji hosei towa nanika?" [What is the emergency legislation?], March 27, 2002, http://www.okazaki-inst.jp/oifront.html (March 17, 2005).

9. *Asahi Shimbun*, April 5, 2002.

10. *Asahi Shimbun*, April 17, 2002.

11. Ibid.

12. *Nihon Keizai Shimbun*, May 28, 2002.

13. *Sunday Mainichi*, June 2, 2002.

14. *Asahi Shimbun*, June 4, 2002.

15. *Kyodo News*, June 13, 2002, http://news.kyodo.co.jp/kyodonews/2002/yuji/news/20020613–175.html (July 9, 2003).

16. *Asahi Shimbun*, September 19, 2002.

17. Among respondents, 73 percent answered "very concerned," and 22 percent said they were "concerned." *Asahi Shimbun*, November 5, 2002.

18. Press conference by Prime Minister Junichiro Koizumi on the issue of Iraq, March 20, 2003, http://www.kantei.go.jp/foreign/koizumispeech/2003/03/20kaiken_e.html (March 9, 2005).

19. *Asahi Shimbun*, March 23, 2003.

20. "Jiritsu shita kojin, jiritsu shita kuni taru tameni" [In order to become an independent individual and make an independent nation], Keizai Doyukai's Kenpo Mondai Chosakai, April 21, 2003, http://www.doyukai.or.jp/policyproposals/articles/2002/pdf/030421.pdf (February 25, 2006).

21. "Yuji kanren hoan no shusei ni kansuru Minshuto to yoto santo tono goi bunsho" [The agreement between the DPJ and the three ruling parties on the emergency legislation], May 13, 2003, http://www.dpj.or.jp/seisaku/gaiko/BOX_GK0115.html (July 10, 2003).

22. *Asahi Shimbun*, May 20, 2003.

23. Ibid.

24. "Yuji hosei shusei kyogi kinkyu intabyu, Minshuto Maehara Seiji shi" [Emergency interview with Seiji Maehara of the DPJ on the conference to revise the emergency legislation], *Asahi Shimbun*, May 15, 2003.

25. "Seiji no shitsu ga towareru, yuji hosei seiritsu" [The quality of politics will be questioned with the passage of the emergency legislation], *Asahi Shimbun*, June 8, 2003.

6   Dispatching the SDF to Reconstruct Iraq

This case study was introduced in Tomohito Shinoda, "Japan's Top-Down Policy Process to Dispatch the SDF to Iraq," *Japanese Journal of Political Science* 7, no. 1 (2006), pp. 71–91.

1. State of the Union address, January 29, 2002.

2. "Bei daitoryo Iraku kogeki wo meigen nigatsu no nichibei shuno kaidan de" [U.S. president clearly mentioned the attack on Iraq at the February U.S.-Japan summit meeting], *Mainichi Shimbun*, June 9, 2002.

3. "Prime Minister Junichiro Koizumi's interview on the issue of Iraq," March 18, 2003, http://www.mofa.go.jp/region/middle_e/iraq/pm_int0303.html (July 8, 2004).

4. Yukio Okamoto, "Toward Reconstruction Aid for Iraq: A Path via the Indian Ocean and the Nile," *Gaiko Forum*, Summer 2003, p. 7.

5. Ibid.

6. *Daily Jimin*, Liberal Democratic Party, May 8, 2003. Available at http://www.jimin.jp/jimin/daily/03_05/08/150508a.shtml (May 19, 2004).

7. "Overview of U.S.-Japan Summit Meeting," Ministry of Foreign Affairs, May 26, 2003, http://www.mofa.go.jp/region/n-america/us/pmv0305/overview/html (May 19, 2004).

8. Tanaka Hitoshi and Tahara Soichiro, *Kokka to gaiko* [The nation and diplomacy] (Tokyo: Kodansha, 2005), p. 121.

9. "Overview of U.S.-Japan Summit Meeting."

10. "Jimin, Komei ni iron mo" [Opposition in the LDP and Komeito], *Kyodo News Service*, June 10, 2003, http://news.kyodo.co.jp/kyodonews/2003/iraq2/news/0611-1140.html (May 19, 2004).

11. "Iraq shinpo giron honkakuka" [Substantial discussion begins on the new Iraq legislation], *Nihon Keizai Shimbun*, June 11, 2003.

12. "Kokyuho motome jokentsuki ryosho" [Approval with conditions to demand a permanent law], *Kyodo News Service*, June 12, 2003, http://news.kyodo.co.jp/kyodonews/2003/iraq2/news/0612-1149.html (May 19, 2004).

13. "Iraku tokuso hoan de han Koizumi wa issei ni hanpatsu" [Strong opposition to the anti-Koizumi camp on the Iraq special measures legislation], *Mainichi Shimbun*, June 13, 2003.

14. "Teiko seiryoku, oshikiri shusei" [The opposition camp wins a revision], *Asahi Shimbun*, June 14, 2003.

15. "Iraku shimpo sanpi kikko" [Sharply divided on the new Iraq legislation], *Nihon Keizai Shimbun*, June 23, 2003.

16. DPJ's Project Team on Iraq, "Iraku fukko shien no arikata ni taisuru kangaekata" [How to deal with reconstruction assistance to Iraq], June 19, 2004, http://www.dpj.or.jp/seisaku/gaiko/BOX_GK01212.html; and "Minshuto no Iraku chosadan hokoku no gairyaku" [Summary of the report by the DPJ research group on Iraq], June 11, 2004, http://www.dpj.or.jp/seisaku/gaiko/BOX_GK0120.html (May 21, 2004).

17. Diet Record, House of Councillors' joint conference of Foreign Affairs and Defense Committee and Cabinet Committee, July 9, 2003.

18. Diet Record, The National Basic Policy Committee, July 23, 2003, http://www.shugiin.go.jp/index.nsf/html/index_kaigiroku.htm (May 21, 2004).

19. "Iraku shimpo jizen no saku to shite seitei isoge" [Rush to enact the new Iraq legislation as the second best option], *Sankei Shimbun*, June 7, 2003; "Iraku sengo fukko shien, ima nani wo subekika" [What we need to do to contribute to the reconstruction of Iraq], *Yomiuri Shimbun*, April 13, 2003; "Iraku hoan no kon kokkai seiritu e giron tsukuse" [Discussion on the enactment of the Iraq legislation during this session], *Nihon Keizai Shimbun*, July 4, 2003; and "Nihon no yakuwari, jindo, fukko e kokusai kyocho toke" [Argue for international cooperation on Japan's role, humanitarian needs and reconstruction], *Mainichi Shimbun*, April 12, 2003.

20. Keizai Doyukai (Japan Association of Corporate Executives) later called for a permanent law that would allow the government to send the SDF overseas for humanitarian reconstruction. "Iraq mondai kenkyukai ikensho" [Opinions by the research group on Iraq], Iraq Mondai Kenkyukai, *Keizai Doyukai*, November 24, 2004, http://www.doyukai.or.jp/policyproposals/articles/2004/041124a.html (March 9, 2006). Rengo

(Japan Trade Union Confederation) issued an official statement against the war on March 18 and 24 but offered no official statement specifically opposing the bill, http://www.jtuc-rengo.or.jp/news/kenkai/index2003.html (March 9, 2006).

21. "Japan-U.S. Summit Meeting," Ministry of Foreign Affairs, October 17, 2003, http://www.mofa.go.jp/region/n-america/us/summit0310.html (May 24, 2004).

22. "Japan's Iraq commitment under pressure after diplomat deaths," *ABC Online*, December 1, 2003, http://www.abc.net.au/am/content/2003/s1000519.htm (September 2, 2004).

23. "Jieitai haken de shusho kankorei" [The prime minister orders secrecy on the SDF dispatch], *Nihon Keizai Shimbun*, December 4, 2003.

24. "Iraku fukko shien ni kansuru chosa hokoku ikeru" [LDP receives report on reconstruction assistance in Iraq], *Daily Jimin*, December 4, 2003.

25. "Setsumei busoku, miuchi mo fuman" [Even supporters complain about lack of explanation], *Asahi Shimbun*, December 5, 2003.

26. MOFA official, interview by author, May 12, 2004.

27. "Jimin haken zentei ni chumon zokushutsu, rikuji tonyu de Komei to masatsu mo" [LDP demands much in return for supporting dispatch, possible friction with Komei on Ground SDF dispatch], *Kyodo News*, December 8, 2003.

28. Press conference by Prime Minister Junichiro Koizumi, December 9, 2003, http://www.kantei.go.jp/foreign/koizumispeech/2003/12/09press_e.html (September 1, 2004).

29. "Naikaku shijiritsu kyuraku" [Sharp drop in cabinet approval rating], *Asahi Shimbun*, December 12, 2003.

30. "Cancel Plan for SDF Dispatch," *Japan Press Weekly*, December 9, 2003, http://www.japan-press.co.jp/2363/cancel.html (September 1, 2004).

31. "Iraku eno Jieitai haken kihon keikaku no kakugi kettei ni tsuite" [On the cabinet decision on the activity guideline for dispatching the SDF to Iraq], December 9, 2003, http://www5.sdp.or.jp/central/timebeing03/danwa1209.html (September 1, 2004).

32. "Statement on the Cabinet Decision to Approve a 'Basic Plan' Based on the Iraq Special Measures Law," December 9, 2003, http://www.dpj.or.jp/english/news/031215/02.html (September 1, 2004).

33. "Haken ni rikai, yoto ando" [General understanding on the dispatch relieves ruling parties], *Asahi Shimbun*, January 20, 2004.

34. General policy speech by Prime Minister Junichiro Koizumi to the 159th session of the Diet, January 19, 2004, http://www.kantei.go.jp/foreign/koizumispeech/2004/01/19sisei_e.html (September 1, 2004).

35. Diet Record, House of Representatives floor meeting, January 21, 2004.

7 Evaluating Kantei Diplomacy

1. Henry Kissinger, *White House Years* (Boston: Little, Brown and Company, 1979), p. 47.

2. I. M. Destler, Leslie H. Gelb, and Anthony Lake, *Our Own Worst Enemy: The Unmaking of American Foreign Policy* (New York: Simon and Schuster, 1984).

3. "Kokuzei yori mizukara no koseki" [Higher priority on self-interest before national interests], *Hokkaido Shimbun,* August 24, 2002.

4. MOFA official, interview by author, May 12, 2004.

5. See Tomohito Shinoda, *Leading Japan: The Role of the Prime Minister* (Westport, Conn.: Praeger, 2000), pp. 106–7.

6. Katsuya Okada, "Koizumi sori no saihocho wo ukete" [On Prime Minister Koizumi's second visit to North Korea], May 22, 2004, http://www.dpj.or.jp/seisaku/kan0312/gaimu/BOX_GAI0006.html (April 12, 2005).

7. "Koizumi hocho hyoka 67%" [67% support Koizumi's visit to North Korea], *Asahi Shimbun,* May 24, 2004.

8. Murata Ryohei, *Naze Gaimusho wa dame ni nattaka?* [Why did MOFA go wrong?] (Tokyo: Fuso-sha, 2002), p. 25.

9. Okazaki Hisahiko, "Imakoso, China School mondai wo, daitan na Gaimusho kaikaku ni mukete no ichi shian" [Now we need to deal with the China School problem: An idea for a bold reform plan for MOFA], *Sankei Shimbun,* July 1, 2002.

10. James Fallows, "Japan Handlers," *Atlantic Monthly*, August 1989.

11. Sassa Atsuyuki, *Shin kiki kanri no nouhau* [New know-how for crisis management] (Tokyo: Bungei Shunju, 1991), pp. 177–78.

12. MOFA official, Kantei, interview by author, June 11, 2004.

13. Sir Harold Nicolson, *Diplomacy* (Washington, D.C.: Institute for the Study of Diplomacy, School of Foreign Service, Georgetown University, 1988), p. 42.

14. Ibid., pp. 47–48.

15. George Kennan, *American Diplomacy 1900–1950* (New York: Mentor Books, 1952), p. 92. The original edition was published by Oxford University Press in 1963.

16. Ibid.

17. Nicolson, *Diplomacy*, p. 49.

18. "Kaeyo! Kawaro! Gaimusho, teigen to hokoku: Uchi karano kaikaku start" [Let's change MOFA! A proposal and report to start reform from the inside], July 12, 2002, http://www.mofa.go.jp/mofaj/annai/honsho/kai_genjo/kk/kk.html (April 14, 2004).

19. "Naikaku fushiji ga gyakuten 42%" [Cabinet disapproval rating surpasses 42%], *Asahi Shimbun,* June 22, 2004.

BIBLIOGRAPHY

English-Language Sources

Aberbach, Joel D., Robert D. Putnam, and Bert A. Rockman. *Bureaucrats and Politicians in Western Democracies.* Cambridge: Harvard University Press, 1981.

Allison, Graham T. *Essence of Decision: Explaining the Cuban Missile Crisis.* Boston: Little, Brown, and Company, 1971.

Angel, Robert C. *Explaining Economic Policy Failure: Japan in the 1969–1971 International Monetary Crisis.* New York: Columbia University Press, 1991.

———. "Prime Ministerial Leadership in Japan: Recent Changes in Personal Style and Administrative Organization." *Pacific Affairs* 61 (Winter 1988/89): pp. 583–602.

Armacost, Michael H. *Friends or Rivals?: The Insider's Account of U.S.-Japan Relations.* New York: Columbia University Press, 1996.

Art, Robert J. "Bureaucratic Politics and American Foreign Policy: A Critique." *Policy Science* 4, no. 4 (December 1973): pp. 467–90.

Barnett, Robert W. *Beyond War: Japan's Concept of Comprehensive National Security: Defense, Diplomacy, Dependence*. Washington, D.C.: Pergamon-Brassey's, 1984.

Belloni, Frank P., and Dennis C. Beller, eds. *Faction Politics: Political Parties and Factionalism in Comparative Perspective*. Santa Barbara, Calif.: ABC-Clio, 1978.

Berger, Thomas. "From Sword to Chrysanthemum: Japan's Culture of Anti-Militarism." *International Security*, Spring 1993.

Blackwill, Robert D., and Paul Dibb. *America's Asian Alliance*. Cambridge, Mass.: The MIT Press, 2000.

Blaker, Michael. *Japanese International Negotiating Style*. New York: Columbia University Press, 1977.

Bryce, James. *Modern Democracy*. New York: The Macmillan Company, 1921.

Buckley, Roger. *US-Japan Alliance Diplomacy, 1945–1990*. Cambridge: Cambridge University Press, 1992.

Budge, Ian, and Hans Keman. *Parties and Democracy: Coalition Formation and Government Functioning in Twenty States*. Oxford: Oxford University Press, 1990.

Burns, James MacGregor. *Leadership*. New York: Harper and Row, 1978.

Calder, Kent E. *Crisis and Compensation: Public Policy and Political Stability in Japan, 1944–86*. Princeton, N.J.: Princeton University Press, 1988.

———. "Japan in 1990: Limits to Change." *Asian Survey* 31, no. 1 (January 1991): pp. 21–35.

———. "Kanryo vs. Shomin: Contrasting Dynamics of Conservative Leadership in Postwar Japan." In *Michigan Papers in Japanese Studies No. 1: Political Leadership in Contemporary Japan*, ed. Terry Edward MacDougall, pp. 1–28. Ann Arbor: Center for Japanese Studies, University of Michigan, 1982.

Campbell, John Creighton. *Contemporary Japanese Budget Politics*. Berkeley: University of California Press, 1977.

Carlile, Lonny E., and Mark C. Tilton, eds. *Is Japan Really Changing Its Ways?: Regulatory Reform and the Japanese Economy*. Washington, D.C.: Brookings Institution, 1998.

Cheng, Peter P. "Japanese Interest Group Politics: An Institutional Framework." *Asian Survey* 30, no. 3 (March 1990): pp. 251–65.

Crabb, Cecil V., Jr., and Pat M. Holt. *Invitation to Struggle: Congress, the President, and Foreign Policy*. 3rd edition. Washington, D.C.: Congressional Quarterly, 1989.

Crossman, R. H. S. "Prime Ministerial Government." In *The British Prime Minister*, ed. Anthony King, pp. 175–94. Durham, N.C.: Duke University Press, 1985.

Curtis, Gerald. "Big Business and Political Influence." In *Modern Japanese Organization and Decision-Making*, ed. Ezra Vogel, pp. 33–70. Berkeley and Los Angeles: University of California Press, 1975.

———. *The Japanese Way of Politics*. New York: Columbia University Press, 1988.

———. *The Logic of Japanese Politics*. New York: Columbia University Press, 1999.

————, ed. *Japan's Foreign Policy After the Cold War: Coping with Change*. Armonk, N.Y.: M. E. Sharpe, 1993.

Destler, I. M. *American Trade Politics*. 3rd edition. Washington, D.C.: Institute for International Economics, 1992.

————. *Presidents, Bureaucrats, and Foreign Policy: The Politics of Organizational Reform*. Princeton, N.J.: Princeton University Press, 1972.

Destler, I. M., Leslie H. Gelb, and Anthony Lake. *Our Own Worst Enemy: The Unmaking of American Foreign Policy*. New York: Simon and Schuster, 1984.

Destler, I. M., Hideo Sato, Priscilla Clapp, and Haruhiko Fukui. *Managing Alliance: The Politics of U.S.-Japanese Relations*. Washington, D.C.: Brookings Institution, 1976.

Drifte, Reinhard. *Japan's Foreign Policy*. London: Routledge, 1990.

————. *Japan's Quest for a Permanent Security Council Seat*. New York: St. Martin's Press, 2000.

Dunleavy, Patrick, and R. A. W. Rhodes. "Core Executive Studies in Britain." *Public Administration* 68, no. 1 (1990).

Frost, Ellen L. *For Richer, for Poorer: The New U.S.-Japan Relationship*. New York: Council on Foreign Relations, 1987.

Fukui, Haruhiro. "Japan: Factionalism in a Dominant Party System." In *Faction Politics: Political Parties and Factionalism in Comparative Perspective*, ed. Frank P. Belloni and Dennis C. Beller, pp. 43–72. Santa Barbara, Calif.: ABC-Clio, 1978.

————. "The Liberal Democratic Party Revisited: Continuity and Change in the Party's Structure and Performance." *Journal of Japanese Studies* 10, no. 2 (Summer 1984): pp. 385–435.

————. *Party in Power*. Berkeley: University of California Press, 1970.

————. "Policy Making in the Japanese Foreign Ministry." In *The Foreign Policy of Modern Japan*, ed. Robert Scalapino, pp. 3–35. Berkeley and Los Angeles: University of California Press, 1977.

————. "Studies in Policymaking: Review of the Literature." In *Policymaking in Contemporary Japan*, ed. T. J. Pempel, pp. 22–59. Ithaca, N.Y.: Cornell University Press, 1977.

————. "Tanaka Goes to Peking." In *Policymaking in Contemporary Japan*, ed. T. J. Pempel, pp. 60–102. Ithaca, N.Y.: Cornell University Press, 1977.

————. "Too Many Captains in Japan's Internationalization: Travails at the Foreign Ministry." *Journal of Japanese Studies* 13, no. 2 (Summer 1987): pp. 359–81.

Fukushima, Akiko. *Japanese Foreign Policy*. New York: St. Martin's Press, 1999.

Funabashi, Yoichi. *Alliance Adrift*. New York: Council on Foreign Relations, 1999.

————, ed. *Japan's International Agenda*. New York: New York University Press, 1994.

Government Section, Supreme Commander for the Allied Powers. *Political Reorientation of Japan*. Washington, D.C.: U.S. Government Printing Office, 1949.

Green, Michael J. *Japan's Reluctant Realism: Foreign Policy Challenges in an Era of Uncertain Power*. New York: Council on Foreign Relations, 2001.

Green, Michael J., and Patrick M. Cronin, eds. *The U.S.-Japan Alliance: Past, Present, and Future.* New York: Council on Foreign Relations, 1999.

Haley, John O. "Consensual Governance." In *The Political Economy of Japan.* Volume 3, *Cultural and Social Dynamics,* ed. Shumpei Kumon and Henry Rosovsky, pp. 32–62. Stanford, Calif.: Stanford University Press, 1992.

———. "Governance by Negotiation: A Reappraisal of Bureaucratic Power in Japan." *Journal of Japanese Studies* 13, no. 2 (Summer 1987): pp. 343–57.

Halperin, Morton H. *Bureaucratic Politics and Foreign Policy.* Washington, D.C.: Brookings Institution, 1974.

Hayao, Kenji. *The Japanese Prime Minister and Public Policy.* Ph.D. dissertation, University of Michigan, 1990.

———. *The Japanese Prime Minister and Public Policy.* Pittsburgh, Pa.: University of Pittsburgh Press, 1993.

Hayes, Louis D. *Introduction to Japanese Politics.* New York: Paragon House, 1992.

Higa, Mikio. *The Role of Bureaucracy in Contemporary Japanese Politics.* Ph.D. dissertation, University of California, Berkeley, 1968.

Hilsman, Roger. *The Politics of Policy Making in Defense and Foreign Affairs: Conceptual Models and Bureaucratic Politics.* Englewood Cliffs, N.J.: Prentice-Hall, 1987.

———. *To Move a Nation.* New York: Doubleday and Company, 1967.

Hine, David, and Renato Finocchi. "The Italian Prime Minister." *West European Politics* 14 (April 1991): pp. 79–96.

Hosoya, Chihiro, and Tomohito Shinoda, eds. *Redefining the Partnership: The United States and Japan in East Asia.* Lanham, Md.: University Press of America, 1998.

Hughes, Christopher W. *Japan's Re-emergence as a "Normal" Military Power.* Oxford: Oxford University Press, 2004.

Igarashi, Takeshi. "Japan's Response to the Gulf Crisis: An Analytic Overview." *Journal of Japanese Studies* 17, no. 2 (Summer 1991): pp. 257–73.

———. "Peace-Making and Party Politics: The Formation of Domestic Foreign-Policy System in Postwar Japan." *Journal of Japanese Studies* 11, no. 2 (Summer 1985): pp. 323–56.

Ikenberry, G. John, and Takashi Inobuchi. *Reinventing the Alliance: U.S.-Japan Security Partnership in an Era of Change.* New York: Palgrave Macmillan, 2003.

Inoguchi, Takashi, and Purnendra Jain, eds. *Japanese Foreign Policy Today.* New York: Palgrave, 2000.

Inoguchi, Takashi, and Daniel Okimoto, eds. *The Political Economy of Japan.* Volume 2, *The Changing Inteternational Context.* Stanford, Calif.: Stanford University Press, 1988.

Irye, Akira, and Warren I. Cohen, eds. *The United States and Japan in the Postwar World.* Lexington: University of Kentucky Press, 1989.

Irye, Akira, and Robert A. Wampler, eds. *Partnership: The United States and Japan 1951–2001.* Tokyo: Kodansha International, 2001.

Jain, Purnendra, and Takashi Inoguchi. *Japanese Politics Today: Beyond Karaoke Democracy.* New York: St. Martin's Press, 1997.

Johnson, Chalmers. "Japan: Who Governs? An Essay on Official Bureaucracy." *Journal of Japanese Studies* 2, no. 1 (Autumn 1975): pp. 1–28.

———. *MITI and the Japanese Miracle.* Stanford, Calif.: Stanford University Press, 1982.

Jones, George W. "The Prime Minister's Power." In *The British Prime Minister*, ed. Anthony King, pp. 195–220. Durham, N.C.: Duke University Press, 1985.

———. "West European Prime Ministers in Perspective." *West European Politics* 14 (April 1991): pp. 163–78.

Kabashima, Ikuo, and Jeffrey Broadbent. "Preference Pluralism: Mass Media and Politics in Japan." *Journal of Japanese Studies* 12, no. 2 (Summer 1986): pp. 329–61.

Kawashima, Yutaka. *Japanese Foreign Policy at the Crossroads: Challenges and Options for the Twenty-first Century.* Washington, D.C.: Brookings, 2003.

Kaplan, Eugene J. *Japan: The Government-Business Relationship.* Washington, D.C.: Department of Commerce, 1972.

Kato, Junko. *The Problem of Bureaucratic Rationality: Tax Politics in Japan.* Princeton, N.J.: Princeton University Press, 1994.

Kawasaki, Tsuyoshi. *The Politics of Contemporary Japanese Budget Making: Its Structure and Historical Origins.* Working Paper Series no. 58. Toronto: Joint Centre for Asia Pacific Studies, 1993.

Kernell, Samuel, ed. *Parallel Politics: Economic Policymaking in Japan and the United States.* Washington, D.C.: Brookings Institution, 1991.

King, Anthony. "The British Prime Ministership in the Age of the Career Politician." *West European Politics* 14 (April 1991): pp. 25–47.

———, ed. *The British Prime Minister.* 2nd edition. Durham, N.C.: Duke University Press, 1985.

Kissinger, Henry. *White House Years.* Boston: Little, Brown and Company, 1979.

———. *Years of Upheaval.* Boston: Little, Brown and Company, 1982.

Kohno, Masaru. *Japan's Postwar Party Politics.* Princeton, N.J.: Princeton University Press, 1997.

Krasner, Stephen D. "Are Bureaucracies Important? (or Allison Wonderland)." *Foreign Policy*, no. 7 (Summer 1972).

Kumon, Shumpei. "Japan Faces Its Future: The Political-Economics and Administrative Reform." *Journal of Japanese Studies* 10, no. 1 (Winter 1984): pp. 143–65.

Kumon, Shumpei, and Henry Rosovsky, eds. *The Political Economy of Japan.* Volume 3, *Cultural and Social Dynamics.* Stanford, Calif.: Stanford University Press, 1992.

Lincoln, Edward. *Japan's Unequal Trade.* Washington, D.C.: Brookings Institution, 1990.

MacDougall, Terry Edward, ed. *Political Leadership in Contemporary Japan.* Michigan Papers in Japanese Studies, no. 1. Ann Arbor: Center for Japanese Studies, 1982.

Maki, John, ed. and trans. *Japan's Commission on the Constitution: The Final Report.* Seattle: University of Washington Press, 1980.

Mann, Thomas E., ed. *A Question of Balance: The President, the Congress and Foreign Policy.* Washington, D.C.: Brookings Institution, 1990.

McFarland, Andrew S. *Power and Leadership in Pluralist Systems.* Stanford, Calif.: Stanford University Press, 1969.

McNelly, Theodore. *Politics and Government in Japan.* 2nd edition. Boston: Houghton Mifflin, 1972.

———. *Politics and Government in Japan.* 3rd edition. Lanham, Md.: University Press of America, 1972.

Mény, Yves. *Government and Politics in Western Europe: Britain, France, Italy, Germany.* 2nd edition. Oxford: Oxford University Press, 1993.

Milford, Paul. "Japan's Response to Terror: Dispatching the SDF to the Arabia Sea." *Asian Survey*, March/April 2003.

Miyawaki, Raisuke. "Difference in the Governing Style between Nakasone and Takeshita." Paper presented at the Johns Hopkins University's School of Advanced International Studies, December 3, 1992.

———. "'Naikaku-Kohokan': Public Relations Advisor to the Prime Minister." Paper presented at the Johns Hopkins University's School of Advanced International Studies, December 3, 1992.

Mochizuki, Mike M. *Toward a True Alliance: Restructuring U.S.-Japan Security Relations.* Washington, D.C.: Brookings, 1997.

Mochizuki, Mike Masato. "Managing and Influencing the Japanese Legislative Process: The Role of Parties and the National Diet." Ph.D. dissertation, Harvard University, 1981.

Mulgan, Aurelia George. "Japan's 'Un-Westminster' System: Impediments to Reform in a Crisis Economy." *Government and Opposition* 38, no. 1 (Winter 2003).

Murakami, Yasusuke. "The Age of New Middle Mass Politics: The Case of Japan." *Journal of Japanese Studies* 8, no. 1 (Winter 1982): pp. 29–72.

Muramatsu, Michio. "In Search of National Identity: The Politics and Policies of the Nakasone Administration." *Journal of Japanese Studies* 13, no. 2 (Summer 1987): pp. 271–306.

Muramatsu, Michio, and Ellis Krauss. "The Conservative Policy Line and the Development of Patterned Pluralism." In *The Political Economy of Japan.* Volume 1, *The Domestic Transformation*, eds. Kozo Yamamura and Yasukichi Yasuba, pp. 516–54. Stanford, Calif.: Stanford University Press, 1987.

Muramatsu, Michio, and Masaru Mabuchi. "Introducing a New Tax in Japan." In *Parallel Politics: Economic Policymaking in Japan and the United States*, ed. Samuel Kernell, pp. 184–207. Washington, D.C.: Brookings Institution, 1991.

Neary, Ian. "Serving the Japanese Prime Minister." In *Administering the Summit: Administration of the Core Executive in Developed Countries*, ed. B. Guy Peters,

R. A. W. Rhodes, and Vincent Wright, pp. 196–222. New York: St. Martin's Press, 2000.

Neustadt, Richard E. *Presidential Power and the Modern Presidents: The Politics of Leadership from Roosevelt to Reagan.* Revised edition. New York: The Free Press, 1990.

Neward, Kathleen, ed. *The International Relations of Japan.* London: Macmillan, 1990.

Okamoto, Yukio. "Toward Reconstruction Aid for Iraq: A Path via the Indian Ocean and the Nile." *Gaiko Forum,* Summer 2003.

Okazaki, Hisahiko. *A Grand Strategy for Japanese Defense.* Lanham, Md.: University Press of America, 1986.

Orr, Robert M., Jr. *The Emergence of Japan's Foreign Aid Power.* New York: Columbia University Press, 1990.

Ozawa, Ichiro. *Blueprint for a New Japan: The Rethinking of a Nation.* Tokyo: Kodansha International, 1994.

Packard, George R. *Protest in Tokyo: The Security Treaty Crisis of 1960.* Princeton, N.J.: Princeton University Press, 1966.

Page, Glenn D., ed. *Political Leadership: Readings for an Emerging Field.* New York: Free Press, 1972.

Park, Yung H. *Bureaucrats and Ministers in Contemporary Japanese Government.* Berkeley: Institute of East Asian Studies, University of California, 1986.

Patrick, Hugh, and Henry Rovosvky. *Asia's New Giant.* Washington, D.C.: Brookings Institution, 1976.

Pekkanen, Robert, and Ellis Krause. "Japan's 'Coalition of the Willing' on Security Politics." *Orbis,* Summer 2005.

Pempel, T. J. "The Bureaucratization of Policy Making in Postwar Japan." *American Journal of Political Science* 18 (November 1987): 271–306.

———. "Organizing for Efficiency: The Higher Civil Service in Japan." In *Bureaucrats and Policy Making: A Comparative Overview,* ed. Ezra N. Suleiman, pp. 72–106. New York: Holms and Meier, 1984.

———. "The Unbundling of 'Japan, Inc.': The Changing Dynamics of Japanese Policy Formation." *Journal of Japanese Studies* 13:2 (Summer 1987): 271–306.

———, ed. *Policymaking in Contemporary Japan.* Ithaca, N.Y.: Cornell University Press, 1977.

Pempel, T. J., and Keiichi Tsunekawa. "Corporatism Without Labor?: The Japanese Anomaly." In *Trends Toward Corporatist Intermediation,* ed. Philippe C. Schmitter and Gerhard Lehmbruch, pp. 231–69. London: Sage Publications, 1979.

Pharr, Susan J., and Ellis S. Krauss. *Media and Politics in Japan.* Honolulu: University of Hawai'i Press, 1996.

Pyle, Kenneth B. "In Pursuit of a Grand Design: Nakasone Between the Past and the Future." *Journal of Japanese Studies* 13, no. 2 (Summer 1987): pp. 243–70.

Reischauer, Edwin O. *My Life Between Japan and America*. New York: Harper and Row, 1986.

Richardson, Bradley M., and Scott C. Flanagan. *Politics in Japan*. Boston: Little, Brown and Company, 1984.

Rose, Richard. "British Government: The Job at the Top." In *Presidents and Prime Ministers*, ed. Richard Rose and Ezra N. Suleiman, pp. 1–49. Washington, D.C.: American Enterprise Institute, 1980.

Rosenbluth, Frances McCall. *Financial Politics in Contemporary Japan*. Ithaca, N.Y.: Cornell University Press, 1989.

Saito, Shiro. *Japan at the Summit: Japan's Role in the Western Alliance and Asian Pacific Cooperation*. London: Routledge, 1990.

Samuels, Richard J. *Machiavelli's Children: Leaders and Their Legacies in Italy and Japan*. Ithaca, N.Y.: Cornell University Press, 2003.

Sartori, Giovanni. *Parities and Party Systems: A Framework for Analysis*. Cambridge: Cambridge University Press, 1976.

Scalapino, Robert A. *Democracy and the Party Movement in Prewar Japan*. Berkeley: University of California Press, 1953.

————, ed. *The Foreign Policy of Modern Japan*. Berkeley and Los Angeles: University of California Press, 1977.

Scalapino, Robert A., and Masumi Junnosuke. *Parties and Politics in Contemporary Japan*. Berkeley: University of California Press, 1962.

Schlesinger, Arthur M., Jr. *The Imperial Presidency*. Boston: Houghton Mifflin, 1973.

Schlesinger, Jacob M. *Shadow Shoguns: The Rise and Fall of Japan's Postwar Political Machine*. New York: Simon & Schuster, 1997.

Schoff, James L., ed. *Crisis Management in Japan and the United States: Creating Opportunities for Cooperation amid Dramatic Change*. Dulles, Va.: Brassey's, 2004.

Schoppa, Leonard J. *Bargaining with Japan: What American Pressure Can and Cannot Do*. New York: Columbia University Press, 1997.

————. "Zoku Power and LDP Power: Case Study of the Zoku Role in Education Policy." *Journal of Japanese Studies* 17, no. 1 (Winter 1991): pp. 79–106.

Schwartz, Frank J. *Advice & Consent: The Politics of Consultation in Japan*. New York: Cambridge University Press, 1998.

Shibusawa, Masahide. *Japan and the Asia Pacific Region*. London: Croom Helm, 1984.

Shinoda, Tomohito. "Japan." In *Party Politics and Democratic Development in East and Southeast Asia*. Volume 2, ed. Wolfgang Sachsenroder, pp. 88–131. Brookfield, Vt.: Ashgate Publishing, 1998.

————. "Japan's Cabinet Secretariat and Its Emergence As Core Executive." *Asian Survey* 45, no. 5 (September/October 2005): pp. 800–821.

————. "Japan's Decision Making Under the Coalition Governments." *Asian Survey*, July 1998, pp. 703–23.

————. "Japan's Political Changes and Their Impact on U.S.-Japan Relations." In *Redefining the Partnership: The United States and Japan in East Asia*, ed. Chihiro

Hosoya and Tomohito Shinoda, pp. 43–58. Lanham, Md.: University Press of America, 1998.

———. "Japan's Political Leadership: The Prime Minister's Power, Style and Conduct of Reform." In *Asian Economic and Political Issues*. Volume 2, ed. Frank Columbus, pp. 1–31. New York: Nova Publisher, 1999.

———. "Koizumi's Top-Down Leadership in the Anti-Terrorism Legislation: The Impact of Institutional Changes." *SAIS Review*, Winter/Spring 2003, pp. 19–34.

———. *Leading Japan: The Role of the Prime Minister*. Westport, Conn.: Praeger, 2000.

———. "LDP Factions: Their Power and Culture." *Bulletin*, The Japan-American Society of Washington, vol. 25, no. 2 (February 1990): pp. 4–7.

———. "Ozawa Ichiro as an Actor in Foreign Policy Making." *Japan Forum* 16, no. 1 (2004): pp. 37–62.

———. "Truth Behind LDP's Loss." *Washington Japan Journal* 2 (Fall 1993): pp. 26–28.

Shinoda, Tomohito, with Ian Holliday. "Governing from the Centre: Core Executive Capacity in Britain and Japan." *Japanese Journal of Political Science* 3, part 1 (May 2002): pp. 91–111.

Sundquist, James L. *The Decline and Resurgence of Congress*. Washington, D.C.: Brookings Institution, 1981.

Taniguchi, Tomohiko. "A Cold Peace: The Changing Security Equation in Northeast Asia." *Orbis*, Summer 2005.

Thayer, Nathaniel B. *How the Conservatives Rule Japan*. Princeton, N.J.: Princeton University Press, 1969.

Tsurutani, Taketsugu, and Jack B. Gabbert. *Chief Executives: National Political Leadership in the United States, Mexico, Great Britain, Germany, and Japan*. Pullman: Washington State University Press, 1992.

Tucker, Robert C. *Political Leadership*. Columbia: University of Missouri Press, 1981.

van Wolferen, Karel G. *The Enigma of Japanese Power*. New York: Alfred A Knopf, 1989.

———. "The Japan Problem." *Foreign Affairs* 65 (Winter 1987): pp. 288–303.

Welfield, John. *An Empire in Eclipse: Japan in the Postwar American Alliance System*. London: Athlone Press, 1988.

Willner, Ann Ruth. *The Spellbinder: Charismatic Political Leadership*. New Haven, Conn.: Yale University Press, 1984.

Woodward, Bob. *Plan of Attack*. New York: Simon & Schuster, 2004.

Japanese-Language Sources

A-50 Nichibei Sengoshi Henshuiinkai. *Nihon to Amerika* [Japan and America]. Tokyo: Japan Times, 2001.

Abe Hitoshi, Shindo Muneyuki, and Kawahito Tadashi. *Gaisetsu gendai Nihon no seiji* [Introduction to contemporary Japanese politics]. Tokyo: Tokyo Daigaku Shuppan-kai, 1990.

Akaneya Tatsuo and Ochiai Kotaro. *Nihon no anzen hosho* [Japan's national security]. Tokyo: Yuhikaku, 2004.

Akiyama Masahiro. *Nichibei senryaku taiwa ga hajimatta* [Japan-U.S. strategic talks have begun]. Tokyo: Akishobo, 2002.

Arai Shunzo and Morita Hajime. *Bunjin Saisho Ohira Masayoshi* [The intellectual Prime Minister Ohira Masayoshi]. Tokyo: Shunju-sha, 1982.

Aruga Tadashi et al., eds. *Koza kokusai, seiji 4: Nihon no gaiko* [Lectures on international politics, volume 4: Japan's diplomacy]. Tokyo: Tokyo Daigaku Shuppan-kai, 1989.

Asahi Shimbun.

Asahi Shimbun Seiji-bu. *Takeshita-ha shihai* [Control by the Takeshita faction]. Tokyo: Asahi Shimbun-sha, 1992.

Asahi Shimbun Wangan Kiki Shuzaihan. *Wangan senso to Nihon* [The Gulf War and Japan]. Tokyo: Asahi Shimbun-sha, 1991.

Asahi Shimbun-sha Seronchosa-shitu. *Naikaku shijiritsu seito shijiritsu* [Approval ratings for cabinets and political parties]. Tokyo: Asahi Shimbun-sha, April 1996.

Auer, James. "FSX kosho wa koshite kecchakushita" [How the FSX negotiation was settled]. *Chuo Koron*, June 1990.

Doi Takako. "Watashi no rirekisho" [My personal history]. *Nihon Keizai Shimbun*, September 1992.

Ebata Kensuke. *Nihon boei no arikata* [How Japan's defense should be]. Tokyo: K.K. Bestsellers, 2004.

Eda Kenji and Ryuzaki Takashi. *Shusho Kantei* [The prime minister's official residence]. Tokyo: Bunshun Shinsho, 2002.

Fujimoto Kazumi, ed. *Kokkai kino ron: Kokkai no shikumi to un'ei* [Arguments for the functional Diet: The mechanism and operation of the Diet]. Tokyo: Hogaku Shoin, 1990.

Fujimoto Takao. *Fujimoto Takao no daijin hokoku* [Report of Minister Fujimoto Takao]. Tokyo: Planet Shuppan, 1989.

Fukuda Takeo. *Kaiko 90 nen* [Memoir of 90 years]. Tokyo: Iwanami Shoten, 1995.

———. "Waga shusho jidai" [My time as the prime minister]. Interview. *Chuo Koron*, October 1980, pp. 291–95.

———. "Watashi no rirekisho" [My personal history]. *Nihon Keizai Shimbun*, January 1993.

Fukushima, Glen S. *Nichibei keizai masatsu no seijigaku* [Politics of U.S.-Japan economic friction]. Tokyo: Asahi Shinbun-sha, 1992.

Funabashi Yoichi. *Domei hyoryu* [Alliance adrift]. Tokyo: Iwanami Shoten, 1997.

———. *Domei no hikaku kenkyu* [Comparative study on alliance]. Tokyo: Nihon Hyoron-sha, 2001.

Furui Yoshimi. *Shusho no shokumu kengen* [The official authority of the prime minister]. Tokyo: Makino Shuppan, 1983.

Furusawa Ken'ichi. *Nicchu heiwa yuko joyaku* [China-Japan peace and friendship treaty]. Tokyo: Kodan-sha, 1988.

Goto Kenji. *Takeshita seiken 576 nichi* [The Takeshita administration: 576 days]. Tokyo: Gyoken, 2000.

Gotoda Masaharu. *Jo to ri* [Emotion and logic]. Tokyo: Kodansha, 1998.

———. *Naikaku kanbo chokan* [The chief cabinet secretary]. Tokyo: Kodansha, 1989.

———. *Sasaeru ugokasu* [To support and mobilize]. Tokyo: Nihon Keizai Shimbun-sha, 1991.

———. *Sei to kan* [Politics and bureaucracy]. Tokyo: Kodansha, 1994.

———. *Seiji towa nanika?* [What is politics?] Tokyo: Kodansha, 1988.

Hanamura Nihachiro. *Seizaikai paipu yaku hanseiki* [My life as a channel between the political and business worlds]. Tokyo: Tokyo Shimbun, 1990.

Hara Yoshihisa. *Kishi Nobusuke: Kensei no seijika* [Kishi Nobusuke: The politician of power]. Tokyo: Iwanami Shinsho, 1995.

Hashimoto Ryutaro. *Seiken dakkairon* [To regain power]. Tokyo: Kodansha, 1994.

Hata Yasuko. *Shusho kotei* [The prime minister's residence]. Tokyo: Tokyo Shimbun, 1996.

Hatakeyama Yuzuru. *Tusho kosho: Kokueki wo meguru dorama* [Trade negotiations: Drama surrounding national interest]. Tokyo: Nihon Keizai Shimbun-sha, 1996.

Hayano Toru. *Nihon seiji no kessan: Kakuei vs. Koizumi* [Japan's political settlement: Kakuei vs. Koizumi]. Tokyo: Kodansha Gendai Shinsho, 2004.

Hayashi Shigeru and Tsuji Kiyoaki, eds. *Nihon naikaku shiroku* [The history of the Japanese cabinet]. Tokyo: Daiichi Hoki, 1981.

Hirano Sadao. *Jiyuto no chosen* [Challenge of the Liberal Party]. Tokyo: President-sha, 1998.

———. *Komeito Sokagakkai to Nihon* [Komeito Sokagakkai and Japan]. Tokyo: Kodan-sha, 2005.

———. *Ozawa Ichiro tono nijunen* [Twenty years with Ozawa Ichiro]. Tokyo: President-sha, 1996.

Hironaka Yoshimichi. *Miyazawa seiken 644 nichi.* [The Miyazawa administration: 644 days]. Tokyo: Gyoken, 1998.

Hirose Michisada. "Gyosei kaikaku to Jiminto" [Administrative reform and the LDP]. *Sekai*, August 1981, pp. 245–57.

———. *Hojokin to seikento* [Subsidies and the government party]. Tokyo: Asahi Shimbun-sha, 1981.

Honzawa Jiro. *Jiminto habatsu* [LDP factions]. Tokyo: Pipuru-sha, 1990.

Hori Shigeru. *Sengo seiji no oboegaki* [Memorandum of postwar politics]. Tokyo: Mainichi Shimbun, 1975.

Hosoya Chihiro and Shinoda Tomohito. *Shin jidai no Nichibei kankei* [A new era of U.S.-Japan relations]. Tokyo: Yuhikaku, 1998.

Ichikawa Taichi. *"Seshu" daigishi no kenkyu* [Study of hereditary Diet members]. Tokyo: Nihon Keizai Shimbun-sha, 1990.

Igarashi Kozo. *Kantei no rasen kaidan* [The spiral staircase of the prime minister's official residence]. Tokyo: Gyosei, 1997.

Ikeda Hayato. *Kinko zaisei* [Balanced budget]. Tokyo: Jitsugyo no Nihon-sha, 1952.

Imai Takeru. *Giin naikaku-sei* [Parliamentary system]. Tokyo: Buren Shuppan, 1991.

Inoguchi Takashi. *Gendai Nihon seiji keizai no kozu* [The composition of the contemporary Japanese political economy]. Tokyo: Toyo Keizai Shimpo-sha, 1983.

———. *Kokka to shakai* [The nation and the society]. Tokyo: Tokyo Daigaku Shuppan-kai, 1988.

———. *Kokusai seiji no mikata* [Perspective on international politics]. Tokyo: Chikuma Shinsho, 2005.

———. *Nihon: Keizai taikoku no seiji unei* [Japan: Political operation of economic power]. Tokyo: Tokyo Daigaku Shuppan-kai, 1993.

Inoguchi Takashi and Iwai Tomoaki. *"Zoku giin" no kenkyu* [Study of "zoku members"]. Tokyo: Nihon Keizai Shimbun-sha, 1987.

Inose Naoki. *Doro no kenryoku* [Power over the road]. Tokyo: Bungei Shunju, 2003.

Iokibe Makoto. *Sengo Nihon gaikoshi* [Postwar Japanese diplomatic history]. Tokyo: Yuhikaku, 1999.

Ishiba Shigeru. *Kokubo* [National defense]. Tokyo: Shincho-sha, 2005.

Ishida Hirohide. *Ishibashi seiken 71 nichi* [The Ishibashi administration: 71 days]. Tokyo: Gyosei Mondai Kenkyusho, 1985.

Ishihara Nobuo. *Kan kaku arubeshi* [The way the bureaucrats should be]. Tokyo: Shogakukan Bunko, 1998.

———. *Kantei 2668 nichi: Seisaku kettei no butaiura* [2,668 days at the prime minister's official residence: Behind the scenes of decision making]. Tokyo: NHK Shuppan, 1995.

———. *Kengen no daiido* [The major transfer of authority]. Tokyo: Kanki Shuppan, 2001.

———. *Shusho Kantei no ketsudan* [Decisions of the prime minister's official residence]. Tokyo: Chuo Koron-sha, 1997.

Ishikawa Masumi. *Deta sengo seijishi* [Data on postwar political history]. Tokyo: Iwanami Shoten, 1984.

Ishikawa Masumi and Hirose Michisada. *Jiminto* [The LDP]. Tokyo: Iwanami Shoten, 1989.

Iwai Tomoaki. *Rippo katei* [The legislative process]. Tokyo: Tokyo Daigaku Shuppan-kai, 1988.

———. *"Seiji shikin" no kenkyu* [Study of the "political fund"]. Tokyo: Nihon Keizai Shimbun-sha, 1990.

Kabashima Ikuo. *Seiji sanka* [Political participation]. Tokyo: Tokyo Daigaku Shuppan-kai, 1988.

Kaminishi Akio. *GNP 1% waku* [GNP 1% ceiling]. Tokyo: Kadokawa Bunko, 1986.

Kan Naoto. *Daijin* [The minister]. Tokyo: Iwanami Shinsho, 1998.

Kanemaru Shin. *Tachiwaza newaza* [Fighting in various ways]. Tokyo: Nihon Keizai Shimbun-sha, 1988.

Kataoka Hiromitsu. *Naikaku no kino to hosa kiko* [The function of the cabinet and supporting organizations]. Tokyo: Seibun-do, 1982.

Kawaguchi Hiroyuki. *Kanryo shihai no kozo* [The mechanism of bureaucratic control]. Tokyo: Kodan-sha, 1987.

Kawauchi Issei. *Ohira seiken 554 nichi* [The Ohira administration: 554 days]. Tokyo: Gyosei Mondai Kenkyusho, 1982.

Kennan, George. *American Diplomacy, 1900–1950*. New York: Mentor Books, 1952.

Kishi Nobusuke. *Kishi Nobusuke kaiso-roku* [Memoirs of Kishi Nobusuke]. Tokyo: Kosaido, 1983.

Kishi Nobusuke, Yatsugi Kazuo, and Ito Takashi. *Kishi Nobusuke no kaiso* [Memories of Kishi Nobusuke]. Tokyo: Bungei Shunju, 1981.

Kishimoto Koichi. *Gendai seiji kenkyu: "Nagata-cho" no ayumi to mekanizumu* [Study of contemporary politics: Development and mechanism of Nagata-cho]. Tokyo: Gyoken, 1988.

Kitanishi Makoto and Yamada Hiroshi. *Gendai Nihon no seiji* [Contemporary Japanese politics]. Tokyo: Horitsu Bunka-sha, 1983.

Kitaoka Shinichi. *Nihon no jiritsu* [Japan's self-reliance]. Tokyo: Chuokoronshin-sha, 2004.

Kiyomiya Ryu. *Fukuda seiken 714 nichi* [The Fukuda administration: 714 days]. Tokyo: Gyosei Mondai Kenkyusho, 1984.

Kobayashi Yoshiaki. *Gendai Nihon no senkyo* [Contemporary Japanese elections]. Tokyo: Tokyo Daigaku Shuppan-kai, 1991.

Kosaka Masataka. *Saisho Yoshida Shigeru* [Prime Minister Yoshida Shigeru]. Tokyo: Chuo Koron-sha, 1968.

Kubo Wataru. *Renritsu seiken no shinjitsu* [The truth of the coalition governments]. Tokyo: Yomiuri Shimbun-sha, 1998.

Kurihara Yuko. *Ohira moto sori to watashi* [Former prime minister Ohira and me]. Tokyo: Kosaido, 1990.

Kuriyama Takakazu. *Nichibei domei: Hyoryu kara no dakkyaku* [The Japan-U.S. alliance: From drift to revitalization]. Tokyo: Nihon Keizai Shimbun-sha, 1997.

Kusuda Minoru. *Shuseki hishokan: Sato sori tono junenkan* [Chief Secretary: Ten years with Prime Minister Sato]. Tokyo: Bungei Shunju, 1975.

———, ed. *Sato seiken 2797 nichi* [The Sato administration: 2,797 days]. Vols. 1 and 2. Tokyo: Gyosei Mondai Kenkyusho, 1983.

Mainichi Shimbun.

Mainichi Shimbun Seiji-bu, ed. *Kensho Kaifu naikaku* [Inspecting the Kaifu cabinet]. Tokyo: Kadokawa Shoten, 1991.

———, ed. *Kensho shusho kantei* [Inspecting the Prime Minister's Office]. Tokyo: Asahi Sonorama, 1988.

Maki Taro. *Nakasone seiken 1806 nichi* [The Nakasone administration: 1,806 days]. Vols. 1 and 2. Tokyo: Gyosei Mondai Kenkyusho, 1988.

———. *Nakasone to wa nandattanoka?* [What was Nakasone?] Tokyo: Soshi-sha, 1988.

Masumi Junnosuke. *Gendai seiji 1955 nen igo* [Contemporary politics after 1955]. Tokyo: Tokyo Daigaku Shuppan-kai, 1985.

———. *Sengo seiji 1945–55 nen* [Postwar politics 1945–55]. Tokyo: Tokyo Daigaku Shuppan-kai, 1983.

Matsuoka Hideo. *Rengo seiken ga hokai shita hi: Shakaito Katayama Naikaku kara no kyokun* [The day the coalition government collapsed: A lesson from the Katayama Socialist cabinet]. Tokyo: Kyoiku Shiryo Shuppan-kai, 1990.

Matsushita Keiichi. *Seiji gyosei no kangaekata* [How to think about politics and government]. Tokyo: Iwanami Shinsho, 1998.

Matsuzaki Tetsuhisa. *Jidai ni totte soshite wareware ni totte Nihon Shinto towa nande attanoka* [What was the Japan New Party to the time and to us]? Tokyo: Free Press, 1995.

Miki Mutsuko. *Shin nakuba tatazu: Otto Miki Takeo to no gojunen* [No rising without his belief: Fifty years with my husband, Miki Takeo]. Tokyo: Kodan-sha, 1989.

Minkan Seiji Rincho. *Nihon henkaku no bijon* [Grand vision of political reform]. Tokyo: Kodan-sha, 1993.

Miyake Ichiro et al. *Nihon seiji no zahyo: Sengo yonjunen no ayumi* [Charts of Japan's politics: Forty years of steps in the postwar period]. Tokyo: Yuhikaku, 1985.

Miyazawa Kiichi. *Sengo seiji no shogen* [Testimony on postwar politics]. Tokyo: Yomiuri Shimbun-sha, 1991.

———. *Shin goken sengen* [New declaration to protect the Constitution]. Tokyo: Asahi Shinbun, 1995.

———. *Tokyo-Washington no mitsudan* [The secret conversations between Tokyo and Washington]. Tokyo: Chuko Bunko, 1999.

Miyazawa Toshiyoshi. *Nihonkoku Kenpo* [The Japanese Constitution]. Revised edition. Tokyo: Nihon Hyoron-sha, 1978.

Mori Kishio. *Shusho Kantei no himitsu* [Secrets of the prime minister's official residence]. Tokyo: Chobun-sha, 1981.

Morimoto Satoshi, ed. *Iraku Senso to Jieitai haken* [The Iraq War and the SDF dispatch]. Tokyo: Toyo Keizai Shimpo-sha, 2004.

Morita Minoru. *Seihen: Jiminto sosaisen uramen anto-shi* [Political upheaval: History of the behind-the-scenes battles for the LDP presidency]. Tokyo: Tokuma Shoten, 1991.

Murakami Yasusuke. *Shin chukan taishu no jidai* [The era of new middle mass]. Tokyo: Chuo Koron, 1983.

Murakawa Ichiro. *Jiminto no seisaku kettei shisutemu* [The policy-making system of the LDP]. Tokyo: Kyoiku-sha, 1989.

———. *Nihon no seisaku kettei katei* [Japanese policy-making process]. Tokyo: Gyosei, 1985.

Muramatsu Michio. *Sengo Nihon no kanryosei* [Postwar Japan's bureaucratic system]. Tokyo: Toyo Keizai Shimpo-sha, 1981.

Muramatsu Michio, Ito Mitsutoshi, and Tsujinaka Yutaka. *Nihon no seiji* [Japan's politics]. Tokyo: Yuhikaku, 1992.

Murata Ryohei. *Naze Gaimusho wa dame ni nattaka?* [Why did MOFA go wrong?] Tokyo: Fuso-sha, 2002.

Murayama Tomiichi. *Murayama Tomiichi ga kataru tenmei no 561 nichi* [561 days of destiny, told by Murayama Tomiichi]. Tokyo: K.K. Best Sellers, 1996.

———. *Sojano: Murayama Tomiichi "shusho taiken" no subete wo kataru* [Murayama Tomiichi tells everything about his experience as premier]. Tokyo: Daisan Shobo, 1998.

———. "Watashi no rirekisho" [My personal history]. *Nihon Keizai Shinbun*, June 1996.

Nagai Yonosuke. "Atsuryoku dantai no Nihonteki kozo" [Japanese structure of interest groups]. *Nenpo Seijigaku*, 1960.

Nagashima Akihisa. *Nichibei domei atarashii sekkeizu* [New blueprint for a U.S.-Japan alliance]. 2nd edition. Tokyo: Nihon Hyoron-sha, 2004.

Naikaku Sori Daijin Kanbo, ed. *Takeshita Naikaku sori daijin enzetsu-shu* [Speeches of Prime Minister Takeshita Noboru]. Tokyo: Nihon Koho Kyokai, 1990.

Nakagawa Hidenao. *Shusho hosa* [Assistant to the prime minister]. Tokyo: PHP Kenkyusho, 1996.

Nakamura Akira and Takeshita Yuzuru, eds. *Nihon no seisaku katei: Jiminto, yato, kanryo* [Japanese policy process: The LDP, the opposition parties, and the bureaucrats]. Tokyo: Azusa Shuppan-sha, 1984.

Nakamura Keiichiro. *Miki seiken 747 nichi* [The Miki administration: 747 days]. Tokyo: Gyosei Mondai Kenkyusho, 1981.

———. *Sori no utsuwa* [Caliber for the prime minister]. Tokyo: Kobun-sha, 1996.

Nakano Shiro. *Tanaka seiken 886 nichi* [The Tanaka administration: 886 days]. Tokyo: Gyosei Mondai Kenkyusho, 1982.

Nakasone Yasuhiro. *Seiji to jinsei* [Politics and life]. Tokyo: Kodansha, 1992.

———. *Tenchi ujo: Gojunen no sengo seiji wo kataru* [Affection in heaven and on earth: Talk on fifty years of postwar politics]. Tokyo: Bungei Shunju, 1996.

Nicolson, Sir Harold. *Diplomacy*. Washington, D.C.: Institute for the Study of Diplomacy, Georgetown University, 1988.

Nihon Gyosei Gakkai, ed. *Naikakuseido no kenkyu* [Study of the cabinet system]. Tokyo: Gyosei, 1987.

Nihon Keizai Shimbun.

Nihon Keizai Shimbun-sha, ed. *Dokyumento seiken tanjo* [Documentary, the birth of an administration]. Tokyo: Nihon Keizai Shimbun-sha, 1991.

———, ed. *"Renritsu seiken" no kenkyu* [Study of "coalition governments"]. Tokyo: Nihon Keizai Shimbun-sha, 1994.

———, ed. *Seifu to ha nanika?* [What is the government?]. Tokyo: Nihon Keizai Shimbun-sha, 1981.

Nonaka Hiromu. *Watashi wa tatakau* [I fight]. Tokyo: Bungei Shunju, 1996.

Nosaka Koken. *Seiken: Henkaku eno michi* [The administration: Road to change]. Tokyo: Suzusawa Shoten, 1996.

Ohinata Ichiro. *Kishi seiken 1241 nichi* [The Kishi administration: 1,241 days]. Tokyo: Gyosei Mondai Kenkyu-sho, 1985.

Ohira Masayoshi. *Watashi no rirekisho* [My personal history]. Tokyo: Nihon Keizai Shimbun-sha, 1978.

Ohira Masayoshi Kaisoroku Kanko-kai. *Ohira Masayoshi kaiso-roku* [Memoirs of Ohira Masayoshi]. Volume 1, *Tsuiso hen* [Reminiscence]; and Volume 2, *Denki-hen* [Biography]. Tokyo: Ohira Masayoshi Kaisoroku Kanko-kai, 1982.

Okada Naoyuki. *Seron no seiji shakaigaku* [Political sociology of public opinion]. Tokyo: Tokyo Daigaku Shuppan-kai, 2001.

Okano Kaoru, ed. *Naikaku sori daijin* [The prime minister]. Tokyo: Gendai Hyoron-sha, 1985.

Okazawa Norio. *Seito* [Political parties]. Tokyo: Tokyo Daigaku Shuppan-kai, 1988.

Okita Saburo. *Ekonomisuto gaisho no 252 nichi: Takyokuka jidai no Nihon gaiko wo kangaeru* [252 days of an economist foreign minister: Talks on Japanese diplomacy in the multipolar era]. Tokyo: Toyo Keizai Shinpo-sha, 1980.

Okubo Shozo. *Hadaka no seikai* [Political world as naked]. Tokyo: Simul Shuppan-kai, 1975.

Osuga Mizuo. *Shusho kantei konjaku monogatari* [The prime minister's official residence: The past and the present]. Tokyo: Asahi Sonorama, 1995.

Otake Hideo. *Gendai Nihon no seiji kenryoku keizai kenryoku* [Political power and economic power in contemporary Japan]. Tokyo: San'ichi Shobo, 1979.

Owada Hisashi. *Sankaku kara sozo e: Nihon gaiko no mezasu mono* [Participation to creation: The goals of Japan's foreign policy]. Tokyo: Toshi Shuppan, 1994.

Ozawa Ichiro. *Kataru* [Talk]. Tokyo: Bungei Shunju, 1996.

———. *Nippon kaizo keikaku* [Japan's reform plan]. Tokyo: Kodan-sha, 1993.

Sakamoto Kazuya. *Nichibei domei no kizuna* [The bond of the Japan-U.S. alliance]. Tokyo: Yuhikaku, 2000.

Sakurada Daizo and Ito Takeshi, eds. *Hikaku gaiko seisaku: Iraku Senso eno taio gaiko* [Comparative study on foreign policy: Iraq War diplomacy]. Tokyo: Akashi Shoten, 2004.

Sakurada Takeshi and Shikanai Nobutaka. *Ima akasu sengo hishi* [The secret postwar history now revealed]. Tokyo: Sankei Shuppan, 1983.

Sankei Shimbun.

Sassa Atsuyuki. *Kiki kanri saisho ron* [On leadership in crisis management]. Tokyo: Bungei Shunju, 1995.

———. *Politico-military no susume* [Politico-military recommendations]. Tokyo: Toshi Shuppan, 1994.

————. *Shin kiki kanri no nouhau* [New know-how for crisis management]. Tokyo: Bungei Shunju, 1991.

Sataka Makoto. *Nihon kanryo hakusho* [White paper on Japanese bureaucracy]. Tokyo: Kodan-sha, 1989.

Sato Seizaburo and Matsuzaki Tetsuhisa. *Jiminto seiken* [The LDP administrations]. Tokyo: Chuo Koron, 1986.

Sejima Ryuzo. *Iku sanga* [So many mountains and rivers]. Tokyo: Sankei Shimbum, 1995.

Sekai Heiwa Kenkyusho, ed. *Nakasone naikakushi* [The history of the Nakasone cabinet]. 5 volumes. Tokyo: Chuo Koron-sha, 1995–97.

Shimizu Masato. *Kantei shudo* [The Kantei initiative]. Tokyo: Nihon Keizai Shimbun-sha, 2005.

Shinkoso Forum, ed. "Nakayama Sohei shi 'Nihon no kiki kanri' wo kataru" [Mr. Nakayama Sohei talks about "Japan's crisis management"]. *Shinkoso Booklet*, no. 1 (September 20, 1991).

Shinoda Tomohito. "Gaiko seisaku kettei actor to shiteno Ozawa Ichiro" [Ozawa Ichiro as a foreign policy actor]. In *Nihon gaiko no naisei yoin* [Domestic determinants of Japan's foreign policy], pp. 25–69. Tokyo: PHP, 1999.

————. "Hashimoto gyokaku no naikaku kino kyokasaku" [Cabinet reinforcement in Hashimoto's administrative reform]. *Leviathan*, Spring 1999, pp. 50–77.

————. *Kantei gaiko: Seiji ri-da-shippu no yukue* [Kantei diplomacy: The direction of political leadership]. Tokyo: Asahi Shimbun-sha, 2004.

————. *Kantei no kenryoku* [The power of the prime minister's official residence]. Tokyo: Chikuma Shinsho, 1994.

————. "Koizumi shusho no ri-da-shippu to anzen hosho seisaku katei: Tero taisaku tokusoho to yujikanrenho wo jirei toshita doshinen bunseki" [Prime Minister Koizumi's leadership and national security policy process: Concentric circles model analysis of the anti-terrorism legislation and the emergency legislation]. *Nihon Seiji Kenkyu* 1, no. 2 (July 2004): pp. 42–67.

————. "Kokunai seiji kozo no henka to gaiko" [Change in the domestic political system and diplomacy]. *Gaiko Forum*, January 2006, pp. 62–67.

————. *Sori daijin no kenryoku to shidoryoku* [The power and leadership of the prime minister]. Tokyo: Toyo Keizai Shimpo-sha, 1994.

————. *Taigai seisaku no kokunai seiji katei: Reisengo no anzenhosho seisaku wo jireini* [Domestic political process in foreign-policy making: Post–cold war national security policy]. Kyoto: Minerva Shobo, forthcoming.

Shiratori Rei, ed. *Nihon no naikaku* [The Japanese cabinet]. Tokyo: Shin Hyoron-sha, 1981.

Shiroyama Hideaki, Suzuki Hiroshi, and Hosono Sukehiro. *Chuo shocho no seisaku keisei katei* [Inside the Japanese bureaucracy]. Tokyo: Chuo Daigaku Shuppanbu, 1999.

Soeya Yoshihide. *Nihon no midoru pawa gaiko* [Japan's middle-power diplomacy]. Tokyo: Chikuma Shinsho, 2005.

Suzuki Kenji. *Rekidai sori sokkin no kokuhaku* [Confessions of close associates of prime ministers]. Tokyo: Mainichi Shimbun-sha, 1991.

Tagawa Seiichi. *Nicchu kosho hiroku* [Secret record of Sino-Japanese negotiation]. Tokyo: Mainichi Shimbun-sha, 1973.

Tahara Soichiro. *Atama no nai kujira: Seijigeki no shinjitsu* [Headless whale: The truth about political plays]. Tokyo: Asahi Shimbun-sha, 1997.

———. *Sori wo ayatsutta otokotachi* [Men who controlled prime ministers]. Tokyo: Kodan-sha, 1989.

Takahama Tatoo. *Nakasone gaiseiron: Sori wa nani o mezashite irunoka?* [On Nakasone's diplomacy: What is the prime minister trying to achieve?]. Tokyo: PHP, 1984.

Takebayashi Masahiko. *Giin kodo no seiji keizaigaku* [The logic of legislators' activities]. Tokyo: Yuhikaku, 2004.

Takenaka Heizo. *Keisei zaimin: Keizai Senryaku Kaigi no 180 nichi* [Governing the world to rescue people: 180 days of the Economic Strategy Council]. Tokyo: Daiyamondo-sha, 1999.

Takeshita Noboru. *Shogen hoshu seiken* [Testimony on conservative administrations]. Tokyo: Yomiuri Shimbun-sha, 1991.

Tamura Shigenobu. *Nichibei anpo to Kyokuto yuji* [Japan-U.S. security treaty and contingency in the Far East]. Tokyo: Nanso-sha, 1997.

Tamura Shigenobu and Suginoo Yoshio. *Kyokasho: Nihon no anzen hosho* [Textbook on Japan's national security]. Tokyo: Fuyo Shobo Shuppan, 2004.

Tanaka Akihiko. *Anzen hosho: Sengo 50 nen no mosaku* [National security: Postwar pursuit for 50 years]. Tokyo: Yomiuri Shimbun-sha, 1997.

———. *Atarashii chusei* [New medieval age]. Tokyo: Nihon Keizai Shimbun-sha, 1996.

———. *Fukuzatsusei no sekai: Tero no seiki to Nihon* [The world of complexity: Japan and the century of terrorism]. Tokyo: Keiso-sha, 2003.

———, ed. *Atarashii senso jidai no anzen hosho* [National security in an era of new war]. Tokyo: Toshi Shuppan, 2002.

Tanaka Hitoshi and Tahara Soichiro. *Kokka to gaiko* [The nation and diplomacy]. Tokyo: Kodansha, 2005.

Tanaka Kakuei Kinenkan, ed. *Watashi no naka no Tanaka Kakuei* [My memories of Tanaka Kakuei]. Niigata: Tanaka Kakuei Kinenkan, 1998.

Tanaka Kazuaki. *Doro kodan kaikaku: Itsuwari no mineika* [Road public corporation: Fake privatization]. Tokyo: Wac. Co., 2004. [[TS: Use full name for pub?]]

Tanaka Kazuaki and Okada Akira, eds. *Chuo shocho kaikaku* [Central government reform]. Tokyo: Nihon Hyoron-sha, 2000.

Tanaka Rokusuke. *Futatabi Ohira Masayoshi no hito to seiji* [More on the personality and politics of Ohira Masayoshi]. Tokyo: Asahi Sonorama, 1981.

Tanaka Shusei. *Sakigake to seiken kotai* [*Sakigake* and political change]. Tokyo: Toyo Keizai Shimpo-sha, 1994.

Taniguchi Masaki. *Nihon no taibei boeki kosho* [Japan's trade negotiations with the United States]. Tokyo: Tokyo Daigaku Shuppankai, 1997.

Tejima Ryuichi. *1991 nen Nihon no haiboku* [Japan's defeat of 1991]. Tokyo: Shincho Bunko, 1996.

Tokyo Daigaku Kokyo Seisaku Daigakuin and Hoshi Hiroshi, eds. *Todai vs.* [University of Tokyo vs.]. Tokyo: Asahi Shimbun-sha, 2005.

Tomita Nobuo. *Ashida seiken 223 nichi* [The Ashida administration: 223 days]. Tokyo: Gyoken, 1992.

Tsuda Tatsuo. *Zaikai Nihon no shihaisha tachi* [The business community: The people who rule Japan]. Tokyo: Gakushu no Tomo-sha, 1990.

Tsuji Kiyoaki. *Shinban Nihon kanryosei no kenkyu* [New edition, study of the Japanese bureaucratic system]. Tokyo: Tokyo Daigaku Shuppan-kai, 1969.

Tsujinaka Yutaka. *Rieki shudan* [Interest groups]. Tokyo: Tokyo Daigaku Shuppankai, 1988.

———, ed. *Gendai Nihon no shimin shakai rieki dantai* [Civil society and interest groups in contemporary Japan]. Tokyo: Bokutaku-sha, 2002.

Tsutsui Kiyotada. *Ishibashi Tanzan: Ichi jiyu shugi seijika no kiseki* [Ishibashi Tanzan: Trace of one liberal politician]. Tokyo: Chuo Koron-sha, 1986.

Uchida Kenzo. *Sengo Nihon no hoshu seiji* [Conservative politics in postwar Japan]. Tokyo: Iwanami Shoten, 1969.

Uji Toshihiko. *Suzuki seiken 863 nichi* [The Suzuki administration: 863 days]. Tokyo: Gyosei Mondai Kenkyusho, 1983.

Wakaizumi Kei. *Tasaku nakarishi wo shinzemu to hossu* [Wish to believe that there was no option]. Tokyo: Bungei Shunju, 1994.

Watanabe Akio, ed. *Sengo Nihon no saisho tachi* [The prime ministers of postwar Japan]. Tokyo: Chuo Koron-sha, 1995.

Watanabe Kensuke. *Anohito: Hitotsu no Ozawa Ichiro ron* [That man: One theory on Ozawa Ichiro]. Tokyo: Asuka Shinsha, 1992.

Watanabe Tsuneo. *Habatsu to tatoka jidai* [Factions and the multiparty era]. Tokyo: Sekka-sha, 1967.

———. *Nagatacho kenbunroku* [Observations on Nagatacho]. Tokyo: Sekka-sha, 1980.

———. *Toshu to Seito: Sono ri-da-shippu no kenkyu* [Party leaders and political parties: A study of their leadership]. Tokyo: Kobun-sha, 1961.

Yabunaka Mitoji. *Taibei keizai kosho* [Economic negotiations with the United States]. Tokyo: Saimaru Shuppankai, 1991.

Yajima Koichi. *Kokkai* [The Diet]. Tokyo: Gyoken, 1987.

Yakushiji Katsuyuki. *Gaimusho: Gaikoryoku kyoka eno michi* [MOFA: The road to strengthening diplomatic power]. Tokyo: Iwanami Shinsho, 2003.

Yamada Eizo. *Shoden Sato Eisaku* [The true story of Sato Eisaku]. Tokyo: Shincho-sha, 1988.

Yamaguchi Jiro. *Igirisu no seiji Nihon no seiji* [British politics, Japanese politics]. Tokyo: Chikuma Shinsho, 1998.

————. *Itto shihai taisei no hokai* [The collapse of the one-party dominance system]. Tokyo: Iwanami Shoten, 1989.

————. *Okura kanryo shihai no shuen* [The end of domination by finance ministry bureaucrats]. Tokyo: Iwanami Shoten, 1987.

————. *Seiji kaikaku* [Political reform]. Tokyo: Iwanami Shinsho, 1993.

Yamaguchi Yasushi. *Seiji taisei* [Political system]. Tokyo: Tokyo Daigaku Shuppan-kai, 1989.

Yamamoto Shichihei. *Habatsu no kenkyu* [Study of factions]. Tokyo: Bungei Shunju, 1989.

Yamawaki Takeshi. *Yusei kobo* [Battles over the postal service]. Tokyo: Asahi Shimbun-sha, 2005.

Yan Jiaqi. *Shunoron* [Theory of national leaders]. Translated from Chinese to Japanese. Tokyo: Gakusei-sha, 1992.

Yano Junya. *Niju kenryoku yami no nagare* [Dual power, current in the dark]. Tokyo: Bungei Shunju, 1994.

Yomiuri Shimbun.

Yomiuri Shimbun Chosa Kenkyu Honbu, ed. *Nihon no Kokkai* [The Japanese Parliament]. Tokyo: Yomiuri Shimbun-sha, 1988.

Yomiuri Shimbun Seiji-bu, ed. *Sori Daijin Nakasone Yasuhiro* [Prime Minister Nakasone Yasuhiro]. Tokyo: Gendai Shuppan-sha, 1987.

————, ed. *Sori daijin* [The prime minister]. Tokyo: Yomiuri Shimbun-sha, 1971.

Yoshida Shigeru. *Kaiso junen* [Memoir of ten years]. 1957; Tokyo: Tokyo Shirakawa Shoin, 1982.

Yoshimura Katsumi. *Ikeda seiken 1575 nichi* [The Ikeda administration: 1,575 days]. Tokyo: Gyosei Mondai Kenkyusho, 1985.